Driving Forces

The Grand Prix Racing World Caught in the Maelstrom of the Third Reich

by Peter Stevenson

A picture worth a thousand words sums up the lengths Berlin would go in using their automobile-based programs to gain popular support. In a specially staged bit of parade ground pomp and circumstance, the race drivers were ordered to display the impressive speed and noise of their cars before a reviewing stand, complete with the hopefully awe-inspiring architectural backdrop of the N.S.K.K. (*Nationalsozialistiches Kraftfahrer Korps*, the National Socialist Motor Corps). Stadtpark, Hamburg, 1938

Driving Forces

Rudi Caracciola and Christian Werner at the 1928 German Grand Prix. Page 30

The start of the Mille-Miglia in Brescia, 1931. Page 53

Caracciola taking the lead in the 1935 Eifelrennen. Page 113

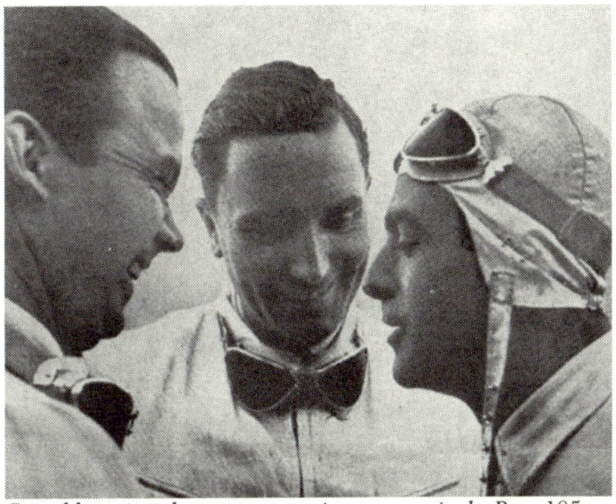
Bernd bursting the pre-race tension among rivals. Page 185

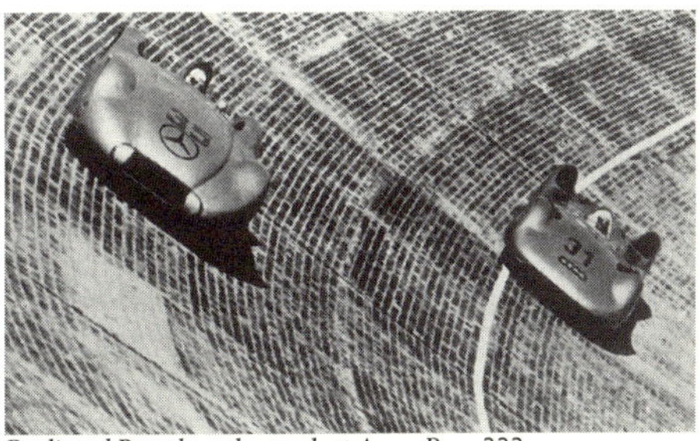
Rudi and Bernd on the track at Avus. Page 222

Bernd aging visibly under the pressure. Page 246

RB BENTLEY PUBLISHERS | AUTOMOTIVE BOOKS & MANUALS

1734 Massachusetts Avenue
Cambridge, MA 02138 USA
800-423-4595 / 617-547-4170

Information that makes
the difference®

www.BentleyPublishers.com

Copies of this book may be purchased from selected booksellers, or directly from the publisher by mail. The publisher encourages comments from the reader of this book. These communications have been and will be considered in the preparation of this and other manuals. Please write to Bentley Publishers at the address listed on the top of this page.
Since this page cannot legibly accommodate all the copyright notices, the caption credits listing the source of the photographs or illustrations used constitutes an extension of the copyright page.

Library of Congress Cataloging-in-Publication Data

Stevenson, Peter, 1941–
Driving forces: the Grand Prix racing world caught in the mealstrom of the Third Reich / by Peter Stevenson.
p. cm.
Includes bibliographical references and index.
ISBN 0-8376-0217-3 (alk. paper)
1. Automobile racing — Germany — History — 20th century. 2. Grand Prix racing. I. Title.
GV1034.49.A1 S74 2000
796.72'0943'09043—dc21

00-034277

ISBN 0-8376-0217-3
Bentley Stock No. GDDF

03 02 01 00 10 9 8 7 6 5 4 3 2 1

The paper used in this publication is acid free and meets the requirements of the National Standard for Information Sciences-Permanence of Paper for Printed Library Materials. ♾
Driving Forces: The Grand Prix Racing World Caught in the Maelstrom of the Third Reich, by Peter Stevenson

Cover Illustrations and fold-out map by Ethan Estes

Cover design by Mary-Margaret Mulligan

Those who worked to put this book together
would like to thank those who were interviewed
and who helped fill in the blanks
about what day-to-day life was like
in Europe before World War II:
Marina Keagy, the late Rene Dreyfus,
and Count Freddie de Broliet.

Foreword

Hans-Joachim Stuck is the second generation of a racing dynasty that has streched its winning streak from the 1920s, when his father drove for Mercedes-Benz, all the way into the 21st century. Hans-Joachim has set an enviable record in gruelling long distance events as a two-time winner of Le Mans, as well as winning the brutal Sebring race three times, driving Formula One, and being very successful in the Racing GT series with Audi and BMW.

photo: BMW Public Relations

My father was lucky enough to enjoy a racing career that saw many colorful eras of competition come and go — from the informal hillclimbs of the 1920s, through the more sophisticated 1930s with their hotly contested battles of the government sponsored teams of Italy and Germany, all the way to the postwar era that led to our present-day age of professionalism and corporate sponsorship.

When we watch films of the sort of racing conditions he and his fellow drivers battled, with the huge unlimited supercharged engines belching clouds of exhaust up into the air; with the racers set off by the cannon fire of the starting gun, ready to fly down narrow, twisting roads on thin, hard rubber tires — often in the rain — it brings a chill when we realize that they were hurtling those beasts around with no cockpit cages, no five-point harnesses, no roll bars, and with gas tanks that could catch fire at the hint of a spark. It was certainly a whole different kind of racing than I have experienced driving both Grand Prix and Formula One cars, and in endurance races like LeMans and Sebring.

My father was in the thick of the action, both on and off the track, during the 1930s, as he watched his beloved sport of racing being commandeered by governments in order to further the popularity of their respective auto industry programs. He tagged along with Dr. Porsche to a meeting with Adolf Hitler, where Porsche's forceful arguments convinced Hitler to split the new government subsidy offered to boost German car racing to create not one, but two rival German teams.

Imagine the enthusiasm of the brand new team — Auto Union — my father headed up as principal driver! They were going to take on Mercedes — at that time the most respected name in racing history, not to mention challenging Mussolini's all-conquering state-backed teams, using a whole new team and radically new race car design created by Dr. Porsche! It was the sort of challenge that competitive people like my father could only dream about. It was a time that brought about the sort of cohesive team spirit that comes along only once in a great while. And at this point, with all their hopes soaring, the possibility that those in power controlling the government funds might eventually want to call the shots on the track for their own purposes was a very remote issue.

But, of course, the time would come when the performance-oriented people and the politicians would find themselves at loggerheads. Drivers who explore the *terra incognita* of new realms speed quickly learn that they have only their own instincts and self-reliance to depend on where there are no set rules to guide them. And when these free spirits, drawn to the truth of performance, had to deal with the conventional world where politicians viewed life as their own private puppet show, the sparks inevitably began to fly.

Driving Forces tells the tale of just such a time, when those who risked their lives for a sport they loved passionately, found themselves on a collision course with social engineers whose dream was to order everyone around, including race-hardened drivers, like toy soldiers.

The accomplishments of my father and his fellow drivers during this period of racing history are legendary, to be sure. They were special people in a special time. But underneath all of that, they were still human beings, with the hopes and fears that we all have. Auto racing gave them an incredible and exciting life. I know they were proud to be a part of it, just as I have been.

Hans-Joachim Stuck

START

Chapter 1

A Tale of Two Drivers

Our story starts back in the early Roaring Twenties, a time when Germany had been devastated by the terms of the Versailles treaty after the First World War and the Belgian army was still patrolling portions of the Rhineland.

We join the first of our heroes as he's riding a motorcycle through a frosty, starlit night wearing nothing warmer than a tuxedo with its lapels turned up against the cold. An icy wind is pulling an endless stream of tears from his eyes, and we can see from his furtive glances behind him that we've caught him in the act of escape. He seems a comely looking young man, with a cherubic, refined sort of devilment to him. But by the concentrated look on his face at the moment, we can see that this is no youthful prank that he's carrying out just to win a bet. He's of good family, we think, but he's obviously running for his life. The young man is named Rudolph Caracciola; he's reached a crossroads in his life through no effort of his own and as a consequence, he's not exactly at his best.

Hillclimbs were an ideal racing venue to test out new designs before subjecting them to the grueling test of full-length grand prix events. Later, the hillclimb cars took on their own specialized look. Here we see Hermann Lang about to make the ascent at the Klausen Pass Hillclimb with a Mercedes sporting a special reduced grill intake for mountain work. Mercedes at times resorted to ice-cooled engines for both hillclimb and record events.

photo: Road & Track

He reaches to unlace a pair of goggles from around the triple-trees of the motorcycle's forks. With a quick, expert movement he grabs the strap, twists backward in the saddle to catch the wind with the lenses, then pulls the strap over his head. They don't fit. The bridge adjustment has been set for the owner of the goggles, a smaller person, not Caracciola. A small person with a small person's name: Karl Kruppke. Good old Kruppke. Who else would force Rudi to take his own faithful NSU, his one claim to mobility, into the night?

On second thought, if it hadn't been for Kruppke's bull-headedness, Rudi wouldn't be fleeing the whole Belgian Army without even a riding jacket to keep him from shivering in the cold. Or *was* it the cold that caused him to tremble?

The thought that any one of the approaching headlights could be a roadblock set to trap the young rider made it hard for him to determine just what was the cause of his tumbling stomach. Headlights from behind brought an involuntary increase in the pace of Rudi's noisy flight into the still darkness.

If it hadn't been for Kruppke they'd still be back in the noisy confines of the Klub Kakadu enjoying some champagne, where Rudi's only worry would be paying the tab instead of evading the Belgian curfew patrols.

And Rudi, a young man with a kind of natural, regal leisureliness, wouldn't have known a character like Kruppke if Rudi's own brother hadn't apprenticed him off to the mechanics' program at the Fafnir Works. And, on further thought, his big brother probably wouldn't have sent him to that apprentice program if Rudi had been able to stand him strutting and posing as the head of the family and director of the family's hotel after Papa died. But whatever the case, here he was fleeing for his life from the Belgians, trying his damnedest to arrive back at brother's hotel safely. What a life.

No, that wasn't true about big brother. He might be an unbearable bore, now that he was wearing Papa's smoking jackets and using his office, but Rudi would never have been able to stick to the hotel business anyway. The phony, forced cordiality. The mother-henning over pennies. To play out his one-and-only life catering to those jumped-up wine salesmen and their doxies was not how Rudi pictured his fate. He wasn't quite sure just how he did picture his fate, but the very thought of the hotel with big brother strutting about brought on a shudder to mix with his other tremblings.

Growing up the youngest had almost certainly foreshadowed Rudi's being thought of as a pest around the place. But then, he hadn't done a lot to dismiss that image either.

Rigging it so that the priest (who had refused on religious grounds to let Protestant Rudi watch the films shown at the church every Saturday) happened to have a power-outage every time he turned on the projector, until he made Rudi projectionist, was just one of a series of pranks and problems caused by Rudi through the long, boring years around the hotel. And with each new offense, big brother had taken another step toward taking over Papa's powers, but without Papa's wise and stabilizing sense of humor.

At each family conference (in which big brother railed, Rudi's mother and sister tried to mitigate, and Rudi only scowled) the group came unconsciously closer to agreeing on one point at least: that Rudi might be happier seeking his fortune elsewhere.

The question that was finally put to Rudi hadn't been unexpected. Still, it took him by surprise. As sometimes happens when people are asked a really searching and important question, a voice will sometimes come from nowhere with an answer that the person had no idea was inside. And when big brother droned on, finally asking, somewhat rhetorically, "And just what do you plan to do with your life, young man?" Rudi heard a strange voice from inside him blurt out, "I want to be a Grand Prix racing driver. If I can't do that, then I don't care what I do."

A stunned silence. He might as well have announced that he wanted to be king of the Barbary Pirates. There followed a roar of laughter, with an accompaniment of female astonishment.

"With a hundred men standing in line for every job and families going hungry, you want to be a Grand Prix driver, eh? Why not be director of Mercedes Benz while you're at it?" big brother chuckled.

"I've heard that the motor industry is becoming a wonderful future for young men." It was a defending sister, Hertha, coming to the rescue.

"And just where did you pick up this news bulletin?" big brother asked with the usual derisive smile.

"From a nice man I met on the train. He said fortunes would be made in automobiles and that any young man couldn't pick a better future to pursue."

"Ah, well then, perhaps it's time Rudi started his pursuit." At this, Rudi looked up at his brother quizzically.

"I have a friend over at the Fafnir plant," his brother went on, with a curious smile Rudi couldn't quite read. "I will call him directly about finding Rudi a place in the auto industry, ... as an apprentice mechanic."

There were squeals of protest. A Caracciola, a mere mechanic! The very idea! Big brother looked over to savor the look of dismay he expected to see on Rudi's face — but instead Rudi was simply thoughtful. He saw that his placement at Fafnir had one goal: to teach him a lesson, once and for all, that would send him back home to the hotel with his tail permanently between his legs when he found he couldn't cut the mustard among the rough lads in the apprentice program. But Rudi, instead, was beginning to find the idea interesting.

He found the boys in the program interesting as well. A little rough, perhaps, but straightforward lads without a duplicitous bone in their bodies. Rudi appreciated that after chafing under petit-bourgeois politeness for all those years. The boys in the program had found Rudi, in turn, amusingly arrogant, which earned him the nickname "the baron" (though mostly because he knew how to hold a knife and fork). But Rudi began to gather friends slowly, nevertheless. And as the months went by, the family (and not least of all, Rudi) was amazed to find that he was sticking to the program and not crawling back to the hotel as planned. For the first time in his young life, Rudi seemed to be following through with what he had started.

The fellow that seemed to get the most sincere amusement out of Rudi's natural regalness was Kruppke. Kruppke had the unfeigned casualness of a pile of dirty laundry. But what Kruppke lacked in grooming he made up for with an honest heart. There never was a better lad to have at your back in a brawl than Kruppke, the kind of fellow who would never leave a friend on his own to sort out a problem by himself. On balance, however, it had to be admitted that it was often Kruppke's short temper that would get that friend into the problem in the first place.

Kruppke loved his motorcycle with a touching, wistful passion that was surprising in such a rough-cut diamond. What was also surprising about Kruppke was the fact that he had somehow convinced a very pretty girl of the solid values that lay beneath his well-disguised surface. Tall and winsomely attractive, she made a strangely contrasting vision when arm-in-arm with Kruppke, the lad who could make a drop-cloth look neat and tidy.

What was more surprising was that this beauty had decided that no man but Kruppke should be her mate, and after the shock of the engagement announcement had passed, there came the tangible proof of the engagement party. For such a visually humorous couple, the lads decided, no effort should be spared to formalize the occasion. They chose the most sought-after club for the party, Klub Kakadu, where on weekends there was a jazz band made up entirely of "American negroes." They could have been Martians, for all anyone knew that night; the Kakadu was so crowded no one could hear a note from the band, which labored on dutifully like silent marionettes behind the din.

As Rudi's party squeezed through the packed, jostling dancers, Rudi and Kruppke spotted a table of Belgian officers sitting and scanning the womenfolk. Rudi and Kruppke traded a meaningful look, then found their table, the size of a trashcan lid, and sat down with one quick glance back at the Belgians. Just a week before, a farmer had been caught out after curfew. The answers he gave the patrol weren't the ones they were looking for, and after a night in jail the farmer was so beaten up that his own wife didn't recognize him. Or so the rumor went. True or not, the story only echoed many others under the Belgian rule. There was little love lost between the neighbor nations, Germany and Belgium.

As the toasts extolled the beauty and obvious saintly compassion of Kruppke's fiancee, Rudi couldn't stop taking quick glances back toward the Belgians. Most of them looked like decent lads, but their captain, an older fellow displaying a proud dueling scar, was staring unabashedly right at Kruppe's fiancee as he drank. Rudi shook off a creeping feeling of dread at the sight of this, and rejoined the jokes made at Kruppke's expense.

Suddenly the banter stopped. Kruppke was staring blankly down at the table before him, and one of the Belgian lieutenants was in their midst. He was asking if mademoiselle would enjoy a dance with a Belgian officer, when there was a sudden explosion of noise like a lion bellowing down at the ground.

"NO." It was Kruppke, his voice sounding eerily disembodied. "No! She's too good for that!"

Kruppke's fiancee looked at him pleadingly. Just a little dance. It wasn't worth throwing away their future. They'd come so close to starting a wonderful life. All that could be wiped out in a split-second mistake.

"What's the trouble here!?" Rudi looked up, startled by this new voice. It was the captain, now at their table with what passed in military circles as a look of amused irony on his face. Kruppke shot to his feet to face the captain. Then Rudi watched as a curious thing happened: the world seemed to rush down around him until he himself was staring into the face of the captain. He could see the irises of the captain's eyes dilate as the moment of action came, he could feel a movement from Kruppke at his side. And then, most curious of all, he could see his own fist flying toward the Belgian's face. Rudi had meant to hit him on the jaw, but his fist landed on the captain's nose, sending him careening back into the crowd.

Pent up mortifications bubbled to the surface to find revenge. A scream, jostlings that were misunderstood, and a fine melee got underway. The band started up again, the lights went out, and Rudi felt a force pulling him down that he fought with all his might to free himself from.

"It's me. Kruppke!" a voice was bellowing in his ear. "You've got to get out of here!"

"Me! You're the one who started it!"

"Well you're the one who hit a Belgian! We'll argue the fine points later." After feeling himself half dragged through the crowd, Rudi smelled the cool clear air of night. They were outside.

"Krause took the girls home. They told me to make you scarce around here." Rudi wondered when all that had happened. By the soreness of both his fists, he guessed some time had passed. They ran through the back streets, ducking into shadowed doorways at every sound that could possibly be a Belgian patrol. They gasped for breath as noiselessly as possible, mouths agape, during their doorway rests. Eventually they made their way back to the street where Rudi roomed.

"Look, it's just a little scrap," Rudi was gasping. "Why are we making such a big — ?"

Kruppke was pointing silently up at Rudi's room. The light was on. They could see the shapes of soldiers going through his things. The truth hit Rudi icily, quieting him in a second.

"Look, you've got to make tracks," Kruppke was saying. " You take the NSU and put as many miles between you and here as you can before dawn."

"I can't take your NSU. It's your bike!" Rudi was saying with an addled logic.

"Here! Here's the money we saved up for the party. At least we didn't have to pay the bill for that." Kruppke tried to force a smile, but it failed and turned into a look of concern that Rudi couldn't ignore. Obediently he grabbed the money.

"This is your engagement money," he said in a distant voice.

"There'd be nobody to be engaged if you hadn't stopped me from hitting that Captain. Now get going!"

Kruppke began the starting routine of the NSU that Rudi knew was necessary from all the times they'd doubled up on it to ride to whatever races could be found around the area on weekends. Kruppke was going through the start-up ritual slowly now, sensing this might well be the last he ever saw of his beloved bike. Then the long ride had begun, the icy night air making Rudi gasp to keep his breath. Slowly, with the help of the cold, the trembling had started.

Then, once in the countryside the ride could almost have been a beautiful, starlit experience if circumstances were different. The sky gradually began to brighten, and with it, Rudi's mood. The countryside was familiar now. He might as well have been returning from one of his youthful nocturnal adventures with the local boys as he neared the family's hotel.

The tires made the familiar old crunch as he turned into the gravel drive — the old sound of having made it back safely. His tremble-muscles had long since given out, and he sat silently on the warm bike after switching it off, savoring the sudden silence, hearing the engine ticking as it cooled from its work. The good old NSU had done its job. A bird was singing loudly, just as it had in the old days when he'd fling gravel its way to shut it up before it woke up the whole hotel. Was it the same bird? Or had other generations taken over the job? His life at the hotel, carefree and full of mischief, seemed like something out of an old fairy tale he'd once heard a long time off. Was he the same boy who had lived here so long, or had he, part by part, been replaced by some other person?

"You've done it this time, young man. Make no mistake!" It was big brother, back at his post as chief inquisitor of pesky younger brothers. "Don't you have the slightest scrap of family loyalty?! Don't you realize" (and he suddenly lowered his voice, as if there were spies at every keyhole) "that at this very moment we have Belgian officers in the hotel?"

He was strutting back and forth in Papa's robe. Suddenly he stopped and motioned Rudi to follow him into Papa's office. He moved toward the safe, and Rudi knew something bigger than the usual ear-scorching was up. Big brother scowled, took out some cash, and then stopped to think — not realizing that Rudi was watching him closely and that he was taking a long time, the way people do when they're about to shortchange someone.

"Papa had set aside a certain amount for you, as you know," brother said, slowly counting out a stack of bills. "What with the cost of your training, wear and tear, and of course inflation ..."

"Inflation, of course," Rudi broke in. Big brother snorted and thrust the small wad of bills toward him.

"I think it's time you were a burden to this family no longer," he said almost sadly, with the regret of someone losing a whipping boy, and some cash.

He went on with his lecture, but Rudi's mind was wandering with a sudden new sense of freedom. Big brother's sleight of hand at the safe had done the trick. Why had he ever been afraid of this pompous fool? Now he only felt disgust.

The womenfolk were wailing supportive suggestions to Rudi, bringing hot food and warmer clothes.

"… And this card is from the man I met on the train from Dresden. He's a manufacturer. See? There's not even a street number. It must be a very large concern…."

Rudi shoved the card idly into his pocket and smiled his thanks. He was grateful for the way they stuck by him. It must have been hard on them too, living under this martinet with no hope of relief. Rudi's relief was still nothing more than a huge question mark standing between him and the rest of his life. But curiously it was a welcome new uncertainty, in view of life around the secure confines of the hotel.

Chapter 2

Tyrant on a Tightrope

In fairy tales people pull swords out of stones and end up ruling kingdoms. In popular histories, army generals with well-publicized commands on the winning side can end up doing much the same thing.

In what we call real life, however, you need more than magic swords and a charismatic smile. You need widespread financial support, and plenty of it. No matter how magnetic their personalities, most leaders arrive at the head of state with big debts to pay — and Hitler was no different.

Thanks a good deal to the chaos created by the terms of the Versailles Treaty following World War I, the Communists had a lot of grievances to capitalize on and were making amazing headway in Italy and Germany with crippling agrarian demonstrations, seized farmlands, factory sit-ins, nationwide general strikes, sabotage. Combined with the vision of the recent revolution in Russia, the term "commie plot" was no laughing matter for mainstream Germany in the 1920s. There were over five hundred thousand Communists signed up and serious in Germany alone.

Business was worried, as business usually is, because parades and strikes and riots and boarded-up windows were all death to trade. Industrialists were worried. Factories had been seized in Russia to pave the way for the people's paradise. What was to stop the same thing from happening in Germany? Bankers were worried. Look at what had happened throughout Russia — the whole banking system decimated and every banker regarded as a persona non grata. Officers in the old-guard army elite were worried. Their counterparts in Russia had been systematically replaced, never to be seen again.

And a vast class of middle-aged war veterans were shocked to find that their nation, which had fought the war largely on French soil, was elected "loser" by the terms of Versailles, an armistice that had called a halt to the fighting only after both sides had come within inches of total collapse and general mutiny. Back home, they found themselves reviled, their country changed, and the values they'd fought four-and-a-half long years for largely a thing of the past. But even those who were capitalizing on this threat of a pan-European Soviet state were finding that this odd-bedfellows-coalition forced to face the Bolshevik menace was not what anyone would call a smooth-running team.

The arrogance of General Hammerstein-Equord was not lost on Hitler when the general told his fellow officers that the regular army would "open fire" the minute Hitler took a step in the direction that they didn't approve. On another front, Hitler's private sources were discovering alarming indications that Hitler's own S.A., his own private army of Brown-shirts, was plotting a coup to topple his new government because they felt Hitler was weakening in his revolutionary resolve. And with the financiers and industrialists in his new coalition openly bragging about sending Hitler "back to his study of architecture," the start of his term as Chancellor was looking more like the end of his career and less like a popular mandate.

"When I took over the government in January 1933," Hitler was to say, "I felt I was marching forward along a broad, well-paved road. But then that road got narrower, and the surface worse. It turned into a narrow footpath — and today I have a feeling that I am inching my way forward, along a tightrope ....They are going to set traps for me, as many as they can. But we will not wait until they act."

In actuality, Hitler had already moved even before taking office to implement a plan to circumvent those who were putting him on that tightrope. He took precious time out during that chaotic period to contact those German Grand Prix racing heroes he thought he could count on to set into motion an idea he'd worked out back in his sequestered days in the Landsberg Prison. The plan centered around the automobile in general and Grand Prix racing in particular.

While political historians can't escape the fact that Hitler spent a lot of time and made a lot of press building the autobahn system, they rarely grasped the power of the automobile to revolutionize life as Hitler grasped it. Most have missed the fact that those who could ride the momentum of the automotive revolution, could gain a popularity to put them far past the reach of the financial kingmakers. And without this key concept, many explanations of Hitler's rise to power are riddled with gaps of cause and effect. The autobahns were just one brick in Hitler's social-motorization bridge to political freedom from the debts he'd built up under the political patronage system — debts Hitler had little desire to repay.

For a man whose schedule was so jam-packed with intrigue during that fateful spring of 1933 that "great issues were being settled in passing on staircases," as he put it, Hitler spent a surprising amount of time on the phone with race drivers and meeting with race-car designers. It seems a strange period in his career to be spending a lot of time on a "hobby" like car racing — if hobby it really was.

Chapter 3

The Round-Table Gang

Rudi arrived at Dresden with little idea about what to do with himself. Then he remembered the card of the manufacturer in his pocket. Why not? What else did he have cluttering up his schedule at the moment? Exactly zero. He took out the card and read it more carefully, "S.T. Rathmann, Manufacturer, Dresden." Not much information to encourage a young man looking for opportunities. But a starting point, perhaps.

As he asked his way toward the Altstadt of this "Rathmann, Manufacturer," the streets became gradually narrower and more wandering. On the street in question there were only sawtooth gabled warehouses with few signs of life. A small temporary placard had been put up on one of the warehouse doors for the benefit of deliveries: "Rathmann, Manufacturing." Rudi looked for signs of automotive activity, some clue linking "Rathmann, Manufacturing" with a bright future in the new Age of the Automobile. In the trash bin he saw only a few discarded doll's legs. He knocked on the door anyway. He'd come all that way. He knocked again and almost instantly the door cracked open. The face of a tow-headed young man with the wild blue eyes of a messiah peered out with an almost burlesque curiosity.

"Ye-es?"

Caught off-guard, Rudi stammered, "I'd like to see Herr Rathmann, if I could."

"And the nature of your business?" the face inquired brightly, as if he were taking a luncheon order at a restaurant.

"It — it has to do with a subject of interest to Herr Rathmann, about a future in the auto industry," Rudi faltered, as the face at the door grew grave with lack of understanding. "Herr Rathmann was discussing this subject with my sister on the train from Dusseldorf," Rudi added, wondering why he had. It was just about all he knew on the subject of Rathmann. The face brightened instantly and the door opened.

"Aha," the face said in triumph. "Now I understand. Yes, I remember your sister well. A charming young lady. You see, I am Rathmann, and you are that curious Italian name, ... ahh, I have it: Caracciola! " And at this Rathmann gestured that Rudi should enter through the narrow door.

Inside it was dark, except for small illuminated areas along workbenches, like a propmaster's backstage shop at a puppet theatre. As his eyes adjusted to the light, Rudi could see piles of bowling pins, newly varnished and striped, croquet balls in bins, and a pile of doll's heads glaring in all directions with the same look of mute accusation.

Rathmann noticed the inquisitive searching of Rudi's eyes and jumped right in,

"Yes. Well. You see, with the state of business being what it is today, one has to take what work comes one's way. I'm a bit shorthanded these days, as you can see. It's better in some ways. Makes us more flexible to work alone. This week it's doll's heads. Next week pine caskets. Then, who knows? Something to do with your precious automobiles, perhaps."

Rudi had been rehearsing his spiel all the way to Dresden, and in his confusion at meeting a specter like Rathmann, he let it begin to slip out, for want of any better conversation,

"Well, yes, at the Fafnir plant I had some experience ..." But Rathmann checked him with an upraised hand.

"Before we go into Caracciola's vast experience in the auto world, he must answer one question which may well have serious bearing on the future of his career." Rudi looked at him blankly. The man moved too fast from subject to subject to follow on an empty stomach.

"And that question is ..." He paused dramatically. "Have you had lunch? No? Then you must follow me at once," Rathmann decided, moving as he spoke to doff his working smock, donning an elegant, if slightly out of date, coat and grabbing a silver-topped cane.

"Now," he announced, "we are ready to settle the future of young Caracciola, lately come forth from the Rhine country. You can leave your bag. The dolls will watch over it for you, the little monsters."

As they made their way toward neighborhoods where an investor might think seriously about placing a restaurant, Rudi let himself be carried along by Rathmann's energetic chatter as it flipped without warning from subject to subject, from real estate to politics to botany to cooking, with equal ease and authority. Here, Rudi realized, would be a guide to Dresden like few others. Rathmann's well-crafted gaiety made the morning seem much more hopeful to a young man without prospects in the depths of Europe's worst economic depression in memory. But with a character like Rathmann around, things seemed suddenly possible, even probable. Big Things.

All at once, as they strode purposefully toward better neighborhoods, Rathmann dove without warning in through a thick door covered with deep old carving. Rudi jumped to catch the door before it closed and found himself in another century.

A dark, low-ceilinged beer hall jammed with equally dark figures bustling about in silhouette carrying huge trays of beer. With arms like pythons the barmaids ferried amazing numbers of steins back and forth with one hand. It was not a place for the uninitiated, Rudi realized as Rathmann made his way expertly through the maze of activity toward a table near the back. They arrived at a well-polished, tobacco-stained, initial-carved table where there already sat a half dozen young men with expectant faces. Rathmann made his entrance.

"Gentlemen, this is Caracciola! A good Rhinelander with an Italian name who has recently made his way from …?

"Remagen," Rudi put in.

"Remagen, where he was engaged in …?"

"I, uh, worked at the Fafnir plant …."

There was an expectant pause. The Student-Prince-operetta atmosphere spurred on by Rathmann's ever so slightly surreal commentary on life, and the first sip of some good beer on a very empty stomach, all worked to loosen Rudi's tongue.

"And then there was … I had a little … trouble."

"Aha!" Rathmann crowed. "Now we're getting to the real saga! Labor-relation problems I guess?"

"No, I hit a Belgian officer."

There was a sudden silence, and Rudi wondered if he'd stuck his foot in his mouth. Who knew what the local politics were? The group exchanged silent looks and then began slamming their beer mugs on the table top with enthusiastic approval.

"Better and better!" Rathmann crowed over the noise. "Now, to earn a rather substantial luncheon we will demand that you tell us the tale without stinting detail, for we are very patient listeners when it comes to stories about bashing Belgian officers and most of us here have the time, unfortunately, for a very leisurely lunch hour."

Given the floor, Rudi told his story, stopping when interrupted for more details by the audience, their mouths generally full. His tale was a great success, broken into repeatedly with shouts of "bravo!" and "encore!" Then it was time for Rudi to meet the group, a mixture of bright young faces, generally in the throes of dealing with their shared fate of not being able to match their careers to the promise of their breeding and education.

There was Kleeberg, whom Rathmann introduced somewhat vaguely as a "businessman"; Scholz, who actually had a job in a bank; and Prickel, whose claim to fame seemed to be that he'd raced a car in a local event.

"And you, Caracciola," Rathmann broke in impatiently, "What do you mean to do with your bright young life?"

And once again Rudi heard that strange far-off voice coming from somewhere inside him, as though he were listening to someone else. "I want to drive Grand Prix," the voice said for a second time. "If I can't do that, I don't care what I do."

No one laughed, as his brother had, but there was a look of serious concern around the table. The lad was either seriously touched in the head, or there was more that they hadn't heard about. Considering his exploit with the Belgian officer, the group gave Rudi the benefit of the doubt and pursued the subject in a serious vein.

"Have you had any racing experience?"

"Well, I drove a Fafnir at the Opel circuit."

"Did you do any good?"

"I won my class."

"A win in his first outing! Gentlemen, we may have a budding Ascari or a Werner here on our hands."

"Prickel came in fourth in a field of six," Scholz announced, slapping Prickel on the back proudly.

"After two of the cars dropped out," Kleeberg added gleefully. "And then in the final, he lost the keys to the car just before the start!"

Rathmann took the floor with a solemn raise of his hand.

"Before our champion of the Opel course, Herr Caracciola, here, can make his impression on the Mercedes team manager, he must have a way to keep body and soul together, in a word — a job. Am I correct?" He addressed this last to Rudi, who nodded gravely.

"If he had connections at Fafnir, why not write to them for a position here in Dresden as soon as he can?" Kleeberg, the practical-thinker, suggested.

"As soon as he can!? He'll write to them now!" Rathmann said, summoning the waitress to bring them pen and paper so a letter could be drafted on the spot.

"My dear General *Direktor*," Rathmann began to dictate, as Scholz took it down.

"Fafnir only has a *Direktor*, not a General *Direktor*," Rudi corrected.

"Never mind. Leave it be. It will flatter the man." And so a letter, with all the tact and flourish of a diplomatic communiqué, was sent to the Dresden office of Fafnir. And in a short time, oddly enough, a reply came back.

"Herr Caracciola, ... So on and so forth, blah, blah, blah." Rathmann read at a later luncheon, editing as he went, "We would be happy to engage your particular sales talents, blah, blah blah ... but since, judging from your letter, you have such well-placed connections in Dresden, we feel that a guarantee or salary would be redundant, due to your obvious sales capabilities."

"Maybe we overdid the local-connections part," Kleeberg muttered.

"Nevertheless, Caracciola now has his foot now firmly in the door. From this point it will be up to his natural tact and courtly good looks to make sure that his sales career flourishes."

Unfortunately, however, a combination of lack of sales experience and natural reluctance to place himself at the whims of potential customers hampered Rudi's progress into the world of sales. He got a cheap room with the money big brother had allotted for just such a purpose, and then he spent the days visiting the homes of the rich to leave his calling card with a polite suggestion that if they ever needed a new Fafnir they should look him up. It wasn't enough, he found, as the weeks went by while his roll of bills from big brother shrank, and still no sales took place.

Then Rudi got word from a butcher that he could use a new Fafnir. Rudi payed him a visit and discovered that sales could be amazingly simple. The butcher was unconcerned about optional extras — or even haggling over the price, for that matter. He seemed anxious to place his order and volunteered to pay full price in cash on the spot. Simple thing, this sales business.

Rudi proudly placed the order on the sales manager's desk. Within minutes he was summoned into the director's office.

"What kind of moron signed a contract setting a price for later delivery?" he shouted at Rudi, who sensed that something had gone wrong from the man's fury.

"Have you never heard of inflation?!" the director continued. "By the time your butcher takes delivery this price you quoted him will just about pay for the headlights! Didn't it seem at all odd that a butcher would want to pay cash for a Fafnir?!"

In further discussions about racing at Rathmann's Round-Table, Rudi steered the conversation away from the possibility of his driving a Fafnir in competition again.

Then one day Prickel arrived at the table with an air of excitement.

"I've got something for you, Caracciola," he said. It was an article about an upcoming local race for small cars, April 3, 1923.

"Unless they make it a foot race, it's not going to do me much good," Rudi moaned.

"I think I can get you a car," Kleeberg chimed in.

"And what will that cost me?"

"Nothing," Kleeberg explained. The car belonged to an old war-buddy. A little sportscar, one of the thousands that are all but unheard of today, called the "Ego."

The next weekend Rudi made his way to Chemnitz to meet Wuesthoff, Kleeberg's army buddy.

Wuesthoff had the manner of a young feudal baron and the financial resources of a paperboy. Still, he was all sportsman and volunteered his little car without hesitation for the race. There was only one problem: the condition that the car was in at the moment made it a contender fit only to race funeral-processions. "Better take it by the factory and have them take a look at it."

Rudi was thoughtful. Where would he be able to drum up money for a refit that could make their car competitive? He began to rehearse his reasons why the factory should rebuild the car on credit.

When Rudi arrived at what was called a factory by the people building the little Egos, the manager had already been called by Wuesthoff and was waiting for him.

"So you're our champion for the Sunday race? You've got courage, I must say. But what about the money?"

Rudi had worked out a plan whereby he would be able to pay back the cost of the work from the prize money he won. He opened his mouth to propose his plan, but the manager broke in, "Never mind. It can happen to all of us." With a wave of his hand dismissing all hope of getting paid properly for their work on the car, the manager explained a plan of his own: if Rudi won, the work would be free. If he did, he'd have to pay for half of the cost of the parts.

Rudi decided to live at the factory through the renovation process to learn what he could and help where he could. One of the mechanics, a cheerful boy named Schultz, who was from Berlin, was appointed his riding mechanic. After a critical turn around Rudi's Ego, Schultz said helpfully, "When you see the other cars in the race, you can sleep in peace. Man … I tell you — iron bathtubs on wheels!"

He was right. The track, an oval-banked affair shaped like a huge bowl, was filled with spidery little cars with strange names like "Coco" and "Omicron."

The drivers were just as fantastically dressed, each in what he imagined was his best approximation of what a really skilled driver should look like. Before the war, the first generation of drivers had not the slightest idea how a race driver should look or dress, and didn't care. That first generation of drivers was, for the most part, adventurers who just happened to be racing one of those new automobile contraptions that day — large, muscle-bound men with a history of taking daring chances in all sorts of pioneering machinery, from transcontinental balloons to fighting off pirates in sailing ships. But this new generation was different. They had grown up with the vision of race drivers in their heads from early childhood. Rudi's generation was as romanced by the vision of "becoming a race driver" as they were by the dream of the actual act of racing. Time would show which ones "wanted to be race drivers" and which ones "wanted to race."

That afternoon the race paddock was filled with both types, all in fantastically romantic garb. Some did not take off their goggles even when stopping for a snack.

The most imposing of the figures around the starting grid was a dark, wiry character with an impudent upturned moustache straight from a moralist's melodrama — Engineer Niedlich. Niedlich's car snarled louder than all the others combined. Niedlich's looks toward newcomers like Rudi were withering, his comments to his hangers-ons, sneering. Niedlich believed wholeheartedly in psyching-out your competition.

Rudi, baby-faced and courtly as always, listened avidly to the talk around the pits, the strategies, the tricks of the course. A "Patzenhofer Brauerei" sign at the rim of the track was where drivers set up their line for the banked turn. Some began their swing down onto the straight at the "P" and some at the "A" in Patzenhofer.

Because of the large turn-out of cars, the race had been divided into two heats with the best cars to run in the final. Niedlich was strutting back and forth like a caged lion, arms folded, waiting for the first heat. He climbed into his car, which, in the interests of aerodynamics, looked more like an upturned boat than an auto, its exhaust pipe pointing backward like a cannon. Rudi was glad he was in the second heat and didn't have to go against this dangerous-looking rival in his first drive.

The cars roared off in a blinding cloud of mixed smoke and steam, Niedlich shooting into the lead and going on the offense at once. The race was Niedlich's all the way, as he made certain everyone understood by strutting around the pits afterwards, talking loudly to his men.

Next it was Rudi's turn. It seemed as if all the city had come out to watch the race. The boys from the Round-Table had arrived, of course. "Just to console you later," as Kleeberg put it.

As he slid behind the wheel Rudi felt strangely like he used to when called on the carpet for some offense or other at school. He had studied how the cars in the first heat, looking like bugs in a bowl, would rise toward the rim of the banked turn, and then swoop down like birds at the straights. Dramatic, Rudi decided, but not smart. Since his car was scarcely capable of today's freeway speeds, he decided to take the shorter route down from the top.

They started, again amid an almost impossible amount of smoke to come from that few cars. Rudi held the accelerator down and steered for the middle, even around the turns. It seemed to work, for lap after lap they powered on past the rest until Schultz was yelling in Rudi's ear to slow down because there was no one left to pass.

They pulled into the pits after the heat. They were cheered by the other pits, and a newspaper reporter came up to find out how to spell "Caracciola." But under the hood, things looked less rosy. Oil was overheating and spraying from the valve stems.

"You're going to have to pump air into the crankcase," Rudi told Schultz, who nodded with resignation.

The starter, looking like a bug on its hind legs in his cutaway coat, readied himself to drop the starting flag for the final. Rudi was next to Niedlich, who refused to return Rudi's friendly nod. It was straight out of a silent melodrama — but real. The bug dropped the flag and they raced off through the starting cloud, Niedlich's car roaring and smoking like a portable volcano, Rudi sticking to the middle line that had made the first win seem so easy. Why hadn't the others taken this shorter line as well?

Schultz sweated and panted at his pumping job. Rudi checked in the mirror — the little Ego was gasping for breath and doing its best. He stepped on the gas harder and a competitor began to fall behind, disappearing in the smoke. Next it was Niedlich falling behind, and then out of sight. Rudi's heart pounded like a drum in his ears, even over the racket. He felt a pounding, then, on his arm. It was Schultz.

"I can't keep it up!"

Niedlich reappeared in the mirror again, hovering menacingly. "You're going to have to!" Seeing Niedlich nearing, Schultz got back to work. They were reaching the "P" in Patzenhofer when Niedlich was at the "A."

Schultz, fading at his task, asked what lap it was. They couldn't agree. The bug walked out at the finish line with the flag. He waved it. Thank God! The finish!

"You see, I told you it was lap thirty-eight!" Schultz was saying, rubbing his arm as they coasted to a stop. Before they had time to crawl out of the Ego a crowd had poured over the car, shaking their hands, patting them on the back. It was too loud to understand anyone, but the message was clear: they'd won the day!

Just then the manager of the Ego factory swam through the crowd and embraced Rudi, "Fabulous, my boy! Just fabulous! If we ever start a racing department, you can come drive for us." Niedlich's car was thundering to a stop near them. Niedlich was grousing loudly about his mechanic leaving the parking brake on. Then he disappeared in the crowd, which seemed relieved that someone could finally beat Niedlich to the finish.

Rathmann and the whole Round-Table arrived. Rathmann started a speech about how Rudi had proved himself to be a real Dresdener that day, but he was carried off by the tide of the crowd, and Rudi was sent off, laden with flowers, to drive a victory lap. Flowers were thrown, hitting Rudi on the head. It was a lap Rudi would never forget, even though few would recognize the names of the cars, the course, or the drivers in just a few years. Schultz said it was the second happiest moment of his life.

The car was waved through a tunnel to the impound area, and it was suddenly quiet. A shadowy figure stepped out of the darkness and stood in the path of the car. “One moment, please,” the figure said. A formal protest had been lodged against their victory.

Rudi was nonplussed. What did he say? Protest? The official was not in a position to say who had lodged the protest, only that they must follow him to where the engine of the Ego could be stripped to check for infractions of the rules. Rudi was not familiar with the rules, nor was he familiar with his car. For all he knew, they might well have been driving under false pretenses.

Measuring devices were lowered into the cylinders, then one of the officials made a motion of regret to someone behind Rudi. Rudi turned and saw a glimpse of Niedlich disappearing around the corner. The officials apologized to Rudi, and, bowing like puppets, disappeared.

From joy to shock — and then back to joy again. They were all very young, with no time for regrets or grudges. And the Round-Table lads had won a whole barrel of beer by betting on their boy’s talents. All the world was mirth and triumph as the men of the Round-Table set off to drink the prize they had won through their faith in their newest member.

Chapter 4

The Motor Show Speech

Hitler had witnessed first hand a lot of changes in warfare in his four-and-a-half years as a frontline courier. He'd seen the difference the tank had made. But he'd also grasped that the tank, as fast and effective an attacker as it is, can just as quickly lose the ground it has just won if it doesn't have close support of supply trucks to replenish it and to carry the infantry at the attacking speed of the tank. Tanks without ample truck support couldn't keep what they had so quickly won.

Hitler also saw that the average German was no match for the average American when it came to keeping those machines running. With a vast number of American soldiers coming from a youth spent tinkering with jalopies and mechanized farm equipment, they often knew just how to jimmy the carburetor or fiddle with the distributor to get the thing running again. Even in the thirties when Hitler took power, there was one car for every six Americans, but only one car for every 211 Germans. The German youth simply hadn't the exposure to get a chance to tinker and as a result, in war, when a German tank or truck faltered and stopped, the typical German soldier threw up his hands in frustration and abandoned it. With the Americans it had been a different story — with some units coming back from battle with forty percent more trucks than they originally set out with. This simple statistic could turn a war, Hitler realized. But there were other ways he could benefit from what Ford had demonstrated with his Model-T.

Without a road system to give drivers a great freedom of choice, the Model-T couldn't have had the impact it did have on America. In this situation, the great boom in the number of cars in the U.S. sparked a popular demand for new pavement.

Freed up under the new maximum-weight formula, the supercharged 1934 Mercedes straight-eight was something to give the Italian teams pause for thought: double overhead cams, four valves per cylinder, 3.36 litres, roller-beaing crank, sodium-cooled valves producing about 314 horsepower (almost 60 horsepower more than the Alfas).

photo: Mercedes Benz

In Germany, Hitler had neither the number of cars nor the popular support for the creation of a freeway network throughout Germany. In fact, there was an established opposition to stop the spread of the auto to the masses, as well as the spread of freeways over Germany.

The automobile could give Hitler other ways to grab the public's undying loyalty as well — the kind of loyal support one would need to pull off a few awkward maneuvers he had in mind, and still keep power. Hitler had long been an avid Grand Prix racing fanatic, and when he had a chance, as time went on, to meet his racing heroes, he astounded them with the wealth of detail he could remember about racing incidents they themselves had often completely forgotten about. He knew at first hand the passions that car racing could raise in a watching public. He knew the immense crowds that Grand Prix racing had drawn, and he recognized an unparalleled chance for Nazi pageantry when he saw one. He had also chafed for years at the sight of Mussolini publicizing the all-triumphant image of Italian technology through the simple and inexpensive means of throwing a little government money at the best racing team in Italy and letting it do the rest.

Mussolini was himself a flying enthusiast, a car-lover, and a supporter of sports. (When the fledgling Auto-Club of Brescia had timidly phoned Il Duce, on a whim, to see if they could shut down a thousand miles of public roads for a race they had planned, Mussolini had answered on the spot, "If you want the roads — take them!") And when his two fastest stars began a rivalry that was wrecking cars and letting other countries walk off with the prizes, he lost no time in sending telegrams reminding them that if they didn't forget their personal problems and start winning for Italy again, there'd be trouble.

When Hitler finally came to power after watching year after year of Italian government-supported triumphs on the track, he knew the time had come for an all-conquering German Grand Prix racing team to appear on the scene and start to accomplish much the same thing. After a steady diet of humiliation, frustration, and mortifying defeats, Germany could well stand to remember what victory tasted like again — even if it were only victories on the race track. A winning team could focus public attention on new heroes, new triumphs, and new Party Programs linked closely with a successful new way of living — in his "New Germany."

There would be another, less talked-about benefit of a Grand Prix racing program — one to which those in the sport of racing are loathe to refer. The Treaty of Versailles had strictly limited aero-science

A package full of new technology desperately needed for fighter aircraft: the Mecredes V-12 racing engine cut new trails in two-stage supercharging, high-load lubrication, metallurgy, fuel delivery, and cooling techniques. The double-row twin cam, four-valve powerplant cranked out about 483 horsepower.

photo: author

development in Germany. Despite all sorts of tricky maneuvering and serial-number-switching programs, Germany's aero-manufacturers were still under close Allied supervision. Anything that looked like a design for an engine that would form the core of a fighter plane was out of the question and would have been spotted immediately by Allied inspectors. The engine is what makes or breaks fighter aircraft, and without a lot of cutting-edge development in metallurgy, high-performance lubricants, supercharging, and streamlined overall packaging, Germany was out of luck as far as developing new fighter planes. Which was just what Versailles had in mind, of course.

But all of these components could be openly developed if the engine were being built for a racecar. Sports historians are hesitant to draw this link, but the fact remains that all of the crucial technologies needed for aero-engines were brought to the highest level yet seen under Hitler's new racing programs. Germany's later successful fighters were powered largely by engines made by the same manufacturers that had participated in Hitler's racing programs. And at least one competition car was powered by an engine that fit directly into a fighter aircraft.

In the spring of 1933 Hitler was taking some broad chances — placing his bets, with the absolute control of Germany as the stakes. Besides his social-motorization plans, Hitler was placing a lot of faith on two other new technologies: the airplane, and the world's first electronic mass medium, the radio.

The airplane he was using as a new way to leapfrog the nation, far outdistancing the traditional campaign-train politicians. However, it was his "Volksradio" that could make or break Hitler's grab for a loyal public, not just in his southland, but across the whole nation.

Here, the future of Social-Motorization, as part of what can be thought of as his "Landsberg Agenda," hung on a single issue: the Volksradio. When we watch films of Hitler's style of speech-making, we can easily see how much of the infectious fervor of his speeches came from his visuals: the slow-burning resentment-scowl, the impassioned pleadings for justice table-poundings, the furious call to action arm-waving. Would these elements translate with only the audio of his spoken word? He'd shown he could rouse huge audiences to a fever in live performance. Could he do the same over the scratchy, low-fi radio speakers of the day?

Normally Hitler preferred to give speeches at night, when the flames of bonfires, spectacular lighting and the dance of shadows added to the magic topspin. How would this croaking voice sound, heard on a warm afternoon in a beer garden with ready hecklers sitting around nearby and no Nazis to knock their heads if they got noisy? Would his message sound over-impassioned or, worse yet, downright silly?

Hitler scheduled his Social-Motorization speech, as soon as he took office, to be given at the Berlin Motor Show only a few weeks into the spring. His Motor Show Speech would tell all.

In the midst of all the purging, nationalizing, parliament-closing, labor-union de-fanging, banker-bashing, Commie-attacking, and "Enabling-Act"-preparing of that spring, Hitler took time out to make sure the setting at the Motor Show was dramatically decorated in the best Nazi pagan-baroque style. There would be an in-person audience at the show. If they were given the full treatment, it was hoped that their passion would then be transmitted over the radios to the folks at home listening in their quiet corners.

He began this pivotal speech by reminding Germany of what a rich culture of arts and technology they possessed, equal to any on the face of the Earth, and that all great civilizations, from the Incas to the Romans, were judged by the sophistication of their communicating road system.

It might be true that in California a new kind of nonstop roadway traffic flowing through on-ramps and overpasses had proved successful. And it was also true that Mussolini had started his Autostrada system ten years before. But for his Motor Show Speech Hitler now drew a picture of a network of autobahns linking the far corners of Germany with fast motor transport — as if it had never been thought of before.

He went on to flesh out this idea with visions of young families able to take their kids for an outing in the fresh country air without the usual rush and confusion of rail travel which, he'd always said since his Landsberg days, left people more tired out after a day of "rest" than they were before.

This brought up the subject of what Germany should be taking these jaunts in. He proposed a people's car: simple, economical, of usable size and speed, and cheap (the price of a middle-level motorcycle). In his concept of the people's car, Hitler would again steal a lot from Henry Ford — emphasizing simplicity, good quality materials, and a reasonably full-scale format. England, France, and Italy had all experimented with people's cars, but these tended to be miniatures of rich men's cars that really weren't cheap to produce and weren't really that usable in real life. Hitler's car should be able to carry a family of two adults and two children plus luggage, safely and economically all day at 100 kilometers an hour. Better aerodynamics than Europe's traditional cars would help this car's gas economy, he declared.

Next on Hitler's docket came the youth of the nation — a motor-starved youth. Because the automobile, even in 1930s Germany, was for the most part still a rich man's toy and convenience, not many of Germany's youth had the opportunity for up-close-and-personal tinkering. Car-fluency was what Hitler wanted, and the N.S.K.K. (National Socialist Kraft Korps) would make this happen by creating a youth-oriented organization to make both cars and motorcycles available for training and hands-on tinkering. The Korps would organize events for chapter members, creating a pipeline for young talent so that a lad could realistically think about joining the Korps and ending up an internationally known Grand Prix champion (or at least, know how to change his own spark plugs). Just as the Hitler Youth had been lured by the chance of owning their own daggers to face the world with, Korps members would be presented with their own crash helmet, a personal, tangible proof of their participation in this romantic new adventure of the motor age.

Then came the announcement that Hitler was taking Germany car racing. In the far-off days before the Great War, Germany (with Mercedes as the standard-bearer) had flourished on the big tracks of Europe, beating the huge Italian Fiats and leaving the previously triumphant French team literally in tears after the German 1, 2, 3 victory at the Grand Prix of France just weeks before war broke out.

But in the upheaval and chaos after the Great War, Germany's racing performance had been spotty at best. Mussolini, grasping the notion that racing not only bred better cars that all Europe wanted to buy, but also sold the high standards of Italian technology through Europe, had spent taxpayer money to make sure Italian talent and technology had a good chance of winning. The high-tech designs of the Italians were making racing an expensive proposition for private auto manufacturers — but it was still chickenfeed compared to a whole nation's tax income. Throwing money at teams like Alfa Romeo — managed by a talent like Enzo Ferrari — had taken hold and was paying back big dividends to the Italian economy.

And by 1933 the Italians were emerging as almost impossible to beat. Mercedes had been forced to cut back its racing schedule as the

Italians escalated their racing budgets and the Depression took hold. And then the unheard-of had happened: Mercedes had dropped out of auto racing altogether. It had been a bitter time for Germany's racing fans — and Hitler had long been one of these.

The new Führer, as he announced in his Motor Show speech, would level the playing field, fund up-to-date new German designs, and develop powerful new German machines to blast the Italians off the track. Driven by the heroic youth of Germany, they would bring the old tradition of German racing excellence back to a long-disappointed public.

New roads (and all the construction contracts that could come from this across the nation), a new car (and all the support industry it could spawn), a new sporting club for the motor-starved youth, and a new team to cheer on the tracks of Europe: it was a full plate of exciting programs, provided anyone bothered to follow through on them. Hitler made it easy for his opponents to see what he was up to, if they'd only open their ears. After he'd outlined his Motorization Plan he added candidly, "Without the automobile programs there is no future for National Socialism."

It was a new kind of speech for Hitler. No scapegoats, no looming threats — just positive step-by-step programs to build an exciting New Germany. "Fear" had always been his favorite motivational tool. How would "hope" do as a substitute?

Chapter 5

Charly

A few weeks after Rudi's victory for the Round-Table gang, the owner of the Rudi's racer did another favor for him by wangling a driver's test at no less than Mercedes Benz.

As a result of Wuestoff's second favor, Rudi was sitting in the outer reception area at Mercedes where a beautiful and efficient receptionist eyed him with distrust as he sat waiting his turn to see Direktor Herzing. Rudi had always had one ambition, to drive for Mercedes — and now Direktors Herzing and Gross were discussing his life's ambition as if it were a new brand of rubber hose to be chosen or discarded.

Rudi finally got up the nerve to imitate Rathmann's approach and push himself forward. "Would you mind, Miss, er ..."

"Schroeder. And no I won't disturb the Direktor. He is never to be disturbed during a meeting."

If Rudi could just be given a chance to plead his own case. Surely they would recognize he was no idle sportsman or fame-seeker. They'd see how much he hungered to drive the big cars. He'd ... The telephone rang, the receptionist made replies with studied ambivalence, without dropping a hint of what the call was about.

"You're to go downstairs to meet Herr Werner at the main entrance."

Werner? The great Werner!? One of the titans of the first generation-drivers who'd battled those high-wheeled old monsters to incredible speeds. When Rudi got to the gate it was raining. Damn. A driver-test in the rain.

The great Werner was solemn, as though he were a man who would never laugh again. He motioned Rudi toward a bare chassis with nothing on it but a steering wheel and a couple of seats sitting in the rain. This would be Rudi's test machine, a bare chassis.

Second time around: Rudi proves his 1926 German Grand Prix win was no accident by repeating it in '28. He's seen here with the great Christian Werner after the event.

photo: Mercedes Benz

With no fenders or windshield, the rain was more than a nuisance. Rudi decided there was little to lose. He'd let the car hang out on the corners, power through the puddles like a tank, and give the old man a ride he wouldn't forget. Werner gave short signals which way to turn, and Rudi just let the car fly, not expecting much from this rainy fiasco.

They pulled up back at the gate. Werner got down and with a simple "Good God!" he headed up to the meeting rooms. Rudi looked around. That was it? He couldn't leave without some indication. He yelled after Werner as Werner made his way up the back stairs. "How was it?"

Werner turned at this impudence and looked down a moment to Rudi. "I'll tell them upstairs," he said, and he disappeared through the back door.

Rudi was beside himself. He couldn't face Fraulein Schroeder again, so he went instead to the guard at the gate and convinced him to call her. She said they were in conference and were not to be disturbed under any circumstance, and that Rudi could wait at the gate. The guard whipped up some hot coffee and began to gossip.

"That Werner is a great fellow. But his wife died not long ago. He's terribly unhappy." Toward closing time the phone rang. The guard turned to Rudi.

"You're to go right up. But hurry. They're closing up."

Rudi ran up the steps and found his way in through the upholstered doors to where Direktors Herzing and Gross were just putting on their topcoats. Gross caught sight of Rudi and boomed in his loud voice, "There's the boy! Well, Werner was quite pleased with you. You can start in Dresden — a hundred marks a month. As a salesman."

Rudi's jaw dropped. Back to salesman! He was about to speak when Direktor Herzing shot him a warning look. Gross slapped Rudi on the back and the party began to make its way down the steps.

"But I wanted to be a race driver!" Rudi whispered to Direktor Herzing.

"Don't be an idiot," Herzing shot back under his breath. "Racing is no profession. First be an employee of Mercedes. Then one day perhaps you can drive as much as you like."

Rudi walked out into the rain, not knowing whether to be elated or depressed. His driving must have impressed Werner, the Great Werner. If he'd only been able to read the future, Rudi would have seen himself hailed in years to come as the "Regenmeister" — the

Rainmaster. Time would show that no one, not even Rudi's racing heroes, would be able to see through the rain and handle a car faster in the wet than Rudi. But that was somewhere in a future that Rudi couldn't read. On the day of his test, Rudi had cursed the rain and was disappointed in his reward for the drive.

Rudi had been pacing the mirror-polished floor of the downtown showroom in his best suit for almost three months and still he'd not made a sale. The showroom was at the best address, right across a fashionable street from the European Hotel. The customers (especially the ladies) seemed to like Rudi's courtly manner and his soft-spoken knowledgeability about cars. But every time he'd get a customer into position for the kill, one of the older salesmen would swoop down and carry off the contract to the manager's office. No one on the staff seemed concerned about Rudi's poor sales record, except Rudi.

The other salesmen were worldly young men of "good family" who were well experienced in the workings of the city. Rudi would listen as they whiled away the slow hours by appraising the women that came by the showroom windows. They seemed to know the talents and challenges of each passing woman at a glance. Rudi wondered at the extent of their experience. They weren't that much older than he was himself, after all.

Almost every day Rudi would see a strikingly beautiful young woman emerging from the European. She would smile at the porter as she got into large cars, walking with an open, graceful gait of confidence past the shops and boutiques, and meeting substantial-looking older men. One day Rudi spotted her gazing idly out of her apartment window up above the showroom, and he fell into a sort of reverie, pausing on every detail of her look — without realizing how long he'd been staring at her. She'd obviously noticed Rudi gaping openly at her as if he'd been behind a one-way mirror. Caught in the act, Rudi flustered for some sort of explanation to account for his stare, but the best move he could think of was to wave stupidly and openly. Amazingly, she waved back and smiled a pretty smile.

Heinz von Berck, one of the older salesmen who seemed to appreciate the same sort of women Rudi liked, knew some facts about this woman: her father owned a popular restaurant in town; she was seeing a number of well-established older men preparatory to the usual sort of marriage into a well-heeled existence that was the norm in

Germany for beautiful young women. Her name was Charlotte, but she was known as "Charly."

That did it. The perfect name for the perfect woman, chic and adventuresome. Rudi put his cards on the table and asked von Berck, how could he meet such a woman? Heinz had a plan ready at his fingertips. Every Wednesday afternoon at the European there was a tea-dance where the young men and women of good families could get together and look one another over. Heinz and Rudi would go to this dance, they would sit near this Charly woman, and Heinz would make appropriate advances toward Charly while Rudi stayed in the background — the man of mystery.

"That's how you do it, if you want to get a girl crazy for you," Heinz said. Rudi listened with the faith of a novitiate. Heinz knew what he was talking about, Rudi was certain. Wednesday it rained, business was nonexistent, and the two young men sneaked off to the tea-dance. Charly was there, and Heinz skillfully got them a table nearby. He played with his gold bracelet, he sat elegantly, he looked over the pickings for that afternoon, he consulted his wristwatch with a sigh.

Eventually Heinz got up and made a gracious request for a dance and Charly, flashing a brilliant smile that sent a pang of envy through Rudi, accepted. They made a chic couple on the dance floor and Rudi sat a little sullenly as it began to dawn on him that just possibly he'd made a terrible mistake enlisting the help of someone as good-looking as Heinz. Then the music stopped, and Heinz sat back down with Rudi, mopping his brow.

"The next dance is yours, Caracciola. Make the most of your big chance."

Rudi got up immediately, before he had a chance to think about it and any fear could set in. Shaky at the knees he made a gruff offer to dance, and then Charly was in his arms. The vision at the window was very close — too close for Rudi to think.

What to talk about? He hadn't even thought of this point. Cars. Cars were his most fluent subject. With luck, she might be interested in cars too.

"Do you drive a car too?" he asked, his voice huskier than he wanted it to be.

"No."

Great start. Better push on, nevertheless.

"But you're interested in the automobile sport?"

She hesitated, teasingly. "A little."

The saxophone player stopped his playing, picked up a megaphone and began crooning words of a love song that seemed to pry into Rudi's most private thoughts. He wondered if Charly could see into his very soul as easily as this saxophone player seemed to.

Charly spoke, so near Rudi's ear it startled him,

"But you're a great racing driver, aren't you?"

"So-so," Rudi heard himself say.

"Your friend told me about you."

"He did?" Why couldn't he think of anything better to say!? He was blowing the whole dance with dull answers. The singer crooned on.

"You're not very talkative," she teased.

Once again, the voice that said what Rudi really thought came out of the blue to surprise him.

"I'd like you to watch me racing some day."

"Why?"

"Because then I think you'd have more regard for me." Great, he thought. That's really staying in the background. The aloof man of mystery.

Charly looked him in the face, astonished. Then she laughed in a way that Rudi couldn't read, and they danced together until the music stopped.

"Well, how did it go?" Heinz asked after the battle. Rudi couldn't muster more than a shrug and a wave of the hand. He was quite beyond speech, just for the moment.

As Direktor Herzing had promised, Rudi had been allowed to drive a Mercedes in local weekend events — hill-climbs and club races. He'd done exceptionally well, winning a raft of silver cups and plaques. But now he needed more. You can't support a woman on cups and plaques.

Whenever he had a chance to see Direktor Herzing, Rudi lobbied for a Grand Prix car to drive, but Herzing always shook his head sadly. The big team cars couldn't be experimented with. They were for the old hands. Gradually, almost painfully slowly, the races that Rudi was offered grew in stature.

His next race was for sportscars, winding through the Eifel mountains over the gusty passes. The power of those gusts of wind won the battle, however, and Rudi lost control of the car, which ended up against a tree looking none the better for it. A mess. His first real wreck with a team car. But no one seemed to notice. The mechanics worked all night and had it ready to race again the next day.

Rudi won the German Tourist Trophy and began to be thought of, even by himself, as a professional racing driver. A trip home to Remagen put the icing on the cake, justifying his sister's faith in Rudi. Big brother only harrumphed from behind his newspapers, but the damage had been done and Rudi could never be the butt of his brother's sneers again.

From then on Rudi was allowed to tag along with the big boys, the drivers of the Age of Titans who (and this is corroborated by several sources) would drive nails through table tops with their bare hands to win bets of champagne. Rudi and another of the younger generation, Alfred Neubauer, would simply sit quietly and watch in awe as the evening activities progressed into the realm of apocrypha.

As reserve drivers in attendance, Rudi and Neubauer passed their novitiate in the world of racing. They learned which drinks the drivers expected to have waiting for them, how to battle the bloodthirsty mosquitoes of cheap Italian hotels, what to expect from the all-conquering Italians gods like Ascari, Campari, and the two young motorcycle rivals turned race car drivers, Nuvolari and Varzi.

As his confidence grew professionally, Rudi saw as much of Charly as he could. Slowly, with unnoticed ease, Rudi was dropping the goddess-worship, while Charly was becoming a confidante and much-needed advisor and companion. And to Rudi's amazement it began to become clear that Charly truly valued the company of such a non-established young man in a very precarious profession.

Then came an opportunity that only a hungry young man like Rudi could see. The German Grand Prix in Berlin had been scheduled the same weekend as a race in Spain. The Direktors were determined to build export sales, so the team had been scheduled to race in Spain. This left not one Mercedes to contend for Germany's big prize — the German Grand Prix. Shocking. Rudi went to the beautiful receptionist this time with a name she could recognize. He got past the upholstered door and into Direcktor Herzing's office, where he harangued for two hours about the disgrace of a German Grand Prix without even one Mercedes trying for the prize.

The Direktor relented. There would be two Mercedes made available for the G.P., but they would be raced as private entries. Rudi would get one of them and another driver, Rosenberger, would get the other. If things went wrong, they'd be on their own.

This was the chance for Rudi to show what he could do with frontline equipment. He took a leave of absence from the showroom (to no one's anguish) and rented a cheap hotel room in Berlin to practice the whole week before the race. It rained the whole week, and every night Rudi would return to his room worn out and depressed. Everyone seemed to be turning in faster lap times than he could manage. The Italians, the French, even Rosenberger was faster.

On the last day of practice there'd been an accident just before Rudi arrived at a certain corner. He pulled up to help, but the driver already lay dead on the track, his eyes staring up unblinking into the rain. They covered him, but the sight of the driver's white tennis shoes poking out from under the blanket in the rain stayed with Rudi like a ghost each night. New possibilities began to crowd into Rudi's mind; not of stealing glory from the champions, but of the distinct chance of a crash.

Charly arrived the evening before the race, and Rudi tried to muster up confidence to match her enthusiasm. She'd only seen and heard about the bright spots in his career so far. Had he been able to keep the evening gay? Could he cover up the miserable forebodings he was facing, and the prospect of her coming all that way just to see him fall on his face in his first real test in the big leagues? And that damned rain that just wouldn't stop!

But Sunday morning, race day, dawned bright and clear. The spectacle of the huge crowd, the flags, the marching bands all flew around Rudi's head almost unnoticed in the tension — but still felt. Dr. Porsche, the head designer of the Mercedes racing department, would be in the pits to help in an "unofficial capacity." This would be one of the last races with riding mechanics on a closed circuit and Rudi's mechanic would be Salzer, an old hand who could probably drive as well as Rudi if need be.

The start was incredibly distracting: the noise of a dozen or more racing engines, the crowd, keeping an eye on the tach, another on the flag. There! It had dropped and the first cars were heading off into the turn. But Rudi's car was sitting still! He'd killed the engine. Salzer's yells to jump out and push rocked Rudi out of his mortified trance. What a gaffe! Here in front of the world, Dr. Porsche, Charly.

He jumped back in and popped the clutch. Nothing. Dead still. Another try, the engine caught, Salzer jumped in and they were rolling at least — with the rest of the race gone from sight. Rudi drove on like a mechanical extension of the car, with no life in his actions, his arms suddenly feeling like cement sacks. Someone else would win that day, and all he could do was finish for the sake of the team. By the fourth lap big rain drops splattered on the track and into the windscreen. That's all he needed to perfect the day. Rain.

Lap after dreadful lap, the rain increased. A car slid and plowed into the press stand right in front of him. Who was it? Who cares? Salzer yelled back, Keep driving! The other cars were slowing. Was there a hazard? Just the rain? Rudi speeded back up and began to pass cars one by one.

Another wreck, this time a car plowed into the crowd. Who was it? Keep driving!

Rudi's car begins to chase the leaders, then suddenly the engine begins to sound off-song. A fouled plug. Rudi pulls into the pits and rushes to unscrew plug number one. Hot, hot, hot! He throws it to Dr. Porsche who inspects it. No problem with this one, and Porsche throws it back. Cars race past. The second plug is unscrewed and thrown to Porsche. Go slowly, hands are fluttering involuntarily with tension. The plug is OK. Screw it back in. Relax, go carefully. Unscrew number three, now unscrew number four while he's checking number three. That's smarter! (What an idiot he felt like!) Cars rush past. It's been over a minute already, and his latter-day challenge seems to be going down the drain with each plug that has to be inspected. There are eight in all. Number eight is the culprit, it's replaced. If he'd only started at the other end of the engine!

No time to think, they tear off. But once again they have little chance of doing anything but finishing.

The rain had increased, not eased since he was out before. Crashes seemed frequent, cars were slowing — slowing more than was needed, it seemed to Rudi. They drove on. One of the Mercedes Direktors, the veteran champion Sailer, was waving from the pits. Waving Rudi to speed up, obviously, but Rudi was already pushing hard as he dared in the wet. With no idea where they stood in the field, Rudi drove just to make a good show of it for Mercedes.

Arms like lead, leg muscles trembling, the final lap of what might well be his final Grand Prix after this performance. They rolled to a stop in the pits — and suddenly Rudi felt sodden, trembling, tired.

Direktor Sailer was waving excitedly. A huge wreath appeared from nowhere and was plopped over the cockpit of Rudi's Mercedes. What was this for? What were they saying? About victory? Rudi and Salzer looked at each other in amazement then burst out laughing hilariously. Everything was hilarious: the people slapping them on the back, Direktor Sailer, Dr. Porsche, everything was another excuse to laugh uncontrollably. A wonderful, marvelous fact was beginning to sink in: he was the winner of the German Grand Prix, winner of the first Grand Prix he was able to drive in. "If I can't drive Grand Prix, then I don't care what I do." Rudi's dream had started — and started with a bang.

As the tumultuous crowd began to quiet down a little, Rudi's eyes began to search for Charly. All his worry about her coming to Berlin was for nothing. He'd not only placed well, he'd walked away with the big prize after overcoming problem after problem. It was a race few who saw it would ever forget. But where was Charly? Did she even see his triumph?

Rudi's mood began to darken, and he excused himself from the victory celebrations, much to the team's puzzlement. He went back to his drab little room for some silence to think. But there, with open arms was Rathmann full of more life than he'd ever seen him.

"Rudi, my boy! We're really proud of you!" Rudi was touched by the lack of joking in Rathmann's manner. He was really nothing but proud of his discovery. But where was Charly? Rudi was less than polite to Rathmann as he rolled on with new dreams, ever bigger dreams.

"That's 17,000 marks you've won today, my boy! Now I'm going to sell the doll factory, that'll be another 17,000. We'll open our own Mercedes dealership on the best street in town, Kurfuerstendamm! With the great Rudolf Caracciola selling cars personally. If that doesn't draw the customers, I don't know my city!"

"I'll think it over," Rudi said in a way that led to an awkward pause. Rathmann, puzzled at this black gloom, pulled back, and left quietly. The phone rang. It was Charly.

"Congratulations." The voice was flat, without emotion.

"What's the matter with you?" Rudi pressed.

"Oh … Nothing."

Rudi set up a meeting at a nearby restaurant. When she arrived Rudi could see that Charly had been crying.

"Charly, what's the matter?!"

"Nothing."

"Why did you leave the race?"

She hesitated, then began relating her story in a flat monotone that Rudi hardly recognized.

"I was sitting next to the wife of that French driver who crashed, Chassagne. When he didn't come by on that lap she just stared. I could tell she was praying. The announcement was made, Chassagne had crashed. Chassagne, seriously hurt. Suddenly she began to cry. I never saw anyone cry like that. No sobbing, not a sound. Just tears running down her face. She was white as a sheet. I … just couldn't stand it anymore. I just left."

Rudi was stroking her hand, listening to every word silently.

"Rudi, must you be a racing driver?"

"Yes," Rudi heard that strange voice of his say, "I must."

That day Rudi knew she would spend the rest of her life with him.

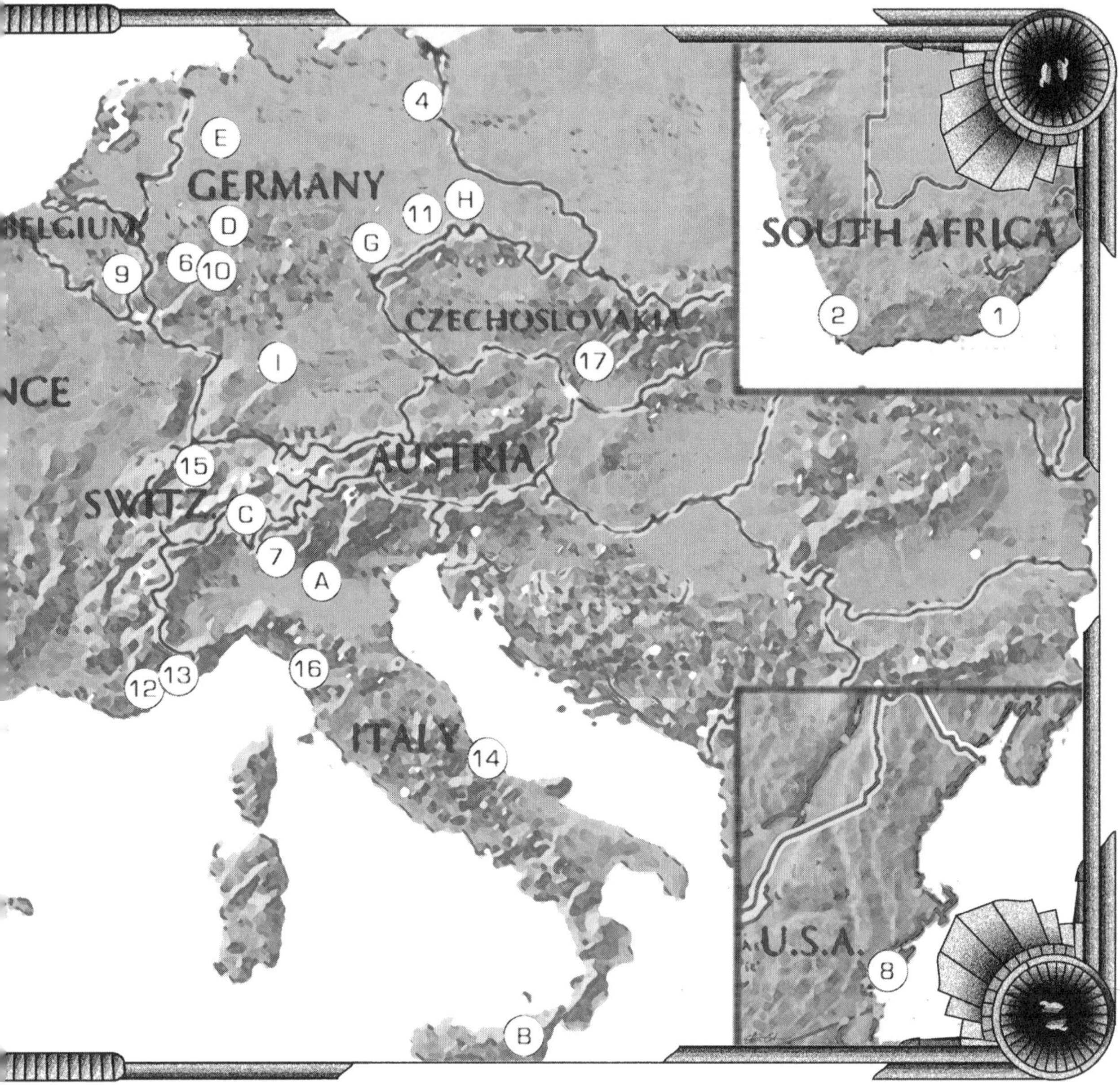

of the Mille Miglia
Florio
eat
ily Hotel
ne Town
se
ory
ind-Table Gang
y
Race

1937 Grand Prix Schedule

1.	January 1:	Grand Prix of South Africa — East London, South Africa
2.	January 16:	Grosvenor Grand Prix — Kapstadt, South Africa
3.	May 9:	Grand Prix of Tripoli — Mellaha, Libya
4.	May 30:	Avusrennen — Berlin, Germany
5.	June 6:	Grand Prix of Rio de Janiero — Gavea, Brasil
6.	June 13:	Eifelrennen — Nürburgring, Adenau, Germany
7.	June 20:	Stadtrennen — Milan, Italy
8.	July 5:	Vanderbilt Cup — Roosevelt Field, New York, U.S.A.
9.	July 11:	Grand Prix of Belgium — Spa, Francorchamps, Belgium
10.	July 25:	Grand Prix of Germany — Nürburgring, Adenau, Germany
11.	August 1:	Deutsche Bergmeisterschaft — Schauinsland, Germany
12.	August 5:	La Turbie Hill Climb — La Turbie, Nice, France
13.	August 8:	Grand Prix of Monaco — Monte Carlo, Monaco
14.	August 15:	Coppa Acerbo — Pescara, Italy
15.	August 22:	Grand Prix of Switzerland — Bremgartenwald, Bern, Switzerland
16.	September 12:	Grand Prix of Italy — Livorno, Italy
17.	September 26:	Grand Prix of Czechoslovakia — Masaryk, Brno, Czechoslovakia
18.	October 2:	Grand Prix of Donington — Donington, England

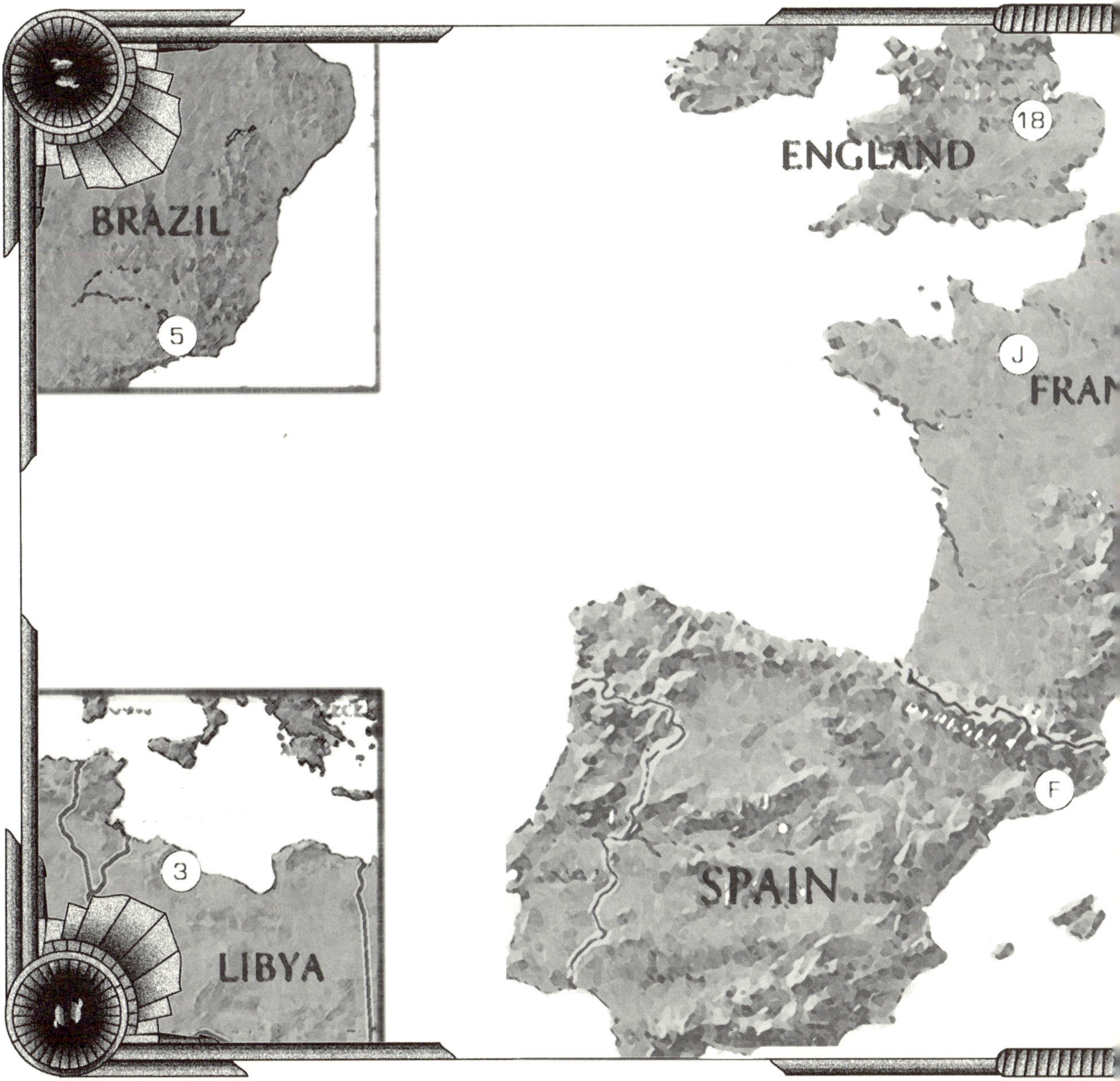

Places in the Book

A.	Brescia:	Start and Finish
B.	Sicily:	Site of the Targ
C.	Lugano:	Caracciola's Ret
D.	Remagen:	Caracciola's Far
E.	Lingen:	Rosemeyer's Ho
F.	Barcelona:	Penya Rhin Cou
G.	Zwickau:	Auto Union Fact
H.	Dresden:	Home of the Ro
I.	Stuttgart:	Mercedes Facto
J.	Le Mans:	Site of 24-Hour

Chapter 6

Casting Call

The morning after the Motor Show Speech, Hitler's severest critics, even the foreign press contingent (including the ever-sensationalist Hearst correspondents) were nonplussed. Something seemed different in the air in Germany, but it was nearly impossible to put your finger on exactly what it was.

Everything looked the same. People still sat at the same cafes reading the same newspapers. The economy was still in shambles, people still out of work, five hundred thousand Communists still carried their cards. Everything seemed pretty much unchanged — except there seemed to be a new look in people's eyes, the look of someone with a secret. Maybe it was the look of a convict quietly planning his jailbreak — the faraway, absentminded look of someone who's just discovered hope, but doesn't want to jinx it by talking about it.

Germany had heard a lot of similar palaver by a lot of well-fed politicians throughout its years of collapse and the public had become gun-shy. Still, it seemed the Motor Show Speech had lit a fuse. Whether there was any powder in the barrel, only Hitler's follow-through would tell. If he really acted on these interesting new promises that seemed to have a lot more life and imagination (and even fun) in them than the usual five-year-plan malarky, then maybe Germany would allow itself to get hopeful. In the meantime, they'd be watching this new Chancellor carefully.

Hitler moved fast while the limelight was still on him, and before his "supporters" had time to mutiny. Meetings with autobahn architect Fritz Todt, cornerstone-laying, ribbon-cutting, all took place quickly and with plenty of press coverage. Hitler's message of quick follow-through was in every newspaper photo, every newsreel sequence, and the message was, "This new guy means business."

Hitler needed someone he could trust, someone with real manhandling abilities to make sure the new N.S.K.K. did its job to keep the motorsports-mad youths in line, to create full blooded racing events, and most of all — to beat the Italians.

At a time when Hitler was discarding old allies of the Munich fiasco-days (sometimes in a very permanent way), he now reached back to call on one of his standbys from the old streetfighting days when the Freikorps was knocking heads with the Communists: Adolf Huhnlein.

Hollywood has spent a lot of effort to perfect the Nazi villain — the brutal linear-thinker who makes us shudder at first sight: a monstrously cool character with unspoken, unspeakable powers of nonrestraint. But one look at Huhnlein's smile tells us that Hollywood still has a long way to go.

Given the chance at an action-based job dealing with the leadership of a spirited slice of Germany's youth, far from a desk, Huhnlein took the job with a fierce loyalty to Hitler's goals. And in this new world of "part-time Nazis," eager to raise their right arm whenever it meant some good would come their way, Huhnlein emerged as one who actually believed in Hitler's early goals. Remaining seemingly forever a lowly major (even though he was often seen in the highest circles), unbribable, energetic, he was everyone's nightmare of the drill sergeant who's really got your number and won't be fooled by any artifice. Huhnlein would be the perfect leader for the N.S.K.K. racing programs — its only leader, as it turned out.

With the autobahns under construction and the N.S.K.K. safely in the hands of Huhnlein, Hitler went car shopping. Specifically, race car shopping. He put through calls to Hans Stuck and Jakob Werlin of Mercedes. It was time to talk technology, and Hitler always loved to show off what he'd learned about cars (though the one thing he never learned about cars was how to drive one).

The summons Dr. Porsche had received in March 1933 was stirring mixed emotions in the renowned designer. It wasn't the first time a head of state had sent emissaries to finesse his technical support. As a buck private in the Great War, young Porsche had been enlisted to drive the Archduke around in a car that young Porsche himself had designed. And more recently had come a call from Stalin. Three Russian engineers had visited Porsche's newly established independent design bureau. Had they come to nose around his tractor designs? (Tractors, a people's car, and race cars were Porsche's three perennial passions.) But the Russians were not the usual idea-beggars that surfaced regularly around the bureau, on the hunt for stray design breakthroughs that might slip out in the natural urge to show off the latest works. They seemed to have something else on their mind. Finally the real reason for their visit surfaced: Stalin wanted Porsche to come to Russia for a look at their plans for huge new industrialization projects. Stalin had no illusions about Russia's position in the world, despite the vast wealth of the Romanovs that had been appropriated. To be a world power Russia had to industrialize at a pace that would make even Japan's rapid catch-up look snail-like. And he needed the best talent to make this dream happen.

Porsche had been shown all, in a tour that would have been the answer to a western spy's dream of thoroughness. He was wined and dined, served sumptuous meals, plied with the finest vodka. And when it came out that he liked beer better, his favorite pilsner was airlifted in by special plane. After he had seen his full, the Russians put their cards on the table: Stalin wanted Porsche as Designer-Supremo to oversee the building of a whole new industrial state — the hydroelectric plants, the car production facilities, the tractor designs. It was the kind of designer's dream that hadn't happened since the Renaissance. An assignment worthy of a Da Vinci. A sure opportunity to make your name part of history.

Porsche had had repeated run-ins with profit-conscious auto-executives who sought to limit his design imagination. In Russia, there would be no profits. No overpreened executives to argue with. No market middle-men to worry about. In Russia there were no bank failures, crippling inflation, market upheavals, or as in Germany, labor strikes. There would be a fine country estate for his family, and plenty of hard currency. With Germany in constant turmoil, car production down, and virtually no racing programs to speak of, Porsche's future in Germany was anything but rosy. He'd been forced to go on his own to escape crippling corporate design restrictions, but business was slow. And now he'd had to hock the family homestead just to keep his small, loyal staff away from starvation.

But then Porsche realized there was one point not mentioned in Stalin's offer. Would there be a racing program to put some muscle into car development? Porsche knew how essential racing had been to the development of safe, dependable cars. Racing was a testbed that laboratory methods simply couldn't equal. Even today we have racing to thank for the rear-view mirror, seat restraints, roll-protection, energy-absorbing frame structures, disc brakes, close-ratio gearing, fuel injection, road-gripping tires, advanced suspension handling — practically everything we demand in cars today. In a racing-conscious country like Germany we have the Audi, the BMW, the Mercedes, the Porsche. Behind the former Iron Curtain, where no manufacturers raced, we had the Trabant, a crude joke of a design.

But the Soviets choked at the image of a People's Grand Prix Team rubbing elbows with the decadent bourgeois idlers at the Monte Carlo Grand Prix. There could be no racing in Russia. And, with a wistful sigh, Porsche allowed there'd be no Dr. Porsche to bring the Soviets into the twentieth century with his designs. Besides, he'd most likely get homesick for the old German *Gemütlichkeit*. So it was back to Germany, with all its industrial problems and highly uncertain financial future.

Ever since his days as this century's first automotive design prodigy, Porsche had had problems with management. As a lad in his twenties he'd designed a forward-looking design for a car that is only now regaining popularity: a hybrid gas-electric four-wheel drive design that is now being revived because of its great low-emissions potential. It was also very smooth with a quiet drive, no gears to shift, and amazing traction. It won the Gold Medal at the 1900 Paris Exposition for the lad, and soon all the right people — the royal family, even the Rothschilds — were driving the early "Lohner-Porsche."

After the Great War the young designer had designed the legendary SSK-Mercedes that is still a collector's dream, a car that made what racing history was made by Germany in the twenties. But he was a man impatient with compromising executives and over-scientific engineers who'd balk at the idea of actually crawling under a car to see what was going on and possibly spoiling their white lab coats. A stocky Austrian with a toothbrush moustache, and a penchant for keeping loaves of bread in his pockets in case he got hungry, he was regarded as somewhat eccentric by the executives who needed him (and most of the time humored him). But Porsche's job (to Porsche) was to design the best possible car design, while Porsche's job to the company directors was to design the most profitable car possible. They reasoned, if only rich people could afford a car these days, why design a people's car?

Clashes were inevitable, as were Porsche's angry outbursts at the short-sightedness of marketing, which concentrated only on the next six-month statement of profits and losses. He was an impassioned arguer and a famous hat-stomper. When his hastily reblocked hat was handed back to him by an aide, it would, as often as not, be stomped flat again within minutes.

Porsche had come up from a world of outdoor plumbing and outside agrarian workshops such as his family of tinkers had used for generations. He'd needed the university training, but lacked the ability to enroll, so he got a job sweeping out the corridors of the university to make it easy for him to slip into classrooms and sit-in on the lectures. But he'd been found out — and then allowed to audit courses after all. But there'd be no degrees. These would have to wait until the whole nation was using his engineering and it was time for the professors to claim him as one of their own.

He'd had so many run-ins with the stratified atmosphere at Mercedes that he'd finally parted company with them, after designing some of their most legendary machines. The Austrian arms manufacturer Steyr had been quick to hire Porsche and put him to work on a brand new design, allowing him much more design freedom to create the best car, not just the bestselling car. The result was something Porsche could really be proud of: the Steyr "Austria," which he decided to drive to the Paris Exposition himself. It won for Porsche another Gold Medal, thirty years after he'd won his first as a new designer on the scene. The celebrations were short-lived, however. Returning to his hotel room after the ceremonies, Porsche caught sight of a newspaper headline that turned his blood cold. In an auto-merger typical of the depression years, Steyr had been taken over by another manufacturer: Daimler-Benz. Porsche's new boss would be Mercedes again. This was when the Porsche Design Bureau came to be. But not many manufacturers were planning to put new designs on the drawing boards in those depression-years markets.

Then came exciting news from France: the international sporting commission controlling Grand Prix racing rules had decided that race car speeds were outstripping the safety of the race courses. To slow the cars back down in the future, they'd made a move to scale-down the cars by restricting them to the weight limit used by a smaller, slower class of race cars called "voiturettes." What the commission forgot to do was to also limit the size of the engine that could be put into these new, lighter cars.

Porsche spotted the opportunities created by this dumbfounding lack of logic instantly and began designing a whole new car on his own time. This was a chance to beat the Italians that shouldn't be missed. With a few clever double-duty uses of components (like using the tubular frame-rails also as oil tanks), by removing a few parts altogether, putting the engine in the back, and by keeping everything elegantly spartan, a designer could plunk in a whopping supercharged engine that would create performance the world had never seen.

Once again a governing body was to demonstrate how easy it is for restrictive rules to accomplish exactly the opposite of what they're supposed to encourage. The cars under these new rules would prove to be so fast, it would take decades for later engineers to match their speeds.

But this performance was still only on paper, done as a design exercise to fill in the slack time between paying customers and to give his staff something exciting to argue about and keep their hopes up about the possibility of Germany returning to Grand Prix racing.

Design accounts had dribbled in. There was a new conglomerate of lesser auto manufacturers called "Auto Union" now on the horizon. The new group, banding together in hopes of surviving the lean depression years, included Horch (well-made luxury cars with not much market share), Audi (mid-price sporty cars with a reasonable following), Wanderer (smaller sporty cars with a youthful clientele), and DKW (small economy cars with innovative engineering, but dubbed "the Kiddiekar" by an ungrateful public).

One of Auto Union's directors, the fiery young Baron Claus von Oertzen, was a motorsports enthusiast who revered Porsche's racing accomplishments at Mercedes. Keenly interested in roping Porsche in to lend impetus to Auto Union's beginnings, von Oertzen recognized the potential of Porsche's new race car design and also knew that racing would be a good way to attract Porsche to Auto Union.

But how could a fledgling new corporation finance the kind of full-blown, international racing effort this design demanded when things were so tight? In Italy, racing teams were mounting more and more expensive campaigns, with more and more sophisticated machines and bigger and bigger budgets. Finances were so tight in Germany that even Mercedes had to cut their racing effort to a shadow of its former self, at a time when Italy was building its attack. They simply couldn't afford to try to keep up with Mussolini's state-backed racing teams with hundreds of mechanics and scores of support trucks.

Chapter 7

Celebrity Status

A win here and there is to be expected even with mediocre drivers when luck goes their way. Their win may come after years of trying, or at the beginning, possibly to be followed by another long dry spell. Whether Rudi would be one of those who found himself regularly in the winner's circle — or only when the competition level was low — had yet to be proved. Only the passage of a few seasons could show what kind of new driver Mercedes had on its hands with this newcomer, Caracciola, despite Rathmann's confidence. As Rudi's fate as one of the promising young comers unfolded on the track, he came in contact with the internationally known champions who defended their countries' honor (and foreign export sales).

As we'd expect, it was a colorful bunch in which teams often fought among themselves as viciously as they fought off competitors. In the Italian corner, three stars shown brightest in the new generation of drivers: Achille Varzi, who was taciturn with the studied arrogance of the new gentry of the Industrial Age, and never seen without a cigarette in his mouth or a woman waiting in the wings; Luigi Fagioli, the "Brigand of Abruzzi," who was short-tempered, paranoid about favoritism, very fast, but also very uncontrollable when his blood was up; and Tazio Nuvolari, quiet, winsomely warm and sportsmanlike, an ethical family-man off the track, a holy terror most often likened to a possessed demon when on the track. The Italian teams were made up of Alfa Romeos racing with the moral and financial support of the ruling Fascist party, and managed by Enzo Ferrari, and Maserati, a smaller family-run team managed by the Maserati brothers and their mechanics in a very egalitarian manner.

Cool, collected, and master of the counterpunch when catching his rivals off-guard, Rudolf Caracciola was one of Germany's few world-class drivers before Hitler's race programs really got rolling. He's seen here listening to a few last-minute tactics from his long-time colleague, Mercedes racing-manager Alfred Neubauer.

photo: Road & Track

The rivalry between Nuvolari and Varzi had slowly escalated from their cycle racing days to the point where whatever one did, the other had to do better. When Varzi had a blue silk driving suit custom-made for him, he took the precaution of paying the tailor extra to keep Nuvolari from finding out about it. But Nuvolari's spies were everywhere, and after paying the tailor twice the price, Nuvolari showed up in blue silk as well. On the track the rivalry was less trivial, reaching a point where both drivers were wrecking an alarming number of Italian cars trying to outdo each other and requiring a telegram from Mussolini to stop.

France fielded mostly Bugattis built in a feudal-style manor-factory, as well as the elegantly engineered Delages, and later the robust Delahayes fielded by an Irish-American woman. From France we have: Louis Chiron, always dapper, soigne, amusing, and a hard competitor; Rene Dreyfus, always charming, always sporting, sometimes temperamental; as well as several other talents like Wimille, Sommer, Williams, and Etancelin, whose stars never reached zenith because of their incompatibility with Germans. (Williams and Etancelin's "incompatibility" growing to the point of becoming fatal when the Gestapo discovered their resistance work.)

Of the group that Rudi was to race against on a regular basis, Louis Chiron was the rival who grew into a friend. In his early days (driving cars owned, for the most part, by wealthy older women) the debonair Chiron took young Dreyfus, shy and obliging, under his wing as his Sancho Panza.

Both Dreyfus and Chiron could get their feelings hurt for imagined slights, and their friendship was limited by occasional misunderstandings and feuds flaring up between them like brush fires. But with Caracciola, Chiron felt less of a big-brother responsibility and more of an admiration between equals. Dreyfus was simply "too nice a guy" for Chiron to really relax with, while Rudi, with all his quiet reserve, had a vicious counterpunch that ranked him among the top contenders and won Chiron's respect as an equal.

The victories were piling up — good news that almost obscured bigger headlines: "American Stock Market Crashes!" Ripple effects were everywhere, and Rudi suddenly found that it was time to shut down the elegant showroom he and Rathmann had set up to sell Mercedes. Banks were failing, unemployment was skyrocketing, and a small splinter party, called the NSDAP or "Nazis" for short, led by a Dr. Goebbels, was winning seats in parliament.

The most shocking news coming from this new situation, from Rudi's standpoint, came from Mercedes itself. It was a letter terminating his contract as a race driver.

By this point in his career, Rudi had little trouble with the elegant receptionist. He was through the upholstered door and into Managing Director Kissel's office in a moment. Charly waited in Neubauer's office as Neubauer tried to ply her with cognac to ease the shock.

They both tried not to look at the clock as two hours dragged by before Rudi returned from Kissel's office looking beaten.

"It's finished," Rudi muttered. "All over."

"Oh no it's not!" Charly said jumping to her feet. "If you can't drive for Mercedes, then you can drive without them!"

Rudi was amused by Charly's loyal outburst. Neubauer was only puzzled. "How so?" he asked.

"Simple. We'll buy our own race car as an independent. Maybe an Alfa Romeo. Their manager Giovannini has already offered us a contract for next year!"

Neubauer was on his feet now. "Good heavens, Rudi. You in an Italian car! You can't do this!"

Rudi had regained his spirit with Charly's defiance. "Why not? My name's Italian."

"This is almost treason," Neubauer wailed.

"My dear Don Alfredo, you can't expect me to give up driving just because Mercedes has taken it into their heads to give up racing!" Through a long sleepless night Neubauer racked his brains for a solution. Giving up racing was just as cataclysmic to Neubauer as it was to Rudi, after all. The next day he called Rudi and Charly for a conference. Neubauer's organizational mind had come up with a possibility.

Neubauer spread out a new contract he'd whipped up on his own. Under its terms Mercedes would provide mechanics, transporter, team manager (Neubauer, of course), repairs, tires, fuel … .

"Fine," Rudi said. "But what about a car to drive?"

This, Rudi would have to buy on his own, but at a very sweet price.

"But what does Mercedes want from this?" Charly broke in. She had become the business manager of the outfit, after all.

Neubauer went on to explain that in exchange for paying all expenses, Mercedes would want to split all prizes and starting money fifty-fifty.

"Stiff conditions," Charly said thoughtfully. "Alfa-Romeo has made us a better offer."

This time it was Rudi who broke in. "Never mind that, Charly. I've grown up with Mercedes. I'll stay with them as long as I'm given a chance to drive a Merc. A few thousand more or less doesn't matter all that much."

They went to see Direktor Kissel. Kissel moaned and groaned about labor problems, rising costs, and falling sales. But in the end he went along with the idea without a fight.

Mercedes would have a one-car racing team that year. Driver: Rudolf Caracciola. Business manager: Charlotte Caracciola. Team manager: Alfred Neubauer. Co-driver: Sebastian. Mechanic: Zimmer. Their first campaign would be to try the impossible: the Mille Miglia.

Neubauer spread out his maps of Italy like Napoleon before Waterloo. When he stopped to think what they were trying to accomplish, he went hot and cold all over. Their one-car assault was up against the legendary Mille Miglia, the race of the thousand miles across all Italy, that was organized by the Brescia Auto Club, which had the brass to call up Mussolini to see if he'd mind shutting down a thousand miles of public roads so they could hold a race. Mussolini realized this would be an all-Italian affair, a perfect time to grab headlines with the story of Italian technological excellence and gubernatorial panache, so he authorized the race.

Local knowledge would be the key to victory in this race, where it was nearly impossible to learn the course enough to memorize its lethal spots in practice. That, and the fact that the Italian teams had never been stronger and would be bringing to bear their best drivers: Campari, Nuvolari, Varzi, Borzacchini. Alfa-Romeo alone would be backing up their drivers with no less than ninety mechanics and seventeen repair trucks, spread over the course running from the plains, through the cities, up among the hill villages, and over the mountain passes all in one day. No one but an Italian had ever won the Mille Miglia, or even posed a threat. The race provided a perfect chance for a fiasco for Mercedes. On the other hand, if the Direktors themselves had been mounting their full attack, they would have been more closely involved and most likely would have eventually scotched the whole idea in the first place as a purely lunatic plan.

They would need four refuelling depots to go this distance, Neubauer had figured out. But they only had personnel for three, even including a volunteer friend of Rudi's, Fritz Kuhnle, and volunteer extra mechanic, Karlo Kumpf, who came along to escape kitchen duties at his wife's country inn. Kumpf, Don Alfredo decided, would have to run two depots. In the early stages of the race Rudi would stop in Sienna to refuel and change tires.

Then while Rudi raced off for Rome, Kumpf would do some racing himself to pack up and make it to Bologna to try to be there when Rudi came back on the second leg.

"If you don't make it, Kumpf, we're sunk," Neubauer said ominously.

The small city of Brescia was tarted up like a spinster to greet the motoring press of the world on race day. It was crowded with a carnival-like market-day atmosphere. The first car, the car with the smallest engine (and probably least-known driver) in the race, was to set off at two o'clock, followed by the next larger car, until the big cars with the legendary drivers took off later in the afternoon. Rudi's Mercedes was to be one of the last to leave, just before the Alfas, the only German in a field of over a hundred and fifty Italian cars.

Neubauer and Charly headed for a trattoria in the Piazza Vittoria to prepare for the long vigil until the cars returned from their tour of Italy early the next morning. Reports started coming in over a loudspeaker. Varzi had fallen out with water pump trouble. The next

The start of the Mille Miglia in Brescia, 1931. Neubauer is standing next to Sebastian in the passenger seat. Charly is reaching out to Rudi with a last good-luck squeeze. Rudi looks like he has other things on his mind: to beat the Italians for the first time in this event — or the possibility of the greatest folly of his career.

photo: Mercedes Benz

announcement brought them out of their chairs — Rudi was leading at a staggering average-speed of over ninety-six miles an hour! Neubauer felt like kissing Charly, while the Italians looked as if they'd somehow been cheated. But then the loudspeaker announced that Campari, the amateur opera singer who drove race cars (or, as some said, the amateur racer who sang), was leading, followed closely by Nuvolari, both in Alfas. No mention of Rudi. Had he put too much strain on the Merc with that blazing start?

They waited for news. Had he crashed trying to keep up that insane pace on the unfamiliar Italian roads? Fifteen minutes went by. Don Alfredo ordered another bottle of Chianti. A half-hour. Then news: Caracciola was still leading! Obviously communications were unreliable. If he could just hold on, Rudi could win the Mussolini Cup for being first at the halfway point — and that in itself would be something to take back to Germany.

Campari was first to Rome, followed still by Nuvolari. Again, no mention of Rudi. At the first depot Kumpf had seen first Campari, then Nuvolari flash past. But no high shriek of the Mercedes supercharger could be heard. Then four minutes later Rudi and Sebastian arrived.

They'd lost an exhaust pipe along the way and had to stop to fix it. Sebastian had burned his hand and wouldn't be much driving help from there on. They refuelled quickly while Rudi took a long drink of water. They changed tires, then the Mercedes shrieked its way southward, while Kumpf threw the tools in the truck and tore off for Bologna. If all went well, Rudi would be there in the early morning hours.

Yard by yard Rudi gained on the Alfas ahead until finally he was closely trailing them. But then they suddenly plunged into a cloud. Fog at this hour? Rudi pulled closer and could see Campari driving along the left-hand ditch and Nuvolari driving in the right. They were raising a billowing screen of dust to slow Rudi's attack and blind him on the straights where Rudi had more speed.

Blocked from passing, Rudi knew he'd have to wait for a town, when the cars were in single file, before pipping them when the road widened out again. But the crowds pushed in on both sides making passing a murderous proposition. Finally a brief opportunity opened up, Rudi kicked in the supercharger and now it was the Italians' turn to drive in Rudi's dust. Rudi realized, however that as long as they stuck to his rear, the Alfas were still ahead on time.

It was Nuvolari, still glued to Rudi's tail light, who won the Mussolini Cup at the halfway point.

When the announcement came to Brescia, Charly was near tears from tension. Giovannini, the jubilant Alfa team manager, popped a champagne cork and kissed an elderly woman who promptly fainted.

After hours of close calls and misjudged turns, the tension was telling on Sebastian, who found himself dozing off in the hurtling cockpit of the Mercedes. Suddenly he sat bolt upright. The song of the engine had gone sour! They ground to a quick stop and Sebastian diagnosed the problem in seconds: a supercharger control had bent. But it took twenty minutes, during which all of the Alfas filed proudly past and into the lead again in a shower of stones and dust, before Sebastian threw his tools back in the Merc and they took out after the Alfas.

Ten hours of razor-edge concentration and now Rudi was the one beginning to show the strain. Finally he began to share the driving with Sebastian; Rudi pulling on the wheel to take the left-handers, and Sebastian pulling on the wheel for the right-hand bends.

At a train crossing Rudi was a fraction of a second slow in correcting. The car hit the rails, and flew into a slide that took Rudi some frightening moments to save. He pulled the car to the side of the road and rolled to a stop. Sebastian was flabbergasted.

"What's the matter? Are you sick?"

"Can't go on," Rudi gasped. "We just about got killed back there! Can't risk somebody else's life."

Sebastian pleaded for Rudi to start the car and get back into the race. But Rudi just shook his head sadly. Then Sebastian began a tirade, storming with rage and pent up adrenalin.

"You can't DO this! All those close-calls will be for nothing, #@&*#@!!"

Rudi gave in. "You win. Here goes ..." With carte blanche given him by Sebastian, Rudi drove like a wild man fighting for his life. No question of Sebastian sleeping now, it was all he could manage just to keep himself from being thrown out.

They gained their old position of threatening the Alfas again after many miles of close ones as they approached the Bologna refuelling depot. Had Kumpf been able to make it in time, or had some trouble on the road held him up? No, there he was waving them to a stop.

Off on the next leg, it was the fast flat plains where the Mercedes could come into its own. But a mist had fallen over the flats, and the three leading Alfas drove three-cars-abreast to make the most of their headlamps (and keep the pesky Mercedes from being able to pass them). Rudi was forced to cruise on their tails along the straights, when, if he could just squeeze past them, he could be shooting off into the lead.

Without warning, the road made a sharp turn to follow the border of a planted field. The three Italians shot straight ahead, however, without slacking their speed, off onto the plowed surface. The tail lights of their Alfas bounced crazily ahead of Rudi warning him that the three Alfas had run out of road and were careening across a field. Rudi only had time to make the bend, then he put his foot down hard, with no Alfas between him and the last leg. Only one of the Alfas was able to keep on racing after their off-road tour.

After fourteen hours Rudi's hands were bleeding through his gloves, his reactions were going on raw nerves alone, and Sebastian was only half-awake, despite the noise, the wind, the ferocious bumps and slides.

Rudi's mechanic, Zimmer, waited at the last depot, worried. He'd worn his white shirt to make himself easier to spot in the early morning gloom, but he knew they'd be exhausted, and any kind of mistake was possible. With a flood of relief Zimmer heard the high whine of the Merc approaching. But then the relief turned to panic, as he realized the whine wasn't easing off — they weren't slowing for the refuelling.

Suddenly Rudi, through his haze, saw a lanky idiot in a white shirt jumping right in the middle of the road. Was this some Italian trick? Then he recognized Zimmer and threw on the binders, bringing the big Merc to a stop just in time.

As the gas gurgled from the cans into the Merc's tank, Rudi and Sebastian began to wake to the fact that they were in the lead, with a mere 120 miles to go! New life flowed into their veins and their minds took on a renewed edge. Rudi drove smoothly now, slithering like an eel through the turns and powering off down the straight — sixty, forty, only twenty miles to go! Dawn was coming on fast. Then a sharp blast announced that a tire had blown only a few miles from the finish! Without a curse, they jumped out, pounded the old wheel off, slammed the new one on, hammered it tight, threw the hammer to the winds and tore off, leaving their tools where they sat on the roadside.

Neubauer was still sitting, cold and stiff in the outdoor restaurant. Charly looked pale from lack of sleep. Then a familiar sound made their backs go ramrod straight, snapping them to attention. It was a sound the Italians around them didn't recognise and, at first,

Tazio, in full flight in his sports Alfa, with "aerodynamic" headlight covers for long races like the Mille Miglia. When things were going his way, Tazio could be seen jumping up and down in his car, patting its sides, and urging it on verbally. On longer races like these, he and his faithful mechanic Decimo Compagnoni would take occasional nips from brandy flasks hung around their necks or munch an orange to keep the blood up.

photo: Shell Oil of London

didn't react to: the screaming shriek of a German car winning the Mille Miglia.

At the Mercedes factory a very special open tourer was being prepared for delivery in late spring of 1931. The installation of pistol cubbies next to the seats and bulletproof windows had taken longer than expected, and Direktor Kissel was half-afraid the customer might not take delivery because of the delay. But since the buyer was an avid car-racing fan, perhaps it would be a nice touch to get them off the hook if Rudi Caracciola, their new white-haired hero, were to deliver the car in person. Rudi didn't mind. It put a seal of approval on his new position at Mercedes as a positive figurehead to be called in for such chores after all.

He drove the car to the address given him, pulling up in front of what he realized was the mansion called "the Brown House" in honor of its new owner, Adolf Hitler. Rudi hadn't payed much attention to the Nazis — laughable guys in jackboots who took themselves pretty seriously when no one else seemed to want to. Just another one of the crazy splinter groups jockeying for position amid the post-Versailles ruin of Germany, he thought (when he took time from his own exciting life to think about politics at all).

Rudi watched with fascination as the guards outside snapped to attention like extras in an operetta. A thin, sharp-looking young man man named Hess came out to greet him. Hess seemed affable enough, and extremely articulate, which surprised Rudi for some reason he didn't take time to examine. Rudi was led through the outer office with its prominent graphic portraying Henry Ford, up flights of stairs, and into a high-ceilinged office where he could see, peeking over a large desk, a short man with a toothbrush moustache and trailing locks over one side of his forehead. This had to be the Adolf Hitler he'd seen photos of in the newspapers — the man everyone seemed to be talking about all of a sudden.

"The Chief" was in a bubbly mood that afternoon. He rose from his huge, dramatically placed desk to greet Rudi. Rudi's exploits on the track had obviously made a deep impression on Hitler. In a deep, broad accent the little man began.

"I must congratulate you on showing the Italians how to drive on their own roads, Herr Caracciola!"

"Thank you, Herr Hitler. I'm pleased to say that the Mercedes tourer you have ordered is now ..."

But the fledgling Führer of this growing political movement had his own conversation all planned out in advance.

"How did you find Italy? Are the people behind Mussolini, do you think? How does the economy look to you? Does Mussolini have the heart of his people on his side?" and a thousand and one other questions about the state of Mussolini's rival fascist state. Rudi found it nearly impossible to get a word in edgewise, the Führer seeming to answer his own questions before Rudi could slip in the fact that most of the Italy he'd seen had flown past his windshield at over a hundred miles an hour.

"Herr Hitler, the Mercedes ..." But once again Hitler took the floor.

"You must see the Brown House while you're here, Herr Caracciola." He was like a boy anxious to show his projects to a favorite uncle. Hitler led Rudi into an enormous room, the so-called Hall of the Senators, with the seats were raised in tiers and covered in expensive red leather. Next, he led Rudi down to the basement where he showed Rudi huge steel safes built into the walls. Another short man with a short moustache greeted them, a Herr Schwartz, national treasurer of the Nazi party.

"My Führer, I wish to report that today the name of the five hundred thousandth member has been entered." They explained to the wide-eyed Rudi that each safe contained file cards, cross-referenced for each party member, detailing his military capabilities, schooling, family status, date of entry to the party, and so on.

"Give me a membership card," Hitler ordered Schwartz, "say, number 1866." Schwartz unlocked the files and pulled out the card in question.

"Now then," Hitler said, grinning like a new father, "give me the name-card of this man." Schwartz pulled this card and, corroborating the data on the two cards, Hitler handed the cards for Rudi's inspection.

Rudi thought, "Well what do you know? A lot of people in this party … Now I've got to get this delivery made." Rudi spotted a lull in the Führer's patter and jumped in.

"Herr Hitler, the big Mercedes you ordered is now ready. I've come to demonstrate it for you. It turned out to be a very beautiful car and I'm sure you will like it."

Hitler thought a moment, as if a little surprised by the change of subject.

"I'd prefer to look at it at the Mercedes garage. Expect me there in half an hour."

Thirty minutes later Hitler appeared at the garage accompanied by two men and his driver, Schreck. While Jakob Werlin explained the options and extras built into the Mercedes (which would resurface in our enlightened age to become the world's most outrageously overpriced collector classic), Schreck took Rudi aside and said in an undertone, "Under no circumstance is the Führer to be driven faster than 30 kilometers an hour. The enemies of our party would jump on the chance to use any accident for counter-propaganda purposes."

Hitler ran his hand over the car, beaming like a child savoring a Christmas gift. The men got in the car and Rudi slid behind the wheel, and drove off as if they were in a funeral procession. He felt like he could get out and walk beside the car, but the men in the back seemed highly satisfied with the "test." As Rudi headed the big car slowly back to the garage, Hitler leaned forward toward the front seat.

"Herr Caracciola, I have a request," Hitler said in a happy tone, "I'd like my niece to see this car. Would you drive her around the block just once?"

Rudi drove on at the glacial pace to the address Hitler had given and stopped in the street. Hitler and the two men went into the apartment house and reappeared shortly with a rather pretty young blond, who got in next to Rudi as the Führer watched them take off. Rudi thought, "Too bad it's just once around the block."

When they returned and pulled up in front of the Führer's entourage, the girl got out of the car and ran to Hitler. "Uncle Dolf, it's such a magnificent car!"

Uncle Dolf beamed with delight. As Rudi drove him away, the girl seemed to wave for a long, long time. Rudi could sense an overenthusiasm in her that rang true to no one but Uncle Dolf.

Driving back to report to Werlin that all had gone well, Rudi had time to think. Perhaps he should pay more attention to what's happening on the political page of the paper. Five hundred thousand Nazis. His thoughts wandered to a village in Switzerland that he and Charly had been returning to more and more often. Perhaps a Swiss refuge would be a good idea in the long run. A half-million Führer-followers. Rudi had had the chance to say, "My Führer, allow me to become number five hundred thousand and one!" but he hadn't. He'd just changed the subject back to the car. But the Führer didn't seem to hold it against him. If Hitler had been a trifle more regal and prepossessing, like a Mussolini, perhaps Rudi would have been swept up in the hypnosis. But somehow Rudi simply couldn't picture this little man as leader of a country, much less one who would hold life or death control over an empire.

Rudi had other crises on his mind: the coming race at Nürburgring. It would take every trick in the book to stay ahead of the quick and nimble little Bugatti in the hands of Louis Chiron on that track. The Mercedes was a wonder at long fast straights, but there was hardly a straight spot in the entire fourteen miles around Nürburgring. The Bugattis would be in their element against Rudi's little team.

In practice Zimmer and Sebastian had taken the car out for a run and hadn't come back for a long time. When they reappeared they looked like two cats who'd eaten the canary. At one tight hairpin on the course — "the Karussel," where cars were forced to slow down to thirty miles an hour — the two mechanics had tested out a new trick. There was a ditch on the inner part of the turn that was slanted at a higher angle to duct water away from the pavement. Yard by yard Zimmmer had inched the big Mercedes around the Karussel driving it down in the banked culvert, while Sebastian checked for clearance to make sure the car would fit before they tried it at speed. Next lap Zimmer took the banked ditch fast as he could, while Sebastian watched the speedometer.

"Forty miles an hour!" Coming out of a curve faster would give a higher speed all the way down the ensuing straight, meaning a real advantage every lap with this new technique.

The battle with Chiron was a real ding-dong affair with only feet separating the two cars all the way to the finish. Rudi had won it, but the afternoon's race had been so exciting, Louis stopped his car at the finish, jumped out and ran to give his rival a big, Gallic hug, the start of a long mutual admiration friendship. The uniqueness of the Caracciola-Chiron relationship was that it came directly out of their competitions on the track. They respected each other's methods of battling it out, as differing as they might have been. After this race at

During the lean years Manfred von Brauchitsch carried on for Germany with this win at the Avus track in 1932. Otherwise, German racing efforts were struggling against Italian subsidies and wealthy private entries from France, as Bugattis, Maseratis, and Alfas ran the show.

photo: Mercedes Benz

Nürburgring, Rudi was starting to win his way into the record books and was establishing himself as a driver capable of beating the world's best in an even fight — a driver any team manager would sign in a minute, if Rudi hadn't been so loyal to his mother-hen, Mercedes Benz.

The same Sunday of the race, lines started to form at the nation's largest banks. People had lost faith in the economy altogether, and there were runs at the bank in the ensuing panic.

Since this race had wound up the season, the party to celebrate the year's victories had gone on late into the night. Neubauer and Rudi sat on a balcony, their feet on the balustrade, watching the sun emerge over the mountains. Neubauer was finding that his new role as team manager suited him perfectly, changing him from what had been a rather mediocre driver into racing's most legendary team manager. Rudi's head was mellow with the hour and the champagne, and he even managed a little speech under the circumstances. "We must have many more victories ..." he began.

Neubauer was silent. Then he spoke quietly.

"Next year, my boy, Mercedes won't run any races. We're short of money. We'll have to go easy." The early morning light looked suddenly gray and lifeless. Rudi thought back to that morning when he'd pulled up on Kruppke's motorcycle at the family hotel. It had been quiet and gray then too. And he'd been given a pat on the back then too, and then sent packing to find his own way in the world.

Chapter 8

Italian Interlude

Rudi and Charly had celebrated the winter holidays at their new villa in Arosa, in Switzerland, south of Lichtenstein — about as far away from urban cares as they could get. Neubauer, meanwhile, had been relegated to a desk job at Mercedes and was constantly miserable without his "babies" to herd toward victories on the track. To console their friend they'd invited Neubauer and his wife to Arosa for the holidays.

Then on New Year's eve of 1932 another guest appeared: Giovannini, the Alfa team manager. Neubauer flinched visibly seeing his Italian counterpart making an unannounced appearance at the villa. At dinner, however, Neubauer made a monumental effort and was more amusing than ever, sending even Giovannini into gales of laughter with the tales of their triumph over the Alfas at the Mille Miglia .

Then Giovannini asked to talk to Rudi, "in private, please."

When he and Rudi were alone in Rudi's study, Giovannini pulled out a contract. Rudi looked it over. It was all filled in. All he had to do was sign it. The conditions were fair, the guarantees adequate. But there was one clause that made Rudi stop dead in his tracks: he was to race for Alfa, but not as one of the regular team. His car would be painted a different color from the traditional Italian red. Rudi's Alfa would be German white.

After all his wins, Rudi was still not "one of the boys" — just as he'd been kept outside the team at Mercedes. How many races did he have to win before people would start taking him seriously as a driver?

"What's this for?" he asked simply. Giovannini seemed embarrassed.

"I don't know. The other drivers, Nuvolari and Campari always share the winnings. They think that with your experience only in the heavy Mercedes, you may not adapt to our little Alfas. Not right away, at least."

"And who thought this up? Nuvolari?"

"No."

"Campari?"

"No. Don't keep asking these questions, Signor Caracciola. Please!"

Rudi slammed the contract down and strode off to get some cigars. In the hall, Neubauer grabbed Rudi by the lapels.

"Rudi! Rudi, you're not going over to the other side, are you?!"

"But I've got to drive, don't you see?"

Neubauer didn't say a word, but couldn't let go of Rudi's lapels until some sort of understanding was built between them. They'd been like brothers through a lot of long, long racing days. Rudi felt miserable — almost sorry for Don Alfredo. Finally Neubauer said in a hoarse whisper, "Promise me one thing, Rudi. Promise me that if Mercedes goes racing again, you'll come back to us." Rudi smiled and shook on it, and then went back to Giovannini and signed the contract that sent Germany's greatest driver over the Alps to the land of Mussolini.

In Italy Rudi found a new way of life, new friends, and a few old foes still smarting from his becoming the first foreigner to break into the ranks of Mille Miglia winners. At this year's Mille, he'd had engine trouble with his Alfa and dropped out without even finishing.

Tazio Nuvolari at Monte Carlo in his Alfa. Tazio's racing outfit was anything but conformist. He had shirts of special colors for good luck, an eighteenth-century-style leather jerkin, different colored windcaps indicating his mood for the day, and a special tortoise-pin given to him by the poet Gabriele d'Annunzio, his constant mascot.

photo: Shell Oil of London

The successful Alfa Romeo Grand Prix team of 1932. They all have Italian names, but can we spot the one with the German passport? (Would an Italian wear knickers?) Rudolf Caracciola, Tazio Nuvolari, Mario Borzacchini, and Giuseppe Campari, the amateur opera singer.

photo: Shell Oil of London

Campari was strutting around saying, "See? Didn't I tell you that one wouldn't make it?" with his satisfied smile.

At the Monte Carlo race, around the tight corners of the town, Rudi had made his nimble Alfa handle like a ballerina. Compared to the big lumbering Mercedes, it seemed child's play and he'd ridden right up on Nuvolari's tail, ahead of the rest of the field without an effort.

The custom was that drivers were not to challenge a team member who had established a good lead by the halfway point. But was Rudi bound by this after they hadn't accepted him on the team? It was a question that could distract you from your business of maintaining regular accuracy to a few inches, a few miles an hour around the unyielding stonework barriers.

He was frustrated at not being able to let his Alfa out to its potential as he followed Tazio. Then on the last lap he shot past the Italian champion as Tazio slowed to fiddle with a balky fuel valve. Rudi glanced over at Tazio and saw the look of bewildered anguish on his face at Rudi's pass.

Now running on instinct only, with no time to mull the ethics, something told Rudi to slow. He would make an enemy for life, perhaps three, if he took advantage of Tazio's last-lap fuel problem. Tazio shot past into the lead again, his fuel line cleared and ran for the finish. Rudi pulled up at the finish feeling miserable. Fans were booing him, mechanics openly asking, "Why did you do that, Signor Caracciola?!"

Tazio was by his side in an instant, clasping him on the shoulder with a warm, heartfelt thanks. Rudi knew now he'd done the right thing. Tazio had dominated the race up to the last laps. It had been Tazio's race, really, and now Tazio wasn't about to forget Rudi's sporting gesture.

"That was decent of you, Caracciola, really decent. I'm going to ask you on behalf of the others if you'll join the team." From then on Rudi's car was painted Italian racing red like the other team cars, and Rudi was given his share of the team's collective wins.

It turned out to be a good season for Alfa, with Rudi justifying all of Tazio's faith in him. Between them they won a lot of cups and newspaper space for Italian technology. There were a few dark days, of course. When one of their teammates, Arcangeli, was killed in practice, the whole Alfa team had decided to withdraw from the upcoming race.

But then one of those telegrams came from Rome. It was, as they feared, from their biggest fan, Benito Mussolini, and it wasn't a telegram of condolence. It ran only to three words (the Duce didn't waste them, after all). "RACE ... AND WIN." They raced. And they won.

At season's end, Rudi and Charly ran to the mountains at Arosa and their beloved villa. Waiting for them was a letter of dismissal from Alfa. They were turning their racing operation over to Ferrari and wished Rudi luck finding work under the new arrangement.

Waiting for them also was Louis Chiron. He'd come for the skiing, and also because he had some time on his hands now that he'd been fired from Bugatti. His track record had been good, but his relations with the race manager had run on the rocks: a woman was at the bottom of it (as they often were with Louis) — the woman he'd brought with him skiing.

She was known as Baby Hoffmann around racing circles, a brilliantly beautiful young blonde who spoke so many languages so well no one was ever quite sure what her native tongue originally had been. She'd married an industrialist, and to give the couple entree into the exciting world of car racing, he'd bought a sparkplug company. Baby had taken to pit management so well she'd become a legend at timing and lap scoring, a process that baffles the best of minds. They'd hired Chiron as driver and it didn't take the unstoppable Louis long to become much more than a driver to Baby, who subsequently divorced the industrialist in a very quiet, continental manner. And through that winter holiday Louis, Baby, Rudi and Charly had become an inseparable, if unemployed, foursome.

One day Louis came into the villa, his spirits even higher than usual. He'd figured everything out for their future. "Rudi, why should we win all that money for other people? We are the ones the spectators come to see. We take all the chances with our skin and they sit back and rake in the rewards. We should better start our own company."

He had it all figured out on an envelope: the starting money, prizes, and endorsements on one side; the costs of mechanics, cars, transport, and repairs on the other. To Rudi's surprise, the plan looked good even when broken down expense by expense. They'd call their two-man team "Scuderia C.C." (Carraciola-Chiron or Chiron-Caracciola, depending on whom you were talking to). Pooling their prize money from the previous seasons, Rudi and Louis bought two brand new Alfa P-3's, painting Louis' Alfa French racing blue with white stripes, and Rudi's German racing white with blue stripes. Their first tilt at the world would be at the G.P. of Monaco next spring.

Since Louis had never raced one of the Alfas, the quartet arrived in Monte Carlo a full week before the race so Rudi could coach him in the new cars. They set out on a twenty-five-lap practice run with Louis following Rudi to see how it's done Alfa-style. Rudi was astonished at how quickly Louis mastered the car. It was as if he'd been driving an Alfa for seasons, clinging right on Rudi's tail. On the last lap Louis slowed, and Rudi, not seeing him in the mirrors, braked as well, but only one brake grabbed, and then wouldn't let go, and the Alfa went into a quick spin. Rudi steered hard against the spin and downshifted mercilessly to reduce speed as a sharp turn toward the sea approached.

He knew he couldn't make it and his last choice was between the harbor and a solid stone parapet. He chose the parapet and hit hard, metal against stone. Everything fell silent. Then a screech of brakes announced that Louis was also stopping. Rudi wanted to jump out quickly to show that he was unhurt, pulling his legs out of the tangled metal mess that was their bright new car just a few seconds before.

But the second Rudi's feet hit the ground a searing pain shot through one leg all the way to his hip, sending him reeling. Louis, with the help of some onlookers who'd rushed up, managed to get

Rudi into the nearby tobacconist's shop where a chair was made available. It was cool and dim in the shop and Rudi had time to calm down and take in the situation. The shop owner, an old man with a dapper goatee, was cheering Rudi up, "We have an excellent hospital, monsieur. Some of the most famous people have died there."

Rudi sweated with the pain as he waited for the ambulance, which seemed to take a long, long time. The drive to the hospital seemed endless, each cobblestone jolt sending an electric current through Rudi's leg.

As he waited for the doctor, stretched out on a table like a loaf of bread, Rudi's shock began to wear off, to be replaced by dizzying pulses of scorching pain. He pressed his head against the pillow hard and dug his nails into his clenched hands. Outside, after the endless x-rays and mumbled consultations, Charly was hearing the words Rudi wanted never to hear, "The thigh and entire tibular bone are smashed. Your husband will never drive again."

Doctors came and went. "When can I get up again?" he would ask, but got only shrugs in response.

"Do you think this thing will come out all right?" Shrugs. A short, sallow doctor bounced in with the kind of birdwalk that vain people sometimes affect.

"I won't be able to drive again, is that it?" Rudi asked, trying to force an answer of some sort.

"Oh, no." The little doctor smiled. "I wouldn't say that. There are such things as miracles."

Giovannini came in his best cheerful manner. "Well Rudi, bent an axle, eh? Well, I brought some special oil to help things along," and he pulled out a bottle of brandy.

"No, I don't feel like drinking. They want to put a saw to my leg," he said somewhat desperately.

Giovannini's face dropped all its forced cheeriness.

"No! They mustn't think of that! There's only one man to help you. Professor Putti of Bologna. I'll bring him here if I have to get him myself!" And he was gone. Putti arrived the next morning, and Rudi liked him immediately. He took a long time examining Rudi, with the little yellow-faced doctor at his side like a suspicious duenna.

"Do I have to have to be cut?" Rudi asked at last, like a child.

"Who said you needed to be?"

Rudi motioned toward the little doctor. Putti looked at the man hard, but said nothing. The little doctor's face turned yellower than ever.

"I don't want you worrying about that, Signor Caracciola. But it would be better if you were to come to my clinic."

The pain through the next day was just as insistent, grabbing Rudi's attention every minute. But with Putti, at least there was hope. On the car ride to Bologna, they ran into their mechanics in Genoa.

It was a sad reunion. Rudi looked at his smashed car — just as sick as he was. Rudi thought of his youth suddenly as a completed unit, viewed as a thing of the past now.

Putti's clinic was in an ancient convent, and it was cool, quiet, serene. Putti came every day with his humor and energy to pump Rudi up after the pain had deflated his hopes through the night. Only another month in the cast, he had said, as if it were an amusing predicament they'd all laugh over later. Still another month! Charly was there every day, playing cards, reading, sharing the ordeal to dilute the pain.

The cast was removed. "Only one more cast, and we'll be all right!" Another cast! What could Rudi say? Five months went by while they listened on the radio to Tazio, Varzi, Dreyfus — all winning the races they'd planned to win. Louis was losing, every race. A bad streak. "Scuderia C-C" was fast becoming a stillborn that would disappear just as other teams had dropped from sight after the expenses gobbled up their hopes.

News from Putti was also disturbing. "The cartilage has shifted. It can't support weight that way. It would be best to operate and put in a pin to hold the stress."

Rudi shook his head.

"Then you'll have to go back in plaster for another period."

Rudi shook his head again. The doctors tried to reason with him, but finally Charly broke in. "Let them operate, Rudi," she said, her body trembling with stifled, fearful crying.

"But what if the joint is stiff? What if I can't drive again?"

She calmed herself and looked straight at Rudi,

"You won't be able to drive in any case. The doctor said that the neck of the femur is completely smashed."

Rudi felt his body stiffen with shock.

"Shouldn't I have told you?"

"Yes, yes." They were both silent, then Charly said in a small voice, "Rudi, must you drive? There are so many things to do in life."

"Please, just stop it!" Instantly Rudi realized he'd hurt her and pressed her hand for forgiveness.

Professor Putti sensed that the time had come for a serious talk with Rudi. He never mentioned lifestyle options or giving up driving. He spoke only of methods of complete cure that were long shots, but still viable bets.

"There are three things, Signor Caracciola, that I have come to believe make men well again: faith, will power, and doctors. I won't insist that we doctors are the greatest force of the three." Rudi sensed that Giovannini had found the one man he needed for this job. They shook hands on what was an unstated contract between them to get this Caracciola character back behind the wheel of a racecar again.

Now the prescription was for rest and sunshine, and to comply Rudi and Charly went back to the Swiss lakes where Rudi, in a new mood of plodding patience, found he never grew tired of watching the clouds mirrored in the blue of the lake below the terrace.

Crutches, progress, setbacks, progress again — but always plodding patience.

Chapter 9

Come to Tea

Porsche got word from von Oertzen that Jakob Werlin was calling a meeting at the Kaiserhof Hotel across from the Chancellery. Von Oertzen needed Porsche and driver Hans Stuck to go along for technical back-up in what promised to be a meeting that had something to do with Hitler's Motor Show speech. The details were unclear and the Auto Union contingent laid odds that Werlin was angling to pick their brains (and their best design talent) before Mercedes launched the official state-backed Grand Prix team to counter Mussolini's Alfas.

The Auto Union party was shown, with a prearranged smoothness, into a conference room, where Werlin was waiting with an air of conspiratorial excitement and references to "something in the air" having to do with a better future for racing in Germany. Porsche was gruff, as if he would have to see the details before getting any hopes up. Tea service appeared, then with an excited flurry, an extra chair was brought in for a late guest. Adolf Hitler was going to join them.

"Of course, we've met before, Herr Professor. At Solitude in 1923, I believe?" Hitler said, recalling a day a decade before when a young political activist named Hitler had managed to meet the world-renowned racing car designer named Porsche.

Then the Führer became all business. There was precious little time to waste and he meant to get his programs underway without delay. His plan was to gather up the best talent in Germany to create a Grand Prix team that would replace Mussolini's in the eyes of Europe as the source of the latest cutting-edge technology. Since the races were drawing crowds regularly above 250,000 with full radio coverage, this was a unique opportunity for pushing German technology. But (demonstrating his knowledge of technical details) they would have to bustle if they meant to make an impact on the 1934 season. The Führer machine-gunned out details and dates of events, expectations, and responsibilities at a dizzying pace. The more the follow-through was talked about, the more obvious it became that Hitler had tacitly elected Porsche as head designer, with Mercedes as the team standard-bearer for Germany.

But Porsche was skeptical. An uncomfortable quiet followed, and aides became nervous as Porsche, the forceful little man from Austria with the toothbrush moustache began to square off against the forceful little man from Austria with the toothbrush moustache: Hitler.

As Porsche took the floor, his design team squirmed. It became obvious that it was Hitler who was being lectured to, this time non-stop for half an hour of point-after-point harangue. Porsche's first Point: Germany should field not one, but two Grand Prix teams because the competitive side-by-side development would actually speed up getting the teams race-ready, not slow it. Point 2: Two teams would not be placing all Germany's eggs in one design-basket. It would also allow freer growth of new ideas and not compromise them just to save reputations and egos. Point 3: Fielding two teams would make better use of talent that doesn't find working with Mercedes congenial. And Point 4: If Germany had two teams, then spectators would still have some exciting competition to watch after the Italians had been well and truly swept off the tracks.

It was Point 4 that seemed to make an impression on the Führer. Point 4 was possibly a concept that he might not have thought about: what happens after they beat the world? Nobody's going to pay to go see a Mercedes parade, and an important marketing audience could be lost. With two teams, they could go on forever providing exciting competitions.

The Führer at first seemed to view Porsche's filibuster with a mixture of surprise and irritation. Egos are unimportant when the state's prestige was at stake. But Point 4 made good sense, and some of the fire went out of Hitler's demeanor. According to those who talked to those who were there, the exchange started to go something like this:

"But Mercedes has always carried the flag for Germany. Who do you see fielding the second team?" Hitler interjected.

"Auto Union," Porsche said, as if it were the most obvious thing in the world.

"Auto Union!" Hitler snorted, possibly picturing the man on the street hearing that the "Kiddie-Kar" company was going to represent Hitler's "New Germany" against Italy's Alfa-Romeos and Maseratis, or even France's Bugattis and Delayhayes.

"I don't fancy their chances are much against Mercedes!" Hitler snorted.

Someone was springing to his feet. It was the lofty figure of von Oertzen in a towering rage at Hitler's thick-headedness.

"And who fancied your chances, Herr Chancellor, when they sent you to Landsberg Prison!?"

The Führer snorted again. It was hard to tell whether it was fury, or to cover a chuckle at von Oertzen's passionate audacity. Such passion could be turned into fiercely uncompromising effort. Hitler was torn. One side of him had always been a Mercedes fan, having a special model ordered for him by the party "for official purposes" when they could ill-afford it. But he also hated the same bourgeois conventional complacency that he at other times cozied up to. When the times called for action, Hitler would doff his comfy middle-class origins and yell, "Do not mistake me for a bourgeois!" It was a logic-gap that had plagued him for years. He admired the accomplishments of the strictly-run Mercedes organization. But on the other hand he hated the spirit of bureaucracy that seemed to reign there. He hated red tape, but exulted in his party's detailed organization. There were times when organization won the day, and other times when inspired instincts and swashbuckling cut-and-run techniques seemed more appropriate.

The new Führer was sitting among his racing heroes that day — men of action who got the job done regardless of frayed feelings. You couldn't expect men of action to be held to the same protocols as bureaucrats. He ignored the impudence of von Oertzen's challenge and pressed on to the point:

"But you're talking about a whole new design. How long would it take to draw up a completely new car?" he said, addressing Porsche.

"I have it right here in my pocket," Porsche countered. It was just the situation he'd been hoping for — to draw the solution from out of his magic pockets. (Hitler was later to complain about those pockets saying, "He never takes his hands out of those damned pockets, even when he's talking to me!")

It's one thing to create a youth club to acquaint young Germans with motor competition, in German cars, on German tracks, with

German officials. But it's quite another thing to take your team on the road and go by other people's rules. Hitler had been used to being able to control the settings and the rules of the games to make sure his own point of view came out triumphant. But in Grand Prix racing he would have to play by rules set by an international governing body in France and, in the majority of races, carried out by foreign officials. With no way to pressure foreign teams or work deals with Mussolini, Hitler would be forced to win honestly, with honestly better machines, backed up by honestly better team management and dependably faster drivers. It was to prove a high-stakes roll of the dice.

Neubauer had found that life without the campaign of racing was not much, and had turned in his resignation, regretfully, to Direktor Kissel. Even a hand-to-mouth existence with a small independent team or a hanger-on job would be better than sitting at a desk knowing exactly to the last detail what the next month, the next year would bring.

Like Rudi, Neubauer had drunk from a headier cup of existence, tasted the romance of something more satisfying than womb-to-tomb protected, guaranteed modern life, and was half a man without the taste of challenge in his mouth. Then came an offer from the new Auto Union group who, surprisingly, was thinking of new racing plans.

Kissel was dumbfounded when Neubauer entered his office and handed his resignation. "What on earth are you thinking of?" he cried, almost pushing Neubauer into one of the deep leather chairs. Neubauer was sitting under a portrait hanging above him not of Hindenburg nor Hitler, but of Rudolf Caracciola. Kissel was at first shocked, and then a little embarrassed. It had never occurred to him how much Neubauer sought the battles of the track, and how long the wait for the next challenge could seem to a man like Neubauer.

Things were moving behind the scenes, Kissel knew, and Mercedes would soon be back in the thick of the battle like never before. But no one had remembered to hint to Don Alfredo to hold on just a little while longer — without, of course, telling all the details of what Hitler had had in mind for the German automotive world since his days at Landsberg. The Landsberg plan had to be kept quiet until the final minutes before implementation to assure that those who would work to dispose of Hitler wouldn't be able to block his way — or take over the plan themselves.

It would be tragic if Neubauer went his own way just weeks before everything was due to change in the New Germany. Kissel didn't know himself all that was afoot, but from Werlin he'd heard promising hints, enough to level with Neubauer and tell him it would be the height of foolishness to quit at this point. Just trust him, and hang on awhile longer. Neubauer got the message and put a call through to Rudi in Arosa. There was a new tone of hope in Neubauer's voice.

"Planning to drive again next season?" he'd asked Rudi after the usual cordialities.

"Of course," Rudi said as truthfully as he could, only fudging a little in his own mind.

"Fabulous. Big things are happening here, Rudi. I can't go into details now," Neubauer said truthfully, for he had no idea what the details were himself. But where there's a desire to believe, two men can con each other with ease. "Would it be convenient if I dropped by next weekend?"

"Wonderful! We'll look forward to it," Rudi said. He didn't add that they'd be looking forward to Neubauer's visit with complete panic.

At once Rudi went to the doctor to have a thinner, less noticeable cast fit to his leg. Then came long painful hours practicing walking so that no one could guess the searing stabs of breathtaking pain that were coursing through him. Charly helped with cosmetics that could lessen the obvious sweat on Rudi's brow when he took more than three steps in succession.

Saturday came, and with it the thunderous stomping of Neubauer running up the stairs.

"Rudi! Good old Rudi, how wonderful to see you in one piece! Feeling fit again?" Neubauer asked, giving Rudi a hug and noticing the cold sweat at the back of the neck.

"Never felt better!" Rudi lied with an open smile.

Rudi offered Neubauer a seat and made the supreme effort to glide casually into the seat next to him.

"The word is, Rudi, that Mercedes is going to go racing again. And in a big way!" He slapped Rudi mercilessly on the injured leg and watched Rudi's eyes closely. Rudi didn't flinch, but a tightening of the neck muscles said all to Neubauer. He was no beginner in trying to get morsels of truth out of drivers with amazing capabilities of covering up pain. "And how about you, Rudi? Would you like to? Can you drive again?"

"Well," Rudi began with elaborate ease, "of course I can drive. It's just a matter of the kind of contract Mercedes is offering these days."

Neubauer's eyes widened with disbelief. "Let's not beat around the bush, Rudi. You know better than I what an ordeal racing can put you through. Look, Rudi, I'm sorry to have to say this. Please don't misunderstand. But what guarantee does the firm have that you won't crack under the strain?"

Charly was on her feet in a second. "What guarantee is there, Herr Neubauer, that your new cars won't crack up in the middle of a race?!"

Neubauer's head was whirling and he beat a quick retreat. "Rudi, you'll have to come to Stuttgart and discuss these things with Dr. Kissel. I actually came just as a friend to spend a few happy hours with you."

The happy hours took ages to pass for Rudi as his defenses against the pain of movement wore down and he knew he couldn't keep the twinges from the hawk-eyes of Neubauer. The next day Neubauer returned to Stuttgart and Dr. Kissel.

"Caracciola is still in bad shape. We can't count on him for the time being."

Behind barbed wire and locked doors, crews were working into the night both at Mercedes and Auto Union to craft what would be the two fastest racers ever to hit pavement.

Chapter 10

The Reich Goes Car Racing

With Hitler's racing effort forming such a large portion of his Social-Motorization programs, and with the Social-Motorization programs being called the sine qua non for the victory of National Socialism, the pressure was on the new racing teams. There was simply no margin for error, no room for foul-ups that might make a joke out of Germany in front of Europe, Hitler, and everybody — especially in front of Mussolini's teams.

At Mercedes, as you would guess, the project was taken very seriously as the wheels of creativity ground ponderously to a start during that spring of 1933. Mercedes was separated into hermetically sealed departments, each under a Direktor, somewhat along military/bureaucratic lines. Everyone seemed to be a "Direktor" this or "Doktor" that, with a rigidly enforced chain of command, even in the actual frontline action of the pits.

Race manager Neubauer had started out as a driver, but moved into management when, after nearly killing himself in an all-out try for victory, he'd found that his time was embarrassingly slow (even his wife commented he looked like a bus driver on the course). As a race-team manager, however, he was without equal, controlling every detail that could help the team win, from finding the right restaurants for his drivers to setting up practice schedules around drivers' sleeping habits, helping out with team members' finances, and keeping tabs on drivers' health habits.

Breaking all the rules of what a successful Grand-Prix car should look like, the new Auto-Unions seemed like they'd wandered off a Fritz Lang futurist movie set when they were first rolled out onto the track.

photo: Auto Union Archive

Neubauer had been the first to use pit signals to communicate with drivers. And every task that he wanted carried out, no matter how small, he would write it down on a note pad and hand to whomever was to carry out the order. He "never told someone to tell someone" — he always stayed no more than one level removed from the action. This way mechanics didn't have to clutter their minds having to remember what had been ordered, and if the order were a mistake, they had proof that it wasn't their fault. Neubauer had seen the many examples of chaos in the otherwise well-equipped Italian teams. A driver would ask a mechanic to have a seat changed in a car, for example. But then another mechanic would come across the change just at the wrong time and confusion would set in, with some adjustments being made twice by two mechanics who each thought it was their job, or worse, being made not at all by two mechanics who each thought it was the other guy's job.

As in a war campaign, the teams would come to a race with a preplanned strategy, then expect this plan to fall apart as soon as the chaos of the race got underway. With Neubauer's written-note method, all changes of plan had to be routed through him, making it easier to catch conflicting orders before they could wreak their havoc.

At Mercedes there was the traditional great German faith in the scientific method, the academy, the pecking order, and the chain of command. Carburetion settings, for example, were dynamometer-tested under strict laboratory control in sealed rooms where the temperature, humidity, and even the air pressure could be set to simulate the conditions at a coming race. In some rooms the walls were made of stainless steel, slightly slanted out at the bottom, with streams of water cascading down constantly to remove dust from the air.

Entering the Mercedes racing department, provided you could somehow pass the security clearance, you would likely find yourself confronted by a disarmingly beautiful and quick-thinking receptionist who instantly had your number and the perfect way to handle the likes of you. No jealously guarded routine behind closed doors could be disrupted. The decor was designed to intimidate; it was carefully furnished to make a visitor feel like his concerns were trifles compared to the ponderous responsibilities of the Direktors.

At Auto Union things tended to be homier. You were likely to be met by a receptionist who looked a lot like somebody's favorite aunt, nestled between filing cabinets used as perches by friendly cats. Chalk bulletin boards betrayed inside jokes for the world to read, and the decor was more functional than intimidating.

At Mercedes the competition design department came up with the cars with which Neubauer had to rally his team to do their best. It wasn't until later that a feedback loop from the drivers back to the designers was established to keep pace with the rapidly developing competition from Auto Union.

The Mercedes design department had, not surprisingly, gone with a fairly conventional, state-of-the-art front-engined racer. Their breakthroughs tended to be less noticeable, hidden-away developments of execution, rather than startling new concepts — like their chassis frame that could be lifted with one hand, with tubes so thin you could flex the sides inward with your fingers, or a suspension that was similar to others to look at, but radically soft and comfortable to ride in (to keep drivers as fresh as possible through a long race).

Neubauer had no direct opposite number on the Auto Union team. The total effort to get their cars across the finish line first tended to be a family affair with everybody getting in on the act. Mechanics made suggestions that were considered, and the designer of the car stayed in the pits through the race, sometimes being able to diagnose a problem by ear, even before the car pulled in to be fiddled with — but most importantly, to be there to see the effects of the design ideas in the heat of action. Dr. Porsche would be prominent in the pits, checking jet-settings, gapping plugs — sometimes even getting the pit action himself — and always listening hard to the song of his engines, hunting for a sour note. He often took movies with his 16 mm camera.

Coming to the Auto Union team were the Sebastian brothers, Wilhelm and Ludwig. The Sebastians' roles were vague, but essential. The nearest term for them would be "mechanic," but they brought a wide variety of helpful talents to the team that they'd honed at Mercedes. They served as acting riding mechanics for Caracciola, performed driving stints when needed, and generally sparked the whole team with their lively geniality. Perhaps the pigeonhole mentality chafed at them in the military correctness at Mercedes. Anyway, they'd come over to the new team with a vigor that everyone appreciated. Also coming to Auto Union was champion driver Hans Stuck. Tall, elegant, and often mistaken for a "von Stuck," this ex-farmer made an easy switch from Dr. Porsche's legendary SSK Mercedes to Dr. Porsche's soon to be legendary rear engined Auto Union.

Two men were set to watch over both teams like hovering angels: Dr. Glaser was the teams' physician who picked up the pieces when things went wrong and a driver was hurt, who dealt with the wives and families when someone was killed, and who tried his best to keep tabs on the drivers' health.

Driver Hans Stuck's expression says it all — about the performance of the new Auto-Unions under test. In these early days of Hitler's racing program, there's hardly a military uniform in sight to spoil the fun.

photo: Auto Union Archive

Watching over the constantly changing tire needs of both teams was a mountain of a man, complete with cropped hair and upturned Hindenburg moustache — Herr Dietrich from Continental Tire. Dressed in his homburg and coat and cane, he was the "ambassador from Transeuropia" in any movie. In the pits, however, dressed in his bib overalls and no shirt, he was the man you stayed friendly with in any bar — for your health's sake. They called Herr Dietrich "Schnurrbiber," the moustached beaver.

The cars of the two teams were as different as day and night. The Mercedes was an evolutionary design based on unlimited faith in the scientific method; the Auto Union, a revolutionary one based on inspired intuitive development through trial-and-error testing. Even though the new cars were roughly evenly matched in ultimate performance, their concepts, their gestation, even their sounds were as different as night and day. The Mercedes, with its superchargers pushing air through their carburetors at high pressure made an otherworldly scream that was unmistakable miles away. The rough-hewn Auto Unions, on the other hand, rumbled your guts with a throaty basso-ostinato, like two huge hotrod V-8's run by a single throttle pedal. Spewing exhaust straight up out of their sixteen exhaust pipes pointed skyward like the barrels of howitzers, the Auto Unions were intimidating just to watch, even before they rolled a wheel in earnest.

A whole starting-grid full of these monsters made giving the "Go" signal problematic. Tachometers had to be watched carefully to prevent over-revving the big, unloaded engines, so visual signals were tough to see. And audio signals were out of the question because of the din. So a system that made use of the shock-wave produced by a starting cannon was used. Drivers could feel the concussion of the cannon blast and know the starting flag had dropped. Watching the films of these beasts being thrown artfully around small mountain roads, and batting around the huge banked "Metropolis"-looking track at over 200 mph leads one to believe the phrase that nearly every eyewitness has echoed, "If you haven't seen the big thirties Grand Prix cars racing, then you just haven't seen car-racing."

Between Hitler's ascension in early 1933, and the 1934 racing season starting a little more than a year later, much was accomplished in both camps. It was obvious from the ultra-fast-paced development of both new cars that much had been done before Hitler's call to arms — on the sly, when it was being rumored that "something was in the wind" about future racing plans for Germany. Otherwise neither team would have been able to make the spring '34 deadline. Mercedes had been making an early start on creating a new car for the new formula because they had the inside line on Hitler's grand plan from Werlin's close contacts with "the Chief," as Hitler was known around his own staff rooms. And Auto Union had jumped the gun on its own, mostly because Porsche simply couldn't resist designing a new racer to fit the new formula where the only restriction was an overall weight limit — leaving the rest of the concept up to the designer's imagination.

In both camps engineers and fabricators strained every creative muscle to insure that every molecule added to the car carried its own weight to make the car go faster. Every part, from the engine block to the brake pedal bracket, was finely sculpted and drilled with lightening holes to minimize weight while maintaining strength. Yet despite the extremes gone to by both teams to cut unnecessary weight, both teams had a seldom-equalled record for structural safety, with very few cars leaving a race because of a rare broken structural part.

The cars had moved into an area of performance that supporting components, like tires and lubricants hadn't quite caught up with. In hot weather the cars would eat up rubber, with exploding tires making the pits sound "like a war zone," as Neubauer put it. To keep the oil from breaking down under the extremes forced by the new engines, thicker and thicker lubricants were used to the point where the oil would arrive in paraffin consistency. The mechanics' first job in the morning was to heat up quarts of oil on a stove until they reached a point where they could be poured into the engine.

At Mercedes, just before an early test carried out under the new formula, a serious glitch had appeared. The new car, it was discovered the night before the scrutineering, was overweight. Somehow, with all that microscopic attention to keeping weight down, their new cars were still two pounds over the limit of 1675 lbs (750 kgs, without tires or fluids).

Neubauer was frantic with frustration. They'd already removed every unnecessary part, drilled out every lever and pedal until they looked like Swiss cheese, hand-filing every tab and welding splatter to remove every iota of unnecessary metal that could add a fraction of an ounce.

Neubauer and his driver, Manfred von Brauchitsch, stared at the car helplessly the night before its first weigh-in.

"Well, take something off the thing!" Manfred suggested helpfully, flipping an ash from his cigarette on the floor of the shop.

"You know we've pared off every gram of unneeded metal, Manfred. And I wish you wouldn't smoke around the cars. "

Manfred chuckled the way he usually did when he saw Neubauer in a sweat. "Well it looks as if the only thing you have left to peel off is the paint!" he said dryly.

"The mechanics see the ashes lying around and they get the wrong idea," Neubauer was going on about Manfred's smoking habits. "I've told them a thousand ..."

Suddenly Neubauer stopped talking like he'd been gagged. Then he gave the astonished von Brauchitsch one of his famous Neubauer-bearhugs.

"The paint! Why didn't I think of that before? Manfred, you're a genius!"

A few phone calls later and the national racing color of Germany was changed from what it had always been (white, as in "the Great

White Team" that had skunked the French back in the days before the War) to what it still is today; silver grey, the color of bare aluminum. The team stayed up all night scraping the paint off the car, and (miraculously to Neubauer's point of view) it narrowly just made it under the weight limit at the next day's scrutineering.

As one would guess under the highly-charged competitive circumstances imposed by Berlin, a certain amount of informal espionage flourished naturally between the two teams. When the Auto Union first rolled out through the compound gates for early-morning preliminary road tests (on actual roads, no less, not special test-tracks) it would be at first light, when no one was around to witness the runs except a stray binoculared early morning birdwatcher or two. When Sebastian noticed the same birdwatchers seemed to appear in the distance every dawn as the tests progressed, he took the precaution to bring along some binoculars of his own. On closer look he saw familiar faces from the Mercedes team under the birdwatchers' bristled alpine hats. After a quick conference it was decided that for the next tests they'd weld on some extra dummy-exhaust pipes in varying numbers so that the Mercedes spies could report back some interesting new engine designs to come from Auto Union. A V-22?

At Mercedes, on the other hand, Neubauer was having a hard time finding a cook that could cope with the varied demands of all the nationalities on the team. An old Mercedes man, now one of the Auto Union team, mentioned to him a fabulous cook who could concoct incredible meals to please a wide variety of national tastes.

The only problem was, this cook was already very busy and only spoke Italian. This didn't stop Neubauer of course, who spoke whatever language was needed at the time, and it wasn't long before the new cook was delighting the whole Mercedes team with his meals.

Then it started to seem like whatever move Mercedes made, the Auto Union team already knew about it. It was only after a number of speed secrets had somehow mysteriously leaked to Auto Union that Neubauer discovered by accident that this "Italian" cook spoke perfect German and was collecting a second paycheck for reporting all the tableside Mercedes scuttlebutt back to Auto Union every week.

Inevitably, as the two teams were thrown together more and more as the season approached, the espionage turned to active practical jokes. Smoke bombs under the hoods of prominent race team figures, tools wired to high-voltage shockers, learner's permit signs fixed onto champion driver's cars — kid stuff, really, but the kind of mischief that kept everyone aware of how easily the opposition could sneak in and out undetected.

Although Huhnlein didn't enjoy his ration of smoke-bombs and pranks, he recognized the high energy-level that the practical joking displayed, and turned a blind eye to it. It was just the sort of thing to diffuse any building animosity between the German teams; the kind of larks that made it easier to stand the repeated all-night deadline-meeting wrench-sessions; easier to stand the times when a much-loved driver goes out for a lap and never comes back again; easier to stand the weekly presence of death which always seemed to lurk a trifle too close for comfort around the world of motor racing.

However, it was just this sort of horseplay that Hitler wanted to see none of when his new teams took center stage for all the world to watch. Hitler, in his own linear-thinking way, could see no use for silliness, especially in front of half-a-million spectators and all the radios at home. Hitler often said that the Nazi movement was essentially a male youth-movement, yet he left precious little room for the kind of horseplay that male youths demand, especially in high-tension contexts.

To provide strong leadership for the N.S.K.K.'s motorsports programs Huhnlein had to call on all his strengths, reaching back to some bitter street-fighting campaigns against the outnumbering Communists. The very nature of the N.S.K.K. programs attracted the most daring youths. And daring youths have a traditional penchant for horseplay that would have to be watched, controlled, channeled. Even with the conflicting agendas, even with the caught-in-the-middle feeling with Berlin breathing down his neck, it was still a dream assignment for the old street brawler.

Huhnlein was not known for hesitating when the time for action came. It might be a challenge to translate his particular style of leadership to the new kind of man of action that was coming onto stage in the thirties, for men like von Brauchitsch and von Oertzen tended to say whatever came into their heads and never cared much for taking orders.

Manfred happened to be the hot-tempered scion of an old Prussian military family, the recent star of a popular movie, nephew of General von Brauchitsch, and infamous playboy who never went to Party meetings, rarely was seen in his SS uniform, and only wore his diamond swastika when it could get him a better table at a nightclub.

On the track, however, Manfred was not a lucky driver. They called him the "Pechvogel" (the bird of bad luck). But he was a steady

SportscorpsFührer Adolf Huhnlein, Hitler's handpicked leader of the N.S.K.K. racing programs brings the military touch to the sport of Grand Prix competition. The occasion is a Nazi demonstration of German Grand Prix might at the Stadtpark in Hamburg.
photo: Auto Union Archive

pusher, a dependable, durable driver whom Neubauer could send off as the "rabbit" to blow his engine by pushing too hard (but also entice the opposition's team leader to blow his engine as well). Often Neubauer's other drivers took the lead at the finish. Part of Manfred's Pechvogel legend had been born of this rabbit role he'd often had to play, and part was the result of his uncontrollable Prussian temper.

But if anyone could tame the high-spirited German youths (and the crusty old campaigners) to turn them into good ambassadors of the New Germany, Huhnlein was likely to be the man to do it.

As the testing progressed toward the start of the new season in spring 1934, it became obvious that the new cars had the potential for the kind of power-performance never before seen on a racetrack. By the time they reached this level of tune, they were pushing only a few pounds for every horsepower (about ten times the power per pound of a passenger car), far outstripping what had been the norm even the season before. In acceleration they were breathtaking — able to spin the rear wheels and leave a black mark at speeds nearing a hundred miles an hour. If we were cruising down the freeway at a hundred and we passed a highway patrolman sitting by the side of the road in an

Auto Union, he would be able to peel out and pass us before we'd gone one more mile (or in less than 45 seconds — hardly time enough to turn on the flashing lights). The torque would prove so amazing that at Monte Carlo, where normally a driver can make 1500 gear changes in a single race, the Auto Union could be left in one gear and still turn in respectable lap times.

But as exciting as this news was to Hitler — that he would very soon have the cars he needed to conquer the world of racing and send the Italians fleeing for cover — there was disturbing news from another part of the program: the drivers. Germany was low on top-rated drivers. Stuck, of course, was of international stature, as was Manfred. But neither had been consistently successful against the Italians. Rudi Caracciola, the German with the Italian name from the Rhineland, had been what Germany needed — a really consistent, professional world-beater against any team. But Rudi had recently been through a hell of accidents and personal setbacks that made his future career in racing a very large question mark. Later in the thirties Germany would have developed a whole platoon of world-class drivers. Then, at one race you could see (along with the French, English, and Italian drivers in German cars) half a dozen or more truly legendary drivers, all of whom were capable of winning the day. But in 1934, just when Germany needed talent the most, the pickings were slim.

It wasn't because of lack of interest from Germany's youth. Ever since Hitler's Motor Show Speech, dreams of leading New Germany's race teams danced through the heads of young Germans from border to border. But, according to Neubauer, most of them began their letters with the phrase, "I'm not afraid to die!" The battlefield ideals of *Ein Heldenleben*, a "Hero's Life" that Hitler was sowing into the romantic minds of young Teutons, was not exactly what race team managers had in mind to build a successful new team.

"It's not dead race drivers that we're interested in," Neubauer would write back, "it's winning race drivers!"

It's here that we run into the first real confrontation between the romantic ideals of the rule-seeking linear-thinker — and the kind of experienced mind that is used to risking its life exploring regions of performance that no one has returned from alive.

Hitler had no concept of what it takes to survive by deliberately throwing your car into a slide so it can exit a corner faster. He not only couldn't drift a car, he couldn't even drive one. He couldn't fly a plane, like Mussolini, and it was possibly this lack of hands-on experience that gave birth to the simplistic, romantic thinking that decided that these new ultra powerful cars should be given to the brave lads of his Hitler-Youth to take Germany to new glory. And the Youth of the nation lined up in impatient queues to try their luck at a hero's life, or a hero's death — whichever came first.

Before we chuckle too much at their eagerness, we should take into consideration what a task driving a really high-tech race car is for anybody bold enough to try it. After much cajoling at a recent press gathering, journalists were given a chance to try their hands at driving a modern Grand Prix car. Very few were able to make the car even leave the starting line, much less make it all the way around the track — and this was the *motoring* press. The situation was much the same in the 1930s. With clutch springs strong as pythons, a narrow powerband that required exact revving to get performance, and wheels that seem to spin uselessly if you let your mind wander for a split second, these monsters needed finesse, not brutal, blind courage, just to get them rolling forward. To persuade one to navigate the fourteen miles of mountainous hairpins around Nürburgring took a bit of practice.

When the first youth of the driver-trials (urged by Berlin to find new talent) was seated in a car staring ahead with glazed determination, Neubauer walked up to the car and gave the lad a friendly, reassuring pat on the cheek (to check for cold-sweat) and a fatherly squeeze of the shoulder (to monitor for trembling). The lad wasn't the only nervous one at these trials. Neubauer and the whole pit crew were standing by watching uneasily. It wasn't fun to see kids get hurt. If Berlin had a better feel for what was really involved in controlling cars like these, they'd never have pushed for putting kids, no matter how brave and well-connected, into these machines without months of preparation.

The engine revved high, then fell too fast as the clutch jerked out when tired leg muscles gave way to the spring pressure. The engine died, as the car lurched only a few feet ahead. Engine restarted, the lad made sure this embarrassment would not recur by keeping the revs too high as he released the clutch. The mechanics standing in attendance knew what this would produce. First the rear wheels would spin madly sending up clouds of bluish white smoke. Then, as the lad discovered he was going nowhere even though the wheels were spinning, he'd ease off on the gas, the wheels would slow, then one would grab pavement and send the car pirouetting until the other wheel grabbed as well. By this time the car was usually pointed toward the reviewing stand and much taking-for-cover would disturb the officials' dignity as the car rocketed toward them, before the engine died again. Since the mechanics sensed this was about to happen they could make simple, but elegant toreador evasions to keep from harm's way. But for officials from Berlin, it was an unnerving display that always ruffled their feathers.

This was enough "racing" for this particular youth, who received little urging to try again. Hard on the cars, and the officials' decorum.

A new Youth took his place and actually made the car get off the starting line, albeit with a few fish-tailing slewings that woke up spectators along the fences. Officials sat back with their stopwatches to be ready to assess the lad's first lap time when he reappeared. But eventually, stopwatches were clicked back to zero again as it became obvious the lad had lost it somewhere on the course. The tow truck was dispatched and preparations were made for the next run.

The next Youth was a huge lad, barely squeezed into his SS uniform, who looked like he "could easily have twisted the steering wheel off like a pretzel," according to Neubauer. Here was a beefy young German who should have little trouble managing mere racing cars. But once again, after he'd taken off on his trial lap, and after he hadn't reappeared on schedule, the somewhat disappointed mechanics started up the tow-truck. When they spotted the car, it was parked off the road in a quiet glen. They found nothing of the SS-Youth except the torn sleeve of his uniform. He'd somehow disappeared into thin air, never to be seen again.

Humorous, of course, but expensive. The driver trials were stopped before more cars were put in danger of being wrecked by overeager, undertrained young lads. In the press coverage, a few phone calls from Berlin made certain that the reason for the hasty cancellation mentioned something about "unprepared equipment" and shifted the blame to the mechanics and designers. The mechanics and designers could have told Berlin that this dangerous waste of time was exactly what they could only expect to happen. But no one had asked their opinion, and a sullen silence came from Berlin.

Then word came: the team managers should seek qualified drivers with the kind of experience needed to beat the Italians, wherever they could find them, regardless of party politics, nationality, ethnic origin, the way they parted their hair, toothpaste preference, anything. Just get drivers who can handle the machines and get the job done. When the name of a very fast driver who also happened to be from a promi-

Dr. Porsche looks pleased with his new creation's performance after taking it for a spin. Interrogating the Professor is Stuck, with a happy-looking Sebastian and Walb looking on. But would it have the stamina to beat Mussolini's teams in the gruelling test of a full-length race?

photo: Auto Union Archive

nent Jewish family was mentioned, word came back from Berlin impatiently, "*We'll* decide who's Jewish!"

Now things started to move. It was like putting out a sign that said, "Available: racing cars that can rub the noses of your worst rivals in the dust. Apply within." Top talent always wants to work on the Big Canvas. It's doubtful if Michelangelo spent a lot of time agonizing over papal atrocities in the New World or the horrors of the Inquisition when the chance to do the Sistine Chapel came his way. And whether

Bach hesitated in taking on new commissions from the king of Prussia in view of his miltary adventurism is hard to imagine. We in our privileged place at the cutting edge of history also don't seem to worry about the lying and treachery of the benefactors who have paid the bills to have our favorite geniuses of our culture put to work either. It's always the age-old balancing act between genius and power, with genius hungering for only the best stage to work on and power buying its way into history by providing the cash to stage the show.

At this point the really talented race drivers of all Europe flocked to the record-breaking cars of Hitler's new teams. It might have taken them awhile to get over their national preferences, but when checkered flags are up for grabs, talent starts knocking on your door. And as in any other talent-based performance group, the ones who answered the call were what might be called a mixed bag.

In this first catch-as-catch-can batch, there was a sprinkling of royalty, minor princes, and shirt-tail aristocracy mixed in among the Italian thugs, Monagasque taxi-dancers, and lowly mechanics with a knack for turning in quick lap times. In later batches would come the British rich-kids, the Swiss Storm-Troopers, the French playboys. A polyglot bunch with about one thing only in common: a talent for driving fast based largely on a spirit of adventurous exploration, and its consequent lack of regard for rules and the bureaucrats who enforce them.

Hitler was in a hurry to prove his motoring plan for Germany, and he wasn't in the mood to care whether those who carried out his plan did things by the book all the time. At least, at this point.

Those who stopped at the border where the comfy rules and catechisms ended and the terra-incognita of unexplored speed began, just wouldn't do the trick. And when those who go beyond the limits return back to Earth among mere mortals again, the old rules and etiquettes often seemed unimportant.

It couldn't have escaped Huhnlein's notice that this new assignment of his might take some clever leadership tricks to keep this adventuresome bunch pointed in the right direction, according to Berlin gospel. This could end up a wild tiger act, with too many cats and not enough stools if he didn't maintain control around the pits. As the spring of 1934 brought their first attempt to beat the Italians closer, the time for Berlin's stirring speeches would soon be over. When the flag drops, as they say, the hogwash stops.

Chapter 11

Rebirth

By winter of 1934, Rudi, in his Swiss convalescence, was coming more and more to the point where he could manage his daily life on his own. Charly's life had come to a stop at Monte Carlo, of course, but now Rudi was determined to start paying her back for her unswerving loyalty. Since Rudi could see she was showing signs of becoming seriously house-bound, and since a party of friends had been planning a ski outing to the glacier, for the first time that season Rudi pushed Charly to go along. Just as he'd lost a big part of his life when the racing had stopped, Charly had missed her skiing trips. A little unsure of herself after the long convalescence that had taken a toll with her as well as Rudi, she hesitated.

But Rudi was adamant. There would be no arguing with him, she knew. He would even pick her up at the station when the party returned that afternoon. Rudi saw with a leap of enthusiasm that the old Charly was beginning to resurface as she prepared her gear and met up with the gathering party. Rudi felt the color coming back into their lives again, with Charly back to her old active life again.

About five in the evening Rudi made his way down to the station to catch a bit of the clamorous good cheer of the returning ski party. But no one was there to meet him. Disappointed, Rudi limped back up to the house and sat in the gathering dusk thinking of the beauty of the evening and all the fun reasons they'd had for missing their train and taking a later one in the past. The telephone rang. It was a stranger saying that the ski party wouldn't be coming until the last train. There'd been an accident that had held them up.

"What kind of accident?"

She didn't know. Just that there was a delay. Rudi had just lit some candles to prolong the soft mood of the twilight into the evening. A skier was walking up the drive. He could hear the solid stomp of the ski boots. He could hear skis being propped in the snow, then a knock at the door? Why would Charly knock?

"Come on up, will you?!" Rudi's voice sounded tight and strange, even to him.

The figure made its way clomping up the stairs. It was one of the young men from the party that was skiing the glacier that day with Charly.

"Good evening Signor Caracciola, I wanted to …."

And then the candlelight fell on the young man's face. He stopped in mid-sentence when he saw Rudi's eyes boring into his own.

"Charly?" Rudi asked.

The lad nodded.

"Dead?" Rudi said, finally forcing the word out of his dry throat.

The lad nodded. They stood gaping at each other stupidly.

"She must have seen the avalanche before it hit her. Heart attack."

Then the lad turned and ran as if the devil were chasing him. Rudi heard the door slam, as if another chapter of his life had been locked away forever. He put out the candles, all except one, and sat staring at it until it guttered out just before sunrise.

No telephone calls, no letters, no telegrams — nothing had been answered.

"I know Rudi," Chiron was saying to Baby. "He'll close up like a crab. He'll just sit in that villa with the blinds drawn until he dies of old age!" He was right, of course. When Chiron had burst into the villa a few days later, unannounced, Rudi was lying on the couch in a darkened room, just as Louis had imagined it.

"Bon Jour, Rudi!" he said, as if they'd only just talked the day before. He threw his coat over a chair, grabbed another, straddled it, and spoke nothing of the cataclysms that had taken place since Monte Carlo. Rudi was grateful for Louis' good sense in these things.

"I was just talking with Faroux about writing to you about doing the lap of honor at the Monte this year. But I said Ah, bah! Why write? Rudi never answers his mail! I'll just go to Arosa and drag him back with me by the scruff of his neck!"

"No," Rudi said softly, "I'd rather not."

"But Rudi! You're still a young man! You can't molder in this cave forever! Just help me arrange this lap of honor thing, eh? Back on the horse, n'est-ce pas?!"

Rudi was no match for Chiron's ebullience, and within a half hour Chiron had won all points. Rudi was going to leave the cave.

At Monte Carlo, where it had all begun, the sun was showing bright as if nothing had happened to change life. The roads shimmered in warmth, the flags snaked in the breeze. Yachts bobbed at their moorings in the harbor. Pretty girls and bright young lads lived their lives playfully, just as if there were no pain anywhere in the world.

Rudi was amazed at the effect, like a tonic, all the colors and aromas and movements were having on him. It was no homage to Charly to let himself grow into a flabby old man in a dark corner. She was not that sort. Charly had known all about her heart condition and had made a secret pact with Baby to make sure Rudi wouldn't do just what he had been doing if it ever overcame her. Chiron had been so right to bring him to Monte Carlo.

And here was all the spectacle that had filled so much of him before. He'd never realized how much of the charm racing had nothing to do with actually driving fast. Here was Tazio, as quietly charming and full of color as ever, just as if no time had passed. And Varzi, gravely chic, like a demon on borrowed time, touring paradise. And Dreyfus — who could keep the stab of pain going when Dreyfus was around making his little quips?

Rudi slipped into the cockpit and felt like he'd found his armor again, his defense against the meaninglessness that all the cynical philosophers went on about. A little girl ran up and dumped a bouquet of roses into Rudi's lap. He laughed gratefully at her pretty formality, and took off around the track slowly on his lap of honor. The president stood and waved to him, and the rest of the crowd followed suit all around the lap, people cheering and clapping. He could hear the splash of the sparkling waves against the quay. How could he have been such a brat sulking in the dark? How many knew the kind of world he knew, and then would dream of turning their back on it? He returned to the pits, his leg twinging with pain, his mind racing with unexpected impressions. Some men were hunters, some were builders. Rudi was a racer, part and parcel of the racing world. The pain from the leg was nothing, he realized, to the unfelt numbing that came from a life without your natural calling. To be the thinking part of a hurtling, beautifully crafted speed machine was worth any kind of waiting and pain.

The old quartet of Rudi and Charly, Louis and Baby, had become the constant trio. There'd slowly surfaced a subtle change in the balance among the three survivors. Rudi was looking at Baby differently these days. Perhaps there'd been more to Charly and Baby's pact than met the eye, for Rudi was hardly the type to go after his friend's mistress without a change of signals about the rules of the game. And Baby seemed to be changing the signals.

Gradually Baby began to take on a role with Rudi that was somewhat different than an angel of mercy. As confusion grew about which man would be her better choice, Baby began to try to pin Louis down about the marriage he had been promising was just around the corner for some time now.

But pinning Louis down, especially about such delicate matters as marriage, well, that was something no one had ever had much success with. Finally driven to distraction by his constant squirming out of the way when a wedding was discussed, Baby sat Chiron down and put it to him. "Louis, look at me. Are you ever going to marry me?"

"But, of course, marriage is a serious subject not to be taken lightly," he began. "When a man thinks of taking a wife he must take into consideration factors other than simple personality attraction," Louis explained. Then he dropped the bomb. "For me, I had always pictured myself with a wife somewhat younger than myself."

"You mean I'm too old for you even though we're the same age?" Baby said as calmly as she could manage.

"Exactly so! I knew you would understand!" In ten more seconds she was out of Chiron's apartment, leaving him to smoke a cigarette in perplexed solitude.

Dreyfus got a call not long after. It was Baby asking him over for dinner. Since Dreyfus's wife Chou Chou and Baby were good friends, Dreyfus was puzzled by the invitation to come alone, but said nothing. When he arrived for the dinner, he was greeted by Baby's bags, all packed and ready to move. Could he give her a lift to the station?

"I'm leaving Louis. I'm going to marry Rudi." Dreyfus, always a little on the innocent side when dealing with the flexibility of loyalties, stood mouth agape.

"Well? Do you think I'm doing the right thing?"

Dreyfus had not known Rudi all that closely. But after a quick think-through, he said, "Well, as a matter of fact, yes I do." Rudi was much better husband material than Louis. Don Juan would be better husband material than Louis.

Dawn the next day Dreyfus heard an impatient knocking at his door. It was Chiron in a fine fury.

"How could she do this to me?!" Louis began without preamble, sitting and lighting a cigarette. "For that matter," he said, looking directly at Rene, "how could he do this to me!?"

"Much the same way you did the same thing to her first husband," Dreyfus said dryly.

"That was different," Louis said, trying fitfully to get a match to light. It was true, it had been different when Louis had taken Baby from Freddy Hoffmann. He'd been coveting another man's wife then, while Baby was nobody's wife now — and not likely to become one as long as she stayed with Louis.

Baby had put one condition on her "Yes" to Rudi: they must first get Chiron's blessing. By the time Louis was asked if he would sanction the marriage, he'd had time to digest the question. Perhaps it was time he started looking for someone a little younger than Baby. Still, he kept his Gallic dignity. "Baby is old enough to know what she's doing," was his reply — a masterpiece of diplomatic knife-throwing, never mentioning Rudi, yet being sure to bring the age-issue back to centerstage.

The cars were passing from their testing programs to the stage when they were put to use setting speed records, a relatively cheap way to gain them publicity without the all-day demands of a full racing competition to overstrain their all-new designs. The Gyon Highway in Hungary was perfect for just such tests. Wide and straight, and away from the prying eyes of the press. In these early runs, there would be plenty of time to inform the press after the fact, just in case things went wrong.

They weren't going particularly right, from Neubauer's point of view, as he sat nursing breakfast in a Budapest hotel. The weather had been steadily miserable, no good for testing anything but umbrellas. Neubauer's only driver available for the test had been Ernst Henne, who was really more of a motorcycle racer than a car driver. But the test had been scheduled, come rain or lack of drivers, so they sat morosely watching the rain dribble down the windows of the cafe. Rudi appeared suddenly, in an immaculate white driving suit.

"Where the devil have you come from?" Neubauer blurted. He wasn't ready for surprises that morning.

"Straight from Switzerland. I thought I'd like to see your record attempts."

"Why the racing suit, if you're just spectating?"

Rudi shrugged. "I always dress for the occasion. Besides, you might need a second driver."

"Hardly likely," Henne broke in. "As you know, I'm driving."

But fate took over in Rudi's favor that day. On the first record attempt, Henne had trouble with the supercharger. On the second run the aerodynamic cockpit-cover loosened and blinded Henne for a split second while he almost disintegrated the timer's hut. Henne climbed out of the new car, a trifle unsteadily, Neubauer thought.

"I've had enough for today," Henne said, stripping off his windcap in disgust. "If you'd like to try your luck, Herr Caracciola, I've no objection."

Rudi nodded, strapped on his windcap, climbed into the Merc, and drove off to hit a top speed faster than any man had driven a Grand Prix car on an open highway. Back in the saddle again.

Neubauer returned to Stuttgart to report to Kissel. Mercedes had some nice new world speed records in their pocket, but most exciting to Don Alfredo, he could face the Direktors honestly about Rudi. They needed him now.

Chapter 12

Teething Problems

In Italy, Germany's new racing threat wasn't underestimated. But when the details of the new cars from Germany became known, the Italians had relaxed a bit. Knowing smiles were traded around racing circles in the Milan trattorias.

The Germans, they believed, were placing too much faith in complete departures from what had been proved won races. The Italians, after all, had become the forefront of racing design with bicycles, motorcycles, cars, and even airplanes, by careful refinement of patiently evolved, tradition-bound designs.

Every once in awhile they would see a competitor, frustrated at not being able to beat them at traditional finish, take off on a completely new tack, hoping for that "X-Factor" that might be found in a completely new approach that could beat the world. That's how Porsche's new design, and even the more traditional Mercedes appeared. The Italians knew how to build cars that won races, and that was that. Radical new changes had been tried before, but they'd rarely met with much success.

Continuity was the watchword of Italy, reaching back with its artisans to the medieval armor makers, the Roman bronze foundries. You can see it all in the exhaust manifold of an Alfa Romeo: peaceful continuity, not barbaric departures, so it was in Tazio Nuvolari's villa at Via Rimembranze, shrouded in tranquil gardens tended by a house-centered wife, his sons overseen by their sports-minded maiden aunt, slippers, hair-net, smoking jacket, and the turtle-pin mascot given to him by the poet Gabriele D'Annunzio. There was the room full of racing trophies from several generations of Nuvolaris, carefully tended by son Giorgio, a budding young motorcylist himself. There was even a gift from that German politician,

Hans Stuck, one of the few tall Grand Prix drivers (he stood 6'2"), dwarfs the Auto Union "Lucca" record-setter. In the late 1920s, he was King of the Hillclimb driving Dr. Porsche's SSK-Mercedes.

photo: Auto Union Archive

Hitler (a nice bronze bust of himself looking severe) as a tribute from one romantic hero to another.

A quiet evening at home where the frantic action of the racing world could be forgotten. Reading the paper, with the radio playing in the background. Suddenly a news item on the radio made Tazio shoot bolt upright in his easy chair.

The announcer was saying that Hans Stuck had just driven his Auto Union over 190 miles an hour. Tazio had to get in touch with Enzo Ferrari at the Alfa Corse racing team at once. If these radical new German machines actually worked, perhaps Italy had better get busy.

The new German teams had survived Hitler's fanciful dream of having his new racers wielded by young Nazi party members, and now with the start of a stable of really professional drivers in each camp, the two teams had settled down to seeing how fast they could come to grips with the Italian cars.

The first driving teams to campaign the new cars turned out to be, for Auto Union: Hans Stuck, ex-Mercedes hill climb master in Dr. Porsche's awesome SSK's, Prince Zu Leiningen, and August Momberger. Rosenberger, the ex-Mercedes driver (and later Auto Union comptroller) had given in to the growing political pressures from Berlin to see to it that the Jews emigrated. Both Stuck and von Oertzen would feel the anti-Semitic ripple effect later for having the thoughtlessness to marry women with Jewish blood. But this would come to bear gradually as pressures increased. The Auto Union team ran its races under the pit management of Willy Walb, another ex-Mercedes old-pro.

Neubauer's team at Mercedes started out its first season with the volatile Manfred von Brauchitsch (of good party pedigree, since his uncle was to become Hitler's Field Marshal); the largely unmanageable Italian, Luigi Fagioli; the cycle racer Henne; and Caracciola as team leader. As the '34 season approached it would be a debut of both the new Grand Prix formula as well as Hitler's new silver rockets. All eyes (especially Berlin eyes) watched how the first races would go in open, international competition, where the very first fruits of Hitler's Social Motorization Programs would show their mettle to the world.

From Hitler's point of view, much of his future political freedom hung on these programs — they had to be successful, especially in the early stages, to prove his follow-through and to build the snowball-effect he was counting on to give him the solid basis of popular support he needed to take a freer hand with his rivals.

Sometimes called "the Brigand of Abruzzi" because of his forceful will to win despite carefully-thought-out-team-plans or Neubauer's orders, Luigi Fagioli nevertheless was instrumental in putting the new Mercedes team back in the winner's circle during that slow, nervous period when teething problems were making victory seem agonisingly far off.

photo: Mercedes Benz

As the season gathered momentum at the Monte Carlo Grand Prix, the race was not won by one of Germany's new-order, futuristic machines driven by one of Germany's young heroes as planned, but by (of all people) an Algerian named Guy Moll in one of the traditional Alfa Romeos. Chiron, also driving an Alfa, came in a strong second, with Rene Dreyfus just behind him in a French Bugatti — an even more tradition-bound design.

Teething problems were to be expected in the new machines. Hitler surely knew this from the vast history of car racing he had at his fingertips. But at Berlin's fabulously futuristic Avus track, a very fast course that would favor the new German giants, Hitler and a full entourage of Nazi nabobs had actually appeared in person to watch their new machines humble Mussolini's teams amid the strange Fascist retro-futuristic pageantry. The Führer was clearly hoping for a better performance than had been seen at the Monte, but then that was a tiny track that favored the nimble Alfas and Bugattis. Here at a real man-sized track like the Avus, Hitler expected more.

But it was "Marcia Reale," the Italian anthem, not "Deutschland über Alles" that was played for the winner, the Algerian Moll coming in first again in an Alfa, followed by Varzi in another Alfa in second place. An Auto Union driven by August Momberger had worked its way to third place, at least. Where were Hitler's champions who had done so well in the past? And where were the German racers that had set such promising, blistering new speed records?

At the French Grand Prix, where Germany hoped to regain the dominance it had shown just before World War I, the world was once again underwhelmed by the much-discussed new rockets from the Reich. Not one of the Mercedes cars was fit to do battle on race day, while the Auto Unions found themselves, once again, trailing Chiron's Alfa in first place, a Bugatti in second, and a Maserati in third. Little problems were crippling the new cars time after time. Porsche knew to expect such frustrations with any new car, but others in Berlin were beginning to shift uneasily in their seats as the season went by with little to show for their efforts.

It was that time of the game when investors start fidgeting nervously and wondering if they've made a big, big mistake. And the investor in this case was Adolf Hitler. His new racing program was to be his first and fastest way to show follow-though to the Social-Motorization plan. But this string of losses was shaping up to be the kind of travesty to make Hitler's centralized planning look like a laughing stock.

Chapter 13

A Tale of Two Drivers II

While this drama was unfolding, with drivers of Caracciola's generation forming the mainstay of Germany's hope for a new assault on Italy's vise-grip on the Grand Prix world, the inevitable was happening: youngsters were coming on stage, eager to topple any champion who happened to have an off-day.

Idolizing drivers like Caracciola and Stuck from the sidelines of a small town called Lingen was a lad named Bernd Rosemeyer. Rosemeyer, much like another of his heroes, Tazio Nuvolari, had grown up around the machinery of his family's garage. Like Nuvolari, he had uncles who'd raced motorcycles successfully and who put their promising young nephew on a machine at an early age. By his teens, Bernd had mastered his motorbike. When a carnival came to town that included a "Wall of Death" act where motorcycles roar around inside a huge, barrel-like circular wall, Bernd had to bribe his way onto the Wall of Death where he amazed the locals by riding it hands-off.

Bernd Rosemeyer, the instant maestro who came from nowhere to surprise Caracciola with the greatest rivalry of his career. Bernd's impish wit and constant grin presented a challenge to more than just his fellow drivers. His antics caused the rival Mercedes team manager, Neubauer to fume at times, but he still couldn't help smiling at Bernd's pranks.
photo: Auto Union Archive

When Bernd was seen riding down the main street of the town standing on top his motorcycle at a respectful military salute, there'd been complaints to the local constabulary. Bernd had been riding around town standing on his head on the gas tank, they complained. Clearly, the boy was becoming a menace to safety and had to be taught a lesson to keep him from riding on the sidewalks all the time. The head of the local police solved the problem with one quick, sure stroke: he took away Bernd's license.

The move was a bigger bombshell in Bernd's life than he'd envisioned. He quickly found he was only half-alive without some sort of motor machine to provide a means for his own peculiar mode of expression. To Bernd, the control of machines could be raised to the level of an art, almost a dance form.

Bernd wrote a piteous letter to the police chief to appeal to the man's humanity, and hopefully reduce this agonizing torture he was going through. Since it was the Christmas season, Bernd didn't hesitate to play on the seasonal sentimentalism and good will that he hoped he could count on at that time of year. The effect was just what Bernd was hoping for, and having learned his lesson (to a certain extent) Bernd started looking toward organized racing as a way to continue building his skills without landing himself in jail.

In 1931, a visitor to his uncle's garage had a bike scheduled for a local race, but his rider was sick. Bernd leapt at the chance and demonstrated some of his motorcycle circus tricks to the man on the spot. He got a ride in the race, a chance to try his hand against other riders in the 250 cc class. He won that and almost beat all of the 500 cc bikes as well.

Impressed, the man hired Bernd to ride regularly, and in one race Bernd demonstrated a quality that stuck with him later in bigger machines, racing for more important sponsors. He'd been well-placed in the field, but then found that his rear tire was leaking, making handling dangerously mushy and unpredictable. There was no way, in those days, for a quick wheel change and for anyone else that would have been that for the day. But Bernd never looked to mechanical problems as an excuse to quit a race. To Bernd, mechanical problems were a nuisance that could cut short his fun for the afternoon if he couldn't find a way around them. He'd find any way to stay in the action, even if he knew he couldn't win. And by staying on the track, he sometimes found others dropping out and leaving the victory to him after all. This day, the best he could do was fourth after his repeated stops to pump the tire back up. But his game approach had impressed some onlookers. Here was a lad who didn't just "want to be a racer" — he "wanted to race." If he won, even better. As a result, he often found himself winning.

Bernd's dream, like that of many young Germans of the time, was to join Hans Stuck in carrying Germany's banner to the world. But unlike all those other young dreamers, Bernd had figured out his own way of making his dream happen, even when no one else agreed with him that he was the obvious choice to be the future champion of Germany.

Bernd was a good looking youth who didn't mind dressing up for the occasion, a bit of a peacock with two heads, as Neubauer would call lads like him. But his constant urge to build new capabilities kept him sensible about performance matters. He was always seen with a trace of a smile, which some saw as arrogance — an expression they'd love to wipe off his face. Others saw it as a much needed dose of fun that could break the spell of fear that could sometimes take over racing.

Track clowns (like Mike Hawthorn in a later era) at first seem to annoy everyone with their constant refusal to take what was very important to the group seriously. But then, as the others come to realize how much personal help they get from an occasional laugh at just the right moment, these clowns become the most valued members of the pits scene.

As soon as he saw that his own arrogant view of his capabilities was backed up by his wins on the motorcycle circuits, Bernd began his long march toward Grand Prix. Huhnlein's N.S.K.K. had been organizing off-road trials for small sportscars — Audis, from the Auto Union group. And Bernd's cycle racing record had been good enough to get him a car to drive at these club-level events, where he competed alongside Dr. Porsche's son, Ferry.

But Bernd had something else in mind. Rather than work his way up step by step through the military-style ranks of the N.S.K.K. events, Bernd began to harass the Auto Union team manager, Willy Walb, into giving him a try-out in the new cars. With no experience at all in single-seat, open-wheeled racers, this seemed a little far-fetched to some.

But Bernd may have sensed that the strange handling of the revolutionary rear-engined car might take a different technique than the one learned by the drivers of traditional front-engined cars. A driver with no "bad habits" built up from years of driving conventional racers might have an edge in these new rear-engined cars.

Bernd had no habits in four-wheeled racers, just those he learned on motorcycles. And history was to show that the ones who learned to handle the Auto Union best, outside of Hans Stuck, all came from a long background of racing motorcycles. But at this point in history, Bernd could only see his lack of experience in race cars as something to be glossed-over and kept quiet, not as a possible advantage in the long run (just as Rudi had cursed his luck that it always seemed to be raining on his early races, before he learned that for his particular style, this was the best luck possible).

Soon, whenever Walb came to work, there on the bulletin board at Auto Union was a message posted prominently, reading: "When is that brilliant new star Rosemeyer going to get a chance to show his stuff in the Auto Union?"

When Walb signed the paychecks, there, scrawled across the ledgers was a reminder, "Rosemeyer is the obvious choice for the Auto Union team!" When Walb took his wife out for a quiet dinner, the waiter would hand him the bill that would read, "If you try Rosemeyer, you won't be sorry!" And looking up from the bill, Walb would see a smiling Rosemeyer in waiter's uniform, towel over his arm.

Bernd's ingenuity outfoxed the factory guards, the secretaries, everyone hired to keep Walb away from pests like Bernd. It became obvious, finally, that the only way to rid himself of this Rosemeyer menace was to give the idiot a chance to make a fool of himself in a driving test and get it over with.

On the morning of the great test Bernd showed up at the track in formal evening attire.

"What's this?" Walb asked, trading an outraged glance with Stuck.

Bernd takes the Auto Union for a dance through the woods. His quick touch with motorcycles gave him the ability to react to the Auto Union's nervous, and sometimes unannounced, handling quirks at speed.

photo: Auto Union Archive

"This is the most important day of my life." Bernd smiled sweetly. "So I thought I'd dress for it."

Walb was not amused. "Get into a driving suit and stop wasting our time!"

Bernd returned ready to drive, slipped behind the wheel, gave the Auto Union a throaty rev, and then took off with not too much fishtailing from tire-spin. Stuck clicked his stopwatch. A while later Stuck and Walb exchanged shrugs. It was obvious the young pain-in-the-neck had run off the course or had some sort of problem. Stuck stopped his watch and reset it to zero, a little disappointed. The lad did have a good bike racing record, he'd learned. And they needed competent new drivers — drivers with a real feel for competition like Bernd.

Then they looked up as they heard a blurping roar of the car being driven back in slowly. Sure enough, as Bernd rolled to a stop, the mechanic began pulling weeds and small shrubs out of the suspension. Walb went over, giving the sign to switch off. But Bernd kept the engine running. He cupped his hands to his mouth to shout to Walb over the din. "Can you imagine? She wanted to take me for a little dance in the woods!" Bernd laughed. "Now I'll take her for one!"

And before Walb could order him to get out, Bernd took off on a second lap. Something about his second start impressed Stuck and he quickly started his watch again. Next time Bernd came past, Stuck's watch showed they weren't wasting their morning with this upstart. Bernd was signed up on the spot.

Bernd's personality became a welcome new addition to the Auto Union team, which were for the most part rebels from the old Mercedes team and naturally inclined toward a certain irreverence themselves. Bernd grew especially close to the Sebastians, who adopted Bernd to become successor to the role Caracciola had played in their lives at Mercedes.

Bernd's exuberance, his spinning the cars in the pits in graceful circles to warm up their tires, his constant prank-playing and total lack of respect for anything but current performance, made him the pet of the mechanic corps. But despite his popularity and obvious delight at being on the team, no drives in the big races were coming his way.

Race after race during that initial, nervously unsuccessful period, while Hitler looked on with gimlet eye at the lackluster performance of his racers on both teams, Bernd chafed for a chance to show his stuff.

"We can't risk cars on new drivers at this point," Walb had said. "We need to chalk up some wins first." Bernd was given a drive at

Avus, but mechanical troubles had placed him back in the field, to no one's surprise. Good to give the lad some experience, though.

It wasn't until June 1935, at the Nürburgring, (Caracciola's personal playground where he'd worked his magic in the rain) Bernd was given another drive, a chance to get the feel of driving against the top men in the world on one of the most twisting, challenging courses.

Soon after the starting gun the crowd knew they were watching racing history. Rudi had shot away from the field, as he so often did at the Nürburgring. But glued to the German champion's tail was a complete newcomer — Rosemeyer. Lap after lap Rudi did everything he knew to shake this new pest off his rear wheels. But lap after lap the crowd gasped to see the newcomer hanging on. The two cars pulled away further from the others, in another race all their own.

Then the impossible. A complete newcomer was leading the entire field at Nürburgring, one of the toughest tracks anywhere, in one of the toughest cars to drive anywhere. The two cars hurtled toward the finish, with Rudi, this time, being the one glued to the back of the car ahead. Rudi was studying the lad's technique. Rough, but effective.

Then Rudi spotted a weak spot, a turn that Bernd simply hadn't yet mastered. Luckily for Rudi, time was running out for the lad to learn how to take that turn and make his shift fast enough to get the jump on the long straight leading to the finish line. Rudi didn't try to pass or regain the lead to lessen the insult of being passed by the newcomer. He just sat back and waited, Rudi-style, for his chance to get in the lethal counterpunch, without telegraphing his plan. Neubauer was signalling furiously to Rudi to speed up and take the lead. But Rudi just waved him off and sat tight on Bernd's tail.

In the final corner, Rudi let it all hang out like he hadn't done before, braking late, making instant gear-changes, and putting his foot down hard for the finish. Bernd, to his astonishment, saw Rudi go deep into the last turn next to him, make a quick shift and then shoot off in front for the finish line to win once again at Nürburgring.

Both German teams heaved a sigh of relief as the Italians were nowhere to be seen in the winner's circle or at a party, the likes of which Neubauer was master at organizing, which took place in the Eifelerhof Hotel situated trackside so drivers and teams could relax without worrying about fighting the traffic jams on the way home.

Rudi's win had been one of the most exciting finishes in a long time. But the name on everybody's lips was the name of this

"Rosemeyer" fellow. This, of course, rankled Rudi, whose brilliant fight back to the top was all but forgotten with the appearance of this youngster. After Neubauer's barrage of humorous toasts and roasts of the Mercedes team's cast of characters, Neubauer even included the Auto Union table in his speech. Germany's future on the track, with such keen inter-team bouts, began finally to look rosy after all.

When Neubauer had quieted down, onlookers noticed Rudi getting up and going over to the Auto Union table, walking right over with his noticeable limp to where Bernd was sitting. Rudi was carrying a swizzle-stick in his hand like a teacher's pointer.

"Well done, young man!" Rudi said, stopping at Bernd's chair. "But in future, don't just drive around the track," he added with a cautionary wave of the swizzle stick. "Use your head!"

For once Bernd was speechless, as Rudi handed him the swizzle stick. "Here. To practice your shifting with," Rudi added.

The room was silent as Bernd gazed at the swizzle stick in astonishment. The story of Rudi's swizzle stick speech made the rounds of the whole racing world before breakfast the next day. For a full year Bernd would wear the swizzle stick in his lapel, and an inscrutable

Rudi, already running away with the 1935 Eifelrennen even as the starting flag falls, shows he's in a hurry to regain his place in the Grand Prix world. This will be Rudi's first solo win after his accident, long convalescence, and after the death of his wife, Charly — the first of what will turn out to be a "Carraciola Year" in G.P. racing with five firsts.

photo: Mercedes Benz

smile on his face when asked about it. Bernd had one of his famous plans in mind.

It wasn't too long (except in Bernd's mind) before he racked up his first Grand Prix win at the Masaryk course near Prague in September 1935. In town to give a lecture to a scientific society about her recent record-setting flights to Asia and Africa was one of Germany's top long-distance record-setting woman pilots, Elly Beinhorn, recent recipient of the Hindenburg Prize. The Hindenburg Prize had come at just the right time for Elly, because she'd had to go into hock to make some of her flights, and she had lectures to give and bills to pay before she could set out on her next adventure.

Elly could hardly guess that her next adventure, probably the biggest in her life, would have little to do with her beloved airplanes. Since she was in Prague for a lecture date she'd been invited as special guest to watch the car race going on that weekend. Elly hadn't much interest in racing in those days. Race car drivers, as she saw them, were not really all that needed in the world — characters very close to carnival hooligans in their lifestyle. During the race, however, she developed a favorite to cheer for: Hans Stuck, with his tall, courtly gentlemanliness and whistle-clean driving style. But at the finish, it was this brash upstart named Rosemeyer who'd won. He was a mere boy, constantly roughhousing with the mechanics, and hardly able to keep a straight face even at the awards ceremony. Elly had been asked to present the trophy, and up close, she noticed a strange manner about the new lad the minute she was face-to-face with him. He seemed to lock on to her eyes, as though he couldn't look anywhere else. Somehow the boy had a strange way of making her nervous. He seemed so ... so unpredictable.

Bernd was hardly noticing. The thrill that comes only once in a lifetime to a driver — of making that first Grand Prix win against the world's best — he had completely forgotten about. He'd just met the woman he was going to marry, and this was much more important. She didn't know it, of course. Bernd couldn't expect other people to see the future the way he saw it, after all. He took the trophy, smiling with appreciation at how perfect Elly looked to him. It was as if he were saying to himself, "Well I'll be damned. So that's what my wife looks like!"

Bernd knew he'd have to move fast to secure a beachhead. He thanked Elly for the trophy and then, before the formalities had time

Elly flew a ME-108 Taifun (Typhoon). Introduced in 1934, the Taifun could carry a useful load over a thousand miles on its wooden frame at a cruising speed of 165 (performance that modern civilian aircraft are still hardpressed to equal). Although at this point Willy Messerschmitt had never designed a warplane, his later ME-109, which was the scourge of the RAF for so many years, owed much of its lines to the Taifun.

to move on, he took the opportunity to add that he'd often wanted a picture of her for his gallery of sports figures and did she have one he could have?

Elly, not so sure she wanted to be this lad's heroine, said that no, she didn't carry around pictures of herself like a movie star.

Then Bernd suggested brightly that he could easily stop by her apartment and pick them up. How could she say no, in front of the world? Curiously, she found herself writing down her telephone number and giving it to this strange young man. She could always turn down his ardor later, if he even followed through with his threat to stop by. She'd long-since learned how to keep men at a distance since she'd become a celebrity pilot.

At her lecture, she found Bernd in the front row, along with Hans Stuck and the whole racing crew, seated all together where they could make irreverent comments through the whole lecture — until Elly had to stop her talk and ask them to be quiet.

Racing drivers, after a successful survival of the day, and especially after a win, often find it nearly impossible to quiet down. They find they can't sleep, they can't follow important rules, they can't take other people's feelings into consideration. The whole proposition of the Human Comedy suddenly looks entirely too amusing to them to keep a straight face. Afterward, of course, when they land back down on Earth, they're apologetic and quite reasonable. But before that, it doesn't do to try to scold them, as Elly was finding out — it has only the opposite effect.

In the years to come as she learned the peculiar rules about the racing life, she would take this effect into account and not see it as a personal affront. But by the end of her lecture she could have cheerfully killed Bernd on the spot given a free shot.

When he showed up in Berlin, as she feared, to collect the promised photograph, the subject of photos never came up. He was full of amusing plans for the two of them, and curiously, Elly found herself tagging along.

The boy was definitely full of fun, and as a performance-person, he understood much about her that her other admirers had no clue about. But he was so impetuous, unpredictable, so full of the devil! Whatever would become of this lad? — she found herself asking herself a little wistfully. Then Bernd became a repeat performance, always arriving with her week well planned out in advance.They'd spend the day hunting down every zoo they could find. Or comparing the performance of their cars or searching out the best place to watch a sunset. Always something active, always something with a zany, senseless quest to it. Not the usual young man with candy and flowers, and not the usual older man with rich dinners and the after-hours expectations.

Elly was taken quite off-guard. Her friends started giggling about "her young race driver." An accomplished young woman like Elly, in the Germany of those days, was expected to be seen with older, established men to whom the future was hardly a gamble. This sort of relationship with a boyish lad like Bernd wasn't taken very seriously by Elly. Or so she thought.

It didn't dawn on her that she was well and truly hooked until one weekend when she was listening to radio coverage of the Monte Carlo Grand Prix that Bernd was driving in. He'd crashed, but then reappeared in the pits carrying a cement flowerpot. The announcer had asked Bernd, not unreasonably, why he was carrying a flowerpot. Bernd said that it had come off the top of the balustrade he'd just smashed with his Auto Union. He said it looked so much like the Rainier Cup that he *wasn't* going to win that year that he'd decided to keep the flower pot as a consolation prize.

Elly couldn't believe she was hearing "her" Bernd's voice all the way from the Riviera, making a joke out of his crash, when others would be cursing their luck or shaking in shock. It was then that Elly realized she was somehow thinking of him as "her" Bernd.

Elly was scheduled to receive a presentation for her contributions to German civil aviation, so Bernd appointed himself Elly's escort to the presentation dinner. When he arrived at her apartment in full black tie and tails, Elly couldn't help giggling and making comments

As Elly Beinhorn, one of Europe's most honored trail-blazing pilots, she was the toast of Germany. As Elly Beinhorn-Rosemeyer, she found herself in a more complicated life that made record-setting flights look easy. Elly had complete faith in Bernd's ability to take care of himself on the track. But when it came to his irreverence around important officials and political figures, she couldn't help but wonder how long he'd last.
photo: Auto Union Archive

about being escorted by a Boy Scout. Bernd was truly hurt, Elly could see by the change of expression. He'd only tried to be supportive, after all, honoring her career (at the same time that his own was shaping up quickly to overshadow hers in the public eye). Elly felt instantly stupid in front of this new, serious Bernd, promising herself never to do such a thing to him again.

"Again?" Did this mean she was thinking of a future with Bernd still on the scene? On second thought, a future without this rich personality in her life suddenly looked empty. Bernd had carved a place in Elly's life as a natural part of the process he'd planned — all part of becoming her husband. It would take time, of course, for Elly to get used to his plan, Bernd realized. Elly was beginning to realize this as well. She decided to slow things down. If things were to get this serious, they were going way too fast. She encouraged Bernd to take an interest in other women. She even arranged for some of her friends to meet Bernd to defuse any star-struck puppy love with a healthy dose of playing the field.

But then when Bernd obeyed, and she began to hear of the good times Bernd was showing her friends, Elly felt a sudden burning jealousy. Slowly, she realized, step by step, Bernd was patiently wearing her down, accustoming her to the inevitable future with him.

Then one day, out of the blue, Bernd announced that he was going to make Elly his wife one day. It was a fair warning, at least. Elly laughed in a motherly way and said something about "seeing how we still feel a year from now." Looking back, some time later she had to laugh at her overconfidence — as if *she* were going to have anything to do with the decision!

Within a year they were getting blood tests and filling out endless forms proving their Aryan blood lines for the bureaucrats. Typically, Bernd had forgotten that he'd been made a SturmFührer in the SS as a result of his racing success. SS officers had to get permission to marry directly from Himmler, and it had slipped Bernd's mind somehow.

When Elly found this barrier, she'd told Bernd she'd marry him even outside the state's blessing. This last-minute glitch had brought a flood of emotion to Elly with the realisation that Bernd was a once-in-a-lifetime chance for a woman like Elly.

The wedding was a quiet affair at the courthouse to sign the papers required by the Reich, with close family in attendance.

An honor guard stood outside the registration office as the married couple filed out. On one side were Bernd's mechanics from Auto Union; on the other, the Shell mechanics that had helped Elly on her record-setting flights.

They went off to a small mountain cabin for awhile to get away from everybody and everything, but the foresters had decorated the cabin with wreaths and a large sign reminding them that, "The whole world celebrates the marriage of Elly and Bernd." Maybe the whole world could let them have a few moments by themselves, then.

Elly's faithful Messerschmitt Typhoon, a quick little monoplane, speedier than many military aircraft and twice as fast as most airliners of the day. In the air, Elly ran the show, holding Bernd to a strict standard of precision — when he was allowed to take over the controls.

photo: Auto Union Archive

Perhaps the happiest gift Elly received was from Willi Messerschmitt: a brand new sleek low-wing monoplane that Elly would come to name "The Typhoon" in honor of her tropical flying adventures. Her Typhoon became the symbol of her independence from total capitulation to Bernd's powerful personality. He might be the master of the Auto Union, but he was still a baby in her Typhoon.

It, perhaps, wasn't the most convenient stage of Bernd's career to get married, but when you meet your wife, you can't take a chance letting someone else win the day. For Elly, there were still public obligations and plans for more exploratory flights to be dealt with. But the strain and worry of the flights had told on Bernd much more than they had on Elly, and Bernd began asserting his role as an old-guard German husband by demanding that only one of them live a life of danger. It was too hard on his nerves. Besides, he'd be needing her to fly him to distant race-dates, now that the international calendar was exploding with new events, some as far away as Cape Town.

Later, in our day of women's lib, Elly took time to assess this role change in her life that Bernd brought with him. She admitted it would be hard for today's modern woman to accept this change, but by the time Bernd had married her, she'd already accomplished much of what she'd set out to do in aviation. And besides, today's modern woman hadn't come up against Rosemeyer, a personality who'd learned early on how to get what he wanted, no matter what the opposition.

Elly had introduced Bernd to flying in her beloved Typhoon (Elly's name for her plane later became the Messerschmitt model-name). Eventually, of course, through their many flights together Bernd had picked up how to fly, and then how to land and take off in the Typhoon.

Fascinated by the freedom of flying, Bernd had soon learned aerobatics, which he couldn't resist showing off over the Nürburgring pits during race practice. He landed on the straightaway for "emergency reasons" and was promptly placed under arrest for violating nearly every rule in the civil aviation code — until it was found out who he was and a few telephone calls had been made to clear things up.

Bernd was changing subtly from the cute little pesky boy Elly had first met into a man who could take care of her better than most men she'd met in her travels on five continents. With this new role came a steadily increasing assumption of power in the Rosemeyer household — a development Elly found she had mixed emotions about. The young Bernd who had prompted Elly to think more than once, "Whatever is going to become of this lad?" while he was busy taking risks and enjoying it, was fast becoming a thoughtful, circumspect man. A man not easy to daunt.

Also adding to Elly's mixed emotions was her own new role as the protected future mother of Bernd's offspring, which he began talking about with growing enthuisiasm. Part of this change rankled her free spirit, almost as much as it satisfied some deeply-planted need.

When the two of them fought it was volatile, flaring, and childish on both sides. When they made up, it was almost as if two other people came out from behind the scenery to have a good laugh at the pair who had just been fighting so adeptly a few moments before. On the other hand they didn't seem to have some of the problems typical with other couples. Bernd would never be interested in "lesser women" and every woman seemed to be a lesser being than Elly. And much the same sort of loyalty borne of simple good taste went for Elly as well.

Elly was becoming accustomed to Bernd's risk-taking, building a trust in him that acted as a barrier between her and the kind of gnawing agony that many of the drivers' wives suffered through at every race. Elly was an action-person herself who had been in many tight spots on her own. She had the ability to judge Bernd's talents

Bernd, Winner of the 1936 German Grand Prix, with his "Dear Uncle Doctor" Porsche looking on like a proud new father.

photo: Auto Union Archive

and recognise that Bernd was his own best help to get himself out of narrow spots on the track and needed no one giving him advice or cautions. Bernd didn't do suicidal things. Stunts, yes. But emotion-driven overreaching, no. He rarely had accidents like the others, relying on a quickly active sense of survival to keep mistakes from growing into tragedies.

But there was one area of risk that worried Elly: politics. As a solitary self-reliant individualist, Bernd was little interested in the theories of the social-engineers spouting various brands of tight government control of life. The Nazi movement had fallen on deaf ears with Bernd. He avoided most of Huhnlein's "pep talk" meetings — half-hearted attempts carried out under orders in the wan hope of convincing these self-generated drivers to be more sympathetic to the idea of subjugating their inborn drive to win to the whims of Berlin.

Elly, with good reason, began to worry that a whole new kind of risk-taking might start to appeal to Bernd; in a state where it was becoming easier every day to offend politically-correct officials, there was a growing risk of Bernd's individuality running afoul of the Nazis — and worse yet, a growing danger that Bernd might enjoy this new risk.

She knew what Bernd would say to her worries: that those things don't affect him, that he lived in a different world than those Nazi idiots, that he'd never had trouble handling bureaucrats. The bureaucrats were quiet, now that they desperately needed drivers to take their cars to victory. But what then? Elly's instincts told her the noose would tighten, and men like Bernd would find themselves having to come to grips with the threat of their own individualism. Even now, Elly thought, Bernd often "forgot" to give the Nazi salute at the victory photos, unlike the other drivers who played along with the operetta act, as long as Hitler bought them the best machines in the world.

He'd even walked out of one Nazi pep talk, calling it a waste of time. And then there was his Hitler routine. Combing his hair down and holding a comb under his nose, Bernd could put on a Hitler-act that left most helpless with laughter. It was only a matter of time before Huhnlein or some Berlin official stumbled onto Bernd's little act.

Not much got past Huhnlein, of course. But so far, with Bernd he'd seemed almost fatherly. His eyes showed he was onto Bernd's political peccadillos, but they also showed an almost sad patience, as though Huhnlein saw individualism only as a childish state of mind to be left behind by grown men. But if Huhnlein were ever caught in the middle between Bernd and Berlin, there was never a moment's doubt which side he would prove loyal to.

Joining the Auto Union team was some new blood. The biggest sensation came when Tazio's long-time rival who had battled so hard with him in Italian and French cars, Achille Varzi, deserted the cause below the Alps and went to Germany to drive for Auto Union. Later another new driver appeared — Ernst von Delius, a shy little man that Bernd appropriated as his side kick.

Another close associate Bernd would attract, oddly, was Tazio Nuvolari. They both had the kind of expressive eyes that won the world over in a minute. It was said of Tazio that if he entered a room where no one knew or cared the slightest about car racing, he'd still be the topic on everybody's lips. There was something magnetic, earthy, unabashedly human about the little man. And much the same could be said about Bernd, with his ever-present inscrutable imp-smile. When these two characters began running into each other through a season of races, a deep bond began to grow, despite the fact that they couldn't really understand one another verbally.

Chapter 14

Blitzrennen

After their shaky start in 1934, the German cars of both teams began to come to grips with the job at hand. Toward the second half of the season they had the Italians well and truly worried. By the end of the season the Italians were scrambling to respond to Germany's wake-up call in time for the following season.

They were the ones, now, resorting to wild design departures in the hopes that one of them would show that "X" factor to regain them the edge. Alfa brought out a new car with two engines sitting side-by-side under the hood. It proved to be too much of a handful on the torturous mountain tracks. And if that weren't radical enough, they brought out a second design with one engine mounted up front in the traditional manner, and a second mounted behind the drive like the Auto Union, combining both of Germany's approaches. It too was a holy terror through the turns and vicious on tires.

Perhaps the wildest, most desperate design of all to come from Italy was a radical new car built by Count Trossi that looked very much like an Auto Union, but with an aircraft radial engine stuck on the front grill. Meanwhile, north of the Alps, the two German teams got down to the job of making the fur fly.

When the German Giants took to the track, crowds saw a kind of fierceness in racing they'd never experienced before. Or possibly since. Eyewitnesses say that later forms of Grand-Prix competition look like kid's play compared the utter abandon of these bellowing beasts, and the films of the races that survive back up this notion.

photo: Auto Union Archive

Back in 1934, Tazio had been so roused by the German challenge that he'd called his faithful mechanic, Compagnoni, to tell him to prepare their car for a Grand Prix he planned to enter the following week. Compagnoni, used to his boss's eccentricities, calmly pointed out that Tazio had just had a bad wreck just weeks before and still had one leg bound up securely in a cast,

"Just get the car ready," Tazio had said to Compagnoni. "Put the pedals closer together so I can reach them. We can't let the Germans walk off with everything, can we?"

Hobbling around the pits with a stiff leg had won Tazio sincere sympathy from his friend Hans Stuck, who knew how frustrating it was to have to be sidelined. But when he saw Tazio crawling into his car with the cast still on, Hans wondered if he was seeing right. How could the old man hope to manage? Tazio was over forty now, in a game usually reserved for young men with lightning-quick reflexes and rubbery bones.

But he'd managed, mounting a challenge to the Germans before being held up by mechanical problems that even Tazio's determination couldn't remedy, and eventually placing fourth. Being laughed at was nothing new to Tazio, who'd once shown up at a motorcycle race so encrusted with plaster casts that he had to be lifted onto his machine, amid a roar of laughter from the crowd. He was so enraged by the crowd's reaction that he won the race, of course, but had to make sure his crew was there to catch him when he stopped his machine before it fell on him.

With the 1935 German Grand Prix coming up, Tazio was quieter than he usually was, as though some new plan was on his mind. He knew the entire Nazi hierarchy of racing would be in their Caesarian tribunes with the highest confidence, now, in their new teams. After all, German cars in 1935 were sweeping the field, and Dr. Porsche's prediction had come true: it was only a matter of which German team would win now. But even that could be counted on as a dogfight. Rudi was back in top form, and had walked away with just about everything so far that season, but Bernd was clearly laying for him at this German Grand Prix.

Tazio had joined up with the Ferrari stable that had entered the old P-3 Alfa anyway. Like Rosemeyer, he liked "to race" better than he liked "being a race-driver." If he didn't win, at least he could have some fun needling the Germans for awhile. Not only that, but Tazio had his own tribune watching: his eldest son Giorgio, and his wife, Carolina, the love of his teens whom he'd married long since and raised the boys with. Asked earlier if he really thought his Alfa stood a chance against the German teams, Tazio only reminded the press, "Our lives are a series of unforeseen events." And when asked by a reporter if he expected to die in a race car, Tazio had admitted it was a probably a safe bet, considering how many crashes he'd had to date. The somewhat shocked reporter mumbled something under his breath about, "I don't see how you have the nerve to get into the cockpit of one, then." Tazio, interested, asked the reporter where he expected to die. The man said, "Well, one day, probably, at home in bed."

"Then I don't see how you have the nerve to get under the covers at night!"

These days, Huhnlein had his speech all written before the race. Only minor modifications would be needed to thank one or the other of the German teams for bringing another resounding victory to the Fatherland. The phone-calls to Hitler after the race to comment on what the Führer had already heard on the radio coverage were getting, happily, to be routine. They were proof that Huhnlein's part of the Social Motorization plan was a success. And every victory for Social Motorization brought the party a little closer to universal popularity, and then perhaps, the popular support to seize still more powers.

The Nürburgring course had been decked in what one Italian called, "The rather vulgar manner of the German Fascists," with swastikas everywhere and the smell of *Wurst* in the air. Before the race the huge crowd was treated to an air show of sorts — one of the Luftwaffe's new "Stuka" dive-bombers was making a flyby overhead. Suddenly it winged over into a nearly vertical dive right at the crowd, while the sirens on its landing gear made an eerie scream before the plane pulled out of its dive, leaving the crowd breathless with shock. Most of the crowd had never seen a Stuka in action before.

The scream of a second siren from a staff car announced that Huhnlein, as SportskorpFührer, was leading in a parade of open Mercedes bearing important Berlin officials to watch the race from their special tribune.

Tazio's P-3 looked truly antiquated in the well-spread-out line up under the snapping banners at Nürburgring. An expectant buzz was running through the crowd of 200,000, many of whom had biked and come by bus to camp out in the woods surrounding the mountainous track — fourteen miles of endless corners, limited passing opportunities, and sometimes unpredictable mountain fogs and rain. Just the sort of limitations Tazio would order up to bedevil the more powerful German rockets.

The marching bands oompahed their last, the cars were started, and the starting cannon's stomach-churning report sent the cars off on their way like a herd of stampeding bulls, slewing forward in broadsides trying their best to grab pavement with their powerful engines and claw their way first into the corner at the end of the straight.

Tazio had grabbed a good start and found himself up in the first group of cars, with Caracciola in the lead, followed by Fagioli's Mercedes, and then Tazio's red car among the silver train.

The German cars were entering the corners wide with their greater power. Tazio kept to the inside, nipping inches away from the inside of the corner. Cutting the shorter route yet keeping the speeds up, Tazio was able to slip past Fagioli into second place. Huhnlein watched Tazio's brave gesture with respect, knowing it had to be an early-race move to grab some newsworthy attention for Italy before his delicate Alfa broke under the strain of trying to match the speeds of the big, sturdy German engines.

Compagnoni, Tazio's mechanic, noticed with a smile that his Maestro seemed to be at the top of his form that day, in complete control of the car, making it dance on ice, taking each turn with exactly the same finesse every lap. Beautifully choreographed precision. Bernd was making an all-out attack now and had worked into

Tazio's P-3 Alfa looking a trifle out of date after the unveiling of the new German giants. The P-3 was perhaps the final development of the race car, following the formats first developed in the pioneer days of auto racing. With its straight axles, forward-mount engine, and rail frame (just to mention a few features it shared with the first cars to race), its days were numbered. For the German Grand Prix, Tazio was running a modified front suspension, at least.
photo: Shell Oil of London

second place, sending the crowds in a frenzy of excitement and kicking Neubauer's race-plan into a cocked hat. But the Auto Union would pay for Rosemeyer's blistering pace, and as the race wore on Bernd's car began to fade.

The other Alfas weren't having such a good time of it either. Tazio's teammate, the genial Count Brivio, had pulled into the pits and doffed his windcap. A broken differential had ended his run for the day. Those differentials were giving the Alfa engineers fits. No matter what they did to modify the set-up, the differentials just couldn't take the power. And the Alfa pits cringed, as Tazio turned in a sizzler of a lap, then slowed and let the German cars through — even letting teammate Chiron past. But then Chiron's differential gave out too, and Tazio was in the only red car left on the track. What a difference a season had made.

Tazio decided it was time to make his attack. When the cars appeared at the end of the straight in front of the grandstands on the next round, the crowd let out something very different from a Teutonic roar: Tazio's red car had somehow appeared first, leading the rest of the silver pack!

Neubauer, in the Mercedes pits, found it nerve-wracking that the little Italian could suddenly appear wherever he wanted to in the pack. Huhnlein kept his eye on the Italian as well, knowing Tazio was grabbing a lot of Volksradio air-time with this frantic suicidal dash. Better he should accept the fate of history and stand aside quietly for the cars of the future instead of this silly gesture. Hopeless gesture! Huhnlein found he was twisting his prewritten victory speech between his hands. Even if Tazio stopped now, Huhnlein would still most likely be on the receiving end of some barbed comments from the Führer in his post-race phone report. He smoothed out his speech again and regained his icy calm "enjoyment" of the race.

In the Mercedes pits a mechanic was reassuring Neubauer, "Within a lap or two the little Italian will be lying in some remote corner with either his gearbox or his head broken." Neubauer realized this had to be right. But he'd seen the little Italian devil do magic before that left the rest of the drivers thinking openly that Tazio had to be "in league with the devil" to pull off what he sometimes pulled off. Still, there were others who called the little man a wrecker — a driver who went for all-out speed, instead of ending up first at the finish.

Neubauer preferred to believe the "wrecker" legend at the moment. At Nürburgring it took over ten minutes for each lap to be completed. Next lap, the red car was incredibly still first to appear. Ten minutes later, again, the red car came around first.

Caracciola and von Brauchitsch both came in for a frantically fast refuelling. Neubauer had offered prizes for the teams who could refuel the fastest. Von Brauchitsch had trained his mechanics the hardest, and today he drove away ahead of Rudi as a result of his faster pit stop.

Then Tazio was due in. He knew his Italian crew had never been as fast as the Germans. But even so, he shouldn't lose more than a few seconds that could drop him down to second place.

Tazio screeched to a stop, took a quick drink from his brandy flask, and then watched in horror as the refuelling pump jammed. After much panic it was decided to use the old churns to refill. Tazio was swearing a blue streak at the hapless mechanics even though it was hardly their fault.

Topped-up, Tazio tore off like a madman, shaving the line of N.S.K.K. guards too close for comfort. The fuelling foul-up had dropped Tazio to sixth place — but it had also changed him from the light-handed gadfly dancer in his little Alfa into a determined challenger obsessed with overcoming his setbacks at any price.

Both Neubauer and Huhnlein noticed with satisfaction that the interval between Tazio and the German leaders was insurmountable. Or — would be insurmountable for most human drivers. With Tazio, they realized a little uneasily, you just never knew.

Tazio was throwing his car now, using the broadsiding technique he'd seen with the American dirt track racers, a technique none of the

Tazio's flubbed pit stop, with the Maestro conducting with his unmistakeable gestures.

photo: Shell Oil of London

other Europeans seemed to master. The crowds filtered to the most difficult corners to watch the Maestro in full flight. Neubauer put out his red "speed-up!" flag to Manfred von Brauchitsch, now in the lead.

Next lap, even after Neubauer's speed-up signal, Tazio had pulled to within sixty-three seconds of the leader. Compagnoni was making some secret signals to Tazio as well. Nuvolari nodded and put his foot down hard. Manfred reacted masterfully by holding Tazio off, keeping his lead intact the next lap. Huhnlein's speech was a twisted mess again. Neubauer was losing his calm again, but breathed a sigh of relief when he realized that Manfred was holding steady, keeping the Italian at bay. Only three laps to go. No one, even an Italian freak in league with the devil, could make up that much time in three laps.

Then a bellow of anguish was heard from the Mercedes pits. Neubauer had spotted the white breaker-strip showing on Manfred's front left-side tire, indicating it was losing its tread.

"We can change one tire in ten seconds," a mechanic was yelling.

"And let the little demon by? He won't be so easy to repass." Neubauer had called in the *Schnurrbiber* — Dietrich from Continental tire. It was true, the tire had not lasted as long as *Schnurrbiber* had predicted. But then being chased to distraction by Tazio hadn't been one of the conditions that *Schnurrbiber* was considering when he made the tire-stop schedule.

"It will hold, it will hold!" Neubauer was yelling to quiet all the clamor. He was mopping his balding head with a handkerchief. The Sebastian brothers in the Auto Union pits, out of the running for this race, exchanged amused grins. It was always a good show to watch Neubauer in full temper.

"Brauchitsch will make it, and so will the tire!" he was bellowing. "It's only a question of a few minutes more."

The Alfa pits were on cloud nine. Even a second place in the German Grand Prix would tell the world Alfa still had what it takes to beat all the Germans but one! Compagnoni took a swig from his flask to calm his nerves. Mechanics were smoking nervously in every corner, and telling the N.S.K.K. fire marshals to go to the devil.

At the Nürburgring a huge lighted map of the course tells exactly where the leaders are during the long lap intervals. It was showing the cars nearing the last turn before the final straight. The announcer was reporting a thirty-four-second lead of von Brauchitsch over the Italian with a hoarse voice. It was an insurmountable lead at this point. The swastika flag was prepped for raising on the flagpole of honor. The "Deutchland Uber Alles" record was put on the record player for the loudspeakers.

Tazio was dancing his car remorselessly close to Manfred, who could see the flashes of red in the mirrors growing larger and larger at each corner. It was as though he could feel Tazio's breath on his neck. Manfred threw the Mercedes into the final corner, and there his Pechvogel, his bad-luck bird, swooped into view. The tire exploded — fortunately, before Manfred had started to gather real speed out of the

Often thought of as being in league with the devil to be able to pull off racing feats that no one else would consider possible, between races Tazio had a modest personal style, completely free of arrogance. However, he never quite agreed that team tactics or team managers really knew the best way to win races. This was the driver that Dr. Porsche (in front of disgruntled Nazi bigwigs) said was the greatest driver "of the past, present or future." An oft-quoted comment about the all-time great drivers ran something like, "Caracciola says he's the greatest, and Rosemeyer obviously thinks he's the greatest. But Tazio knows he's the greatest."

photo: Shell Oil of London

corner. He slewed the car desperately to a standstill within view of the stands, of Huhnlein, and all the Nazi contingent. At the finish straight a roar of disbelief went up, as the red car of the little Italian shot past Manfred and motored on to the checkered flag.

"Too bad," Tazio thought, as he cruised past the skidding Mercedes grinding to its stop. He was sure he could have taken Manfred before the finish anyway. It would have been more exciting that way. But still, a win is a win.

Huhnlein racked his brain to think of a speech on the spot that Hitler would approve of but that would have something to do with the truth. His mind went blank, as he heard someone crying out that there was no Italian National Anthem record for the loudspeaker. They couldn't even find an Italian flag to run up the pole of honor. But then Compagnoni showed up with his own record of Italy's "Marcia Reale." Tazio never went to a race without a record of the Italian Anthem, just in case. With Tazio, you just never knew.

Tazio's amazing battle at the Nürburgring would be talked about for decades. But of course, the reason his drive posed such a heroic example was that it was a "man bites dog" tale. Just two years before the same race results would have caused little more than yawns.

Tazio's drive stood alone as the two German teams, under the watchful gaze of Berlin, gathered the kind of steam Hitler was counting on for his Motorization programs. Out of eleven races in 1935 we find the Italian teams winning one race: Tazio's wild ride. Still, in '35, if we count the twenty-two second and third places, we find the Italians taking up ten of these spots — definitely contenders for the rostrum at the awards ceremonies.

In 1936, however, out of the same thirty-three win, place, and show spots, the Italians could only manage four with no outright wins (except Tazio's brilliant coup at the Vanderbilt Cup in New York). Clearly, the German teams had got the range on the Grand Prix world and all its publicity opportunities, extending as far as the span of Africa from Tripoli to Cape Town, and as far west as New York.

The race action that the ever-growing crowds were streaming in to see these days was the battle between Rudi and Bernd, or as Neubauer put it, "Mercedes versus Rosemeyer." Although their contrasting styles (Rudi smooth and always in control, but mercilessly fast; Bernd hell-bent for leather) resulted in some post-race feuds, Rudi just as often found himself getting a much-appreciated laugh out of Bernd before they set to their next battle.

It was a classic conflict: a king, still in his prime and wanting to stay on his throne a few seasons more, versus the challenger, capitalizing on any show of weakness to race on past to the winner's flag. They both pushed the other as hard as they knew how, not letting up or giving any quarter.

When Bernd had barely made it back to the pits after leaving one Auto Union in the bushes and sprinting a half mile back to take over a slower teammate's car, he looked over to the Mercedes pits. Neubauer had seen Bernd's excursion into the weeds and had written him off as out of the race. Now, he was shocked to see Bernd back in the pits so soon and was making his move to signal Rudi to get a move on. Bernd would soon be back in the race. It was a long course. If Rudi somehow didn't see Bernd in the pits and just cruised along past Bernd's wrecked car, Bernd might stand a chance. But Neubauer's signal sys-

Grand Prix racing in Europe was headline news, and took up long hours of radio time every weekend. With a quarter-million spectators often attending a single race, it was a leading venue of public attention that Hitler was unlikely not to take advantage of. With Motorshow pageantry and official public demonstration of the cars in urban stadium parks, racing was everywhere and it was hard to escape knowing what was going on through the Grand Prix season. Here we see a Mercedes being raced to the top of a remote Alpine pass.

photo: Road & Track

tem would never let that happen, of course. Rudi was approaching and Neubauer got ready to give Rudi his "step-on-it" signal.

Just as Rudi came by, however, Neubauer found that his arms were pinned to his sides, and Rudi went by without a speed-up signal. When Neubauer turned to see who had pinned his arms, he saw Bernd running back to his pit, "Sorry Herr Neubauer, but that was just self-defense!" he yelled over his shoulder.

Neubauer countered at a later race by posting fake lap times that drove Bernd crazy after he made a substantial bet he could top anything the Mercs could put up. But as hard as they fought on the track, Neubauer couldn't help thinking of Bernd as a son, just as he thought of Rudi as his kid brother. Porsche was another part of Bernd's extended racing family, with Bernd calling the Professor "Dear Uncle Doctor" in his usual faux-childlike manner.

It was time, Hitler knew, to start reaping the harvest of his investment, and the drivers began to discover there were other duties in their job description beyond just beating the Italians. Hitler now began to call on his racing heroes to fill a social-propaganda role for his spanking-new Reich.

At every luncheon and awards ceremony, Hitler amazed his racing legends with his knowledge of their track adventures, even the state of their social lives. It was as if he had hidden microphones into their houses — a thought that became less of a paranoid fear and more a distinct possibility as time went on.

Hitler always asked after Rudi's leg and seemed satisfied with only the most optimistic reports. Optimism was the mood-of-choice when talking to Hitler if you wanted to make a sure hit. Unless you were Dr. Porsche, of course. Porsche never bothered to fake up anything for anybody. He never called Hitler by any title other than the same "Herr" he used with his mechanics. Aides cringed at this, but Hitler pretended to take no notice.

Rudi and von Brauchitsch had received a royal summons to a luncheon in Berlin where Hitler wanted to parade his victorious champions in front of the world. As usual, Rudi groused at this interruption to his freedom.

Von Brauchitsch was more philosophic, thinking of what they'd be driving otherwise, with those damned Italians and even the French rubbing their noses in it still if it weren't for the support of Berlin.

Hitler had sent his own Junkers airliner to pick them up. They were the only passengers, and the pilot seemed like a good sort, an action-man who understood Rudi and Manfred's lack of rapture at being invited to dine with a bunch of politicians.

"Tell me. Herr Caracciola; there's a lot of talk flying around," the pilot began to gossip once they were in the air. "Is it true you've become a Swiss citizen?"

Rudi showed him his German passport. Rudi was suddenly pensive. So his private life-decisions were now the property of every coffee-house gossip in Berlin. The villa in Arosa in the Swiss lake country looked like a smarter move to Rudi all the time. On the other hand, it might bring trouble with the N.S.K.K. as time went on.

When they arrived at the Chancellory, Hitler had been detained by important business. As the time went by, it became obvious that something was more pressing to the Führer than this luncheon. Rudi, ever since his first days at Mercedes, had developed a phobia for having to wait. Manfred simply occupied himself scanning the females in Hitler's office staff, but Rudi only paced and chafed. Suddenly he burst out in a voice meant for everyone to hear, "Well Manfred, I can see that the Führer is busy with more important matters." And with that he grabbed his hat and left the office, Manfred tagging along with a poorly-hidden grin.

Manfred told the story of "How Caracciola stood up the Führer" all over Berlin. "Rudi missed his calling. He should have been in the diplomatic corps! After that he even convinced the pilot to fly us back in Hitler's own plane."

As a German victory became more and more of a sure thing, Huhnlein began to get orders to step up the pre-race pageantry and give the crowds an even bigger show — a good Nazi show, of course. The cars were marched out beforehand under rows of swastika flags, their drivers at attention by their side, like good soldiers fighting for the glory of the Reich. It was the usual sort of Nazi pomp seen at all sorts of events these days, from the Berlin Olympics on down to a village parade.

But there was only one problem. These particular marchers were racing cars in a few minutes — about to risk their lives in an afternoon of sport they could just as easily not return from. This wasn't a soccer game they were talking about. Those precious minutes before a race had always been a time of private idiosyncrasies for the driver, just as matadors are allowed some privacy before facing death. Talismans, rituals, upset stomachs, short tempers, horseplay — all are allowed when men are facing an event that includes a reasonable possibility of death. When life is saying, "Any last wishes?", the last thing you want to spend your concentration on is a marching drill routine to please some pompous politico.

For Varzi, whose only existence without a cigarette in his mouth was when he was driving a race car, these pre-race parades were agony. For Rudi they were a mildly mortifying nuisance. For Bernd, they were a time-bomb growing closer to the explosion point with every occurence. They'd all expended the grand effort to get where they were. They'd all risked virtually everything to get to that starting grid. Marching in parades and having to give the Nazi salute was blocking their concentration.

There were those who didn't seem to mind, of course. A new generation of talent had been selected to balance out the teams politically and nationally. Since the only cars that could win came from the Fatherland these days, Huhnlein was getting pressure from Berlin to bring in talent from the rest of Europe to keep the races popular across the continent.

Christian Kautz, a talented young Swiss (and Nazi SS), had joined Mercedes under pressure from Jakob Werlin. Varzi was the token

Neubauer and his boys: Manfred von Brauchitsch leaning on Neubauer. *Der Englischer* Richard Seaman in front of him. Rudi Caracciola resting on the left front wheel, with ex-mechanic Hermann Lang close behind him (as he often was in a race).

photo: Road & Track

Italian on the Auto Union team, later replaced by the switch-hitter Fagioli, who moved from Mercedes to Auto Union when Varzi had "troubles with his health." Rumors were saying those trouble were entirely self-inflicted. Dreyfus, the French half -Jewish ace was invited, but though he had many friends on both teams, he found that when it came right down to it he was still too French to play. He left the big leagues to return to a private team in France run by the colorful Lucy O'Reilly Schell. And a young Britisher, an avid jazz fan and racing devotee from Oxford, Dick Seaman was put on the Mercedes team. Later, Tazio was to join his friends at Auto Union as well.

In time, Hitler would realize with satisfaction, nearly every racing hero of Europe was driving under the swastika. As in ancient times where princes of the outlying barbarians were brought to Rome to learn its ways before returning to the shocking crudeness of their own Nordic tribes again, Europe was becoming once again an empire. This time the Nordics were on top.

Chiron once again found himself driving on the same team with Rudi at Mercedes. Louis shrugged, as if to say, "If you want to paint the Sistine Chapel, you must be prepared to deal with a Pope." As proof that the new Nazi state was one that gave respect to both intellectual and worker-bee alike, one of the Mercedes mechanics, Hermann Lang, was put at the wheel of a Grand Prix Mercedes.

At Auto Union the mood was slightly less political. They were still very much the stepchild team. They refused to supply free staff cars to Nazi officials (possibly an promotional mistake, judging from the holy devotion still paid by collectors to the Grosser Mercedes of the Nazi ruling class). Stuck was fast losing interest in his beloved racing, as his part-Jewish wife received more and more flak from both officials and public. Their treasurer, Rosenberger, had already been forced to flee to America. And even von Oertzen would pay a price for having married a Jewish woman, first exiling himself to South Africa for the sake of his wife (and then interned after the war by the British as a Nazi.) The plot was thickening.

To a politician, reality is endlessly negotiable. A twist of the phrasing regularly changes defeats into victories, foul-ups into carefully-planned strategies. As Huhnlein received orders to beef up the pageantry, efforts were beginning to orchestrate race results to favor political needs of the moment.

The strategists were forgetting one little point: the only reason drivers stick to risking their lives on a regular basis to see who can drive the fastest is that the game is played fair. If it becomes a circus act, the drivers are likely to lose interest in placing their necks on the line.

Not only that, racing is a blood-sport. If a person is drawn to risking his life for it, the sport has long since become a sort of religion in the mind of the driver. If they offer their life up to this holy following, they aren't likely to let outsiders turn it into a cheap political sideshow. When a person returns from the threat of life or death, political threats have to take their place down among the wines and spirits. Not only that, to some, any threat, especially a fresh new one to test their nerve against, can sometimes be attractive — sometimes little less than delicious.

Huhnlein, living with the drivers through thick and thin, seeing them dying and watching them watching their friends die, could have little less than a growing respect for his charges. If not respect, then at least a realistic appreciation of the sort of characters he was dealing with. These were not your ordinary empire-climbing, boot-licking celebrities. But orders are orders.

Already Neubauer had been approached by Berlin to figure out a prearranged winner for a certain race. But, knowing that the drivers would balk at the idea (he could only occasionally get them to do what he wanted for the team, as it was, much less for some politician) and since the order hadn't come until the race had already started, Neubauer was able to stall in the confusion of the battle until the situation sorted itself out on its own. He mopped his brow in relief. That was a close one, and the ominous thought that orders like these might be more insistent next time made him quiver. Didn't Berlin realize what sparks would fly if the drivers thought their beloved sport was being tampered with? There would be no way to keep it from the public, a public very wise to the inflexible characters of those who were driving these monsters. If these inflexible characters suddenly gave in without a fight, it wouldn't fool a schoolboy.

Coming over from England to accompany Dick Seaman in this strangely energetic foreign land was the photographer, George Monkhouse. When Monkhouse first saw the scale that racing had grown to under Mussolini and now Hitler, he was stunned. England was living in its own charming, but essentially intramural, world of clubby racing at Brooklands, where school ties meant more than lap times when it came to setting up a race team. Racing had grown parochial in England — but fun.

The sight of the huge excited crowds filling the stands at Germany's futuristic and incredibly fast tracks and shouting energetic Nazi slogans made Monkhouse ponder in awe. One almost wished one could join the enthusiasm. But of course, one couldn't. Not and keep one's calm British perspective. The Brits were so reserved that after the Germans had come to England and decimated all competition at Donington, the officials failed to play the German National Anthem following the race. Not cricket, of course. But then, foreigners so seldom raced on English soil, you see.

Seaman, estranged from his immensely rich family because of his love for racing, had pulled off some very clever methods of raising himself to international status in the smaller voiturette racers. He'd taken a ten-year old car that he sensed had never been tuned to its potential, hot-rodded it, and walked away with the prizes across the continent. Now an international figure, he further estranged his family by adding another British taboo to his list: that of the friendship he was building with the daughter of the Direktor of BMW, Erika Popp.

Dick, a prototypical Gilbert and Sullivan slave of duty when it came to loyalty to England, was torn severely by the lure of the Mercedes' power and ability to allow Dick to try his talents against the world's best on one hand, and his self-determined hatred of totalitarian states on the other. He sent a letter to the dean of the British racing world, the genial Francis, Earl of Howe (who called himself simply "Earl") for advice about the politics of the issue. The Earl contacted his pals at Whitehall who told him that any friendly contact with Germany should be maintained at all cost. That solved one question, at least. The Mercedes won out over his mother when it came to continuing his racing.

The Erika question was another kettle of fish. His mother could in no way be reconciled to Hitler's New Germany and, to her, the thought of a "mixed marriage" to this German girl, no matter how well placed in the regime, was out of the question.

Dick was a truly fast driver with a real mechanic's feel for his machinery, its limits and its weak-points. Neubauer sensed he had a real history-making driver on his hands with Dick. But appearing side-by-side with this new pan-Europeanism following in the wake of the successes enjoyed by the German teams, came a lessening of team spirit. That certain sense of cohesive, it's-us-against-the-world feeling was beginning to fall apart. The old saying that "Germans are always 'becoming' and never 'being'" seemed to be coming true.

Even when sitting on a tire, Stuck is almost as tall as Nuvolari, seen here with drivers gathered around the Auto Union pits: Nuvolari, Stuck, Kautz, Mueller, and Meier.
photo: Auto Union Archive

Von Brauchitsch, for example, was from an old Prussian military family. And while it was true he might have had little time for the military attitude himself in his quest for the best restaurants and women available to him, he still carried some of Old Prussia with him and continued to balk at "partying with the help." He'd seen little good come of mixing workers and aristocrats, spoiling the servants, and falsifying the nobility with a forced popularism. When mechanic Lang joined the team as a full-fledged Grand Prix driver, Manfred thought it was a mistake. Treat your squire well, but don't put him on your horse or you can expect trouble.

He rode Lang mercilessly, always on the lookout for any pretensions Lang might put forward. But Manfred didn't have much to attack.

Lang was a modest, simple-living family man. Still, von Brauchitsch couldn't resist firing cannon balls across Lang's bow every now and again the minute Manfred suspected Lang was getting above himself. Rudi and Manfred, as a natural matter of course in racing with each other season after season, had had their run-ins as well.

Manfred at times would grow tired of constantly having to play the role of the plodding team-supporter — the hare who was ordered to destroy his car so that others on his team could win. There were times when something snapped in Manfred and he would clear the decks by going straight for checkered flag — to hell with Neubauer's, or Hitler's, or anybody's team orders.

Fagioli, of course, was for Fagioli, and that was that, no matter what the situation. His temper was known far and wide and there was one time when, if Rudi hadn't ducked in time, a wrench thrown at him by Fagioli would have put him in the hospital for another long spell.

Christian Kautz, the handsome young Swiss driver and member of a prominent banking family, might well be counted on to relate any un-Fascist uprisings directly to the top. As the pressure began to build from Berlin to control these drivers and mold them into good ambassadors of the Reich, Neubauer could be seen mopping his brow more often. The situation was nothing less than a time-bomb.

Things were changing, and Neubauer longed for the close racing family he used to guide like a mother hen — those blessed days when their only enemies were the Italians. Berlin, he knew, was a bad enemy to have. More and more N.S.K.K. guards were crowding the pits with every race, eager to poke their noses into everyone's business.

The old casual sophistication around the pits — the beautiful girlfriends, the portable bars, the humor, the high-charged horseplay, was all alien to these linear-thinkers from Berlin. They envied the quick wit of the banter and could see no value in tension-release. The shallow diversions had grown up, almost unnoticed, as a necessary balance to the presence of death. Luftwaffe fighter pilots living a life of combat for long periods also knew what tension-release could mean in terms of a survival tool. But then, they too had nothing but problems with the brass-hats of Berlin.

But by this time it was clearly too late to back out. How could Neubauer leave his life of racing behind? Perhaps it only had to be endured for a while. Perhaps when Berlin had gotten what it wanted, it might move onto new arenas and leave racing alone again.

Otto Skorzeny, Hitler's top commando, had once said that patience was the sine qua non for dealing with Berlin. When Berlin came up with some ludicrous plan, Skorzeny had learned the hard way that the idea was not to oppose the plan and point out all its lunatic contradictions, but rather to agree and then keep postponing things until Berlin got another new brainstorm in its bonnet that made them forget all about the previous one. Patience, Neubauer decided, would be his best friend. Like most well thought-out plans, it didn't last long.

R73

Chapter 15

Hell on Wheels

It all seemed to begin at Nürburgring, quite without warning. The whole Mercedes team had gotten off to a precision start in perfect formation and now were leading the race like a big, silver train. Then suddenly a Nazi official, one Neubauer hadn't seen around the pits before, appeared in front of him looking very serious.

"Herr Neubauer, you must bring in your cars at once!"

Neubauer looked at the man as if he'd asked Neubauer to dance a hula. What on earth did this idiot mean? You don't just bring in a whole team at the same time.

"They're leaking oil and endangering the chances of the others. Nuvolari's already been held up by this!" the Nazi was shouting in a hysterical voice.

Neubauer's blood ran cold. To stop the whole team would lose the race, it was as simple as that. And the Führer, snug in his comfy office in Berlin, was expecting them to win this particular race.

It was nearly impossible to conduct a detailed explanation to a newcomer over the din of the pits with cars rocketing past, but Neubauer knew he had to try.

"This sort of thing is common at this stage of the race. It doesn't last!" Neubauer protested.

"I can't rely on that!"

Neubauer racked his brain for another way out. He'd always been the one to handle balky border guards, enraged innkeepers, and such blots on the human race.

"There will be a tire change in just five laps," he said, brightening, "Then we can put everything right. Please be reasonable!"

"I am being reasonable, Herr Neubauer. That's why I'm ordering you to stop your cars," the Nazi said, suddenly icy.

Signals from the man who invented the pit-signal system (and who was told to leave the track by outraged officials the first time he tried it): Neubauer tells Manfred how he stands in the Donington G.P.

photo: Mercedes Benz

The leaders rushed past at this point, Nuvolari pulling by with plenty of room to pass.

"There! Look for yourself!" Neubauer yelled, beginning to lose control, himself. When Neubauer lost control, it could be dangerous for officials. He'd already been banned from racing in Ireland for physically threatening a whole race committee and calling them "swine" to their faces.

"Nuvolari's not being held up! If he can't pass them it's not because there's oil on the track. It's because his car isn't good enough! There are four Mercedes in the lead and you're asking me to pull them out! You might as well hand Auto Union the race on a silver platter!"

Neubauer saw the Nazi turn white with rage.

"Are you accusing me of favoritism?!" he said, turning to face Neubauer directly.

Neubauer, becoming just as enraged himself, gave the Nazi a disgusted look. The Nazi turned on his heel and marched off, jackboots ringing on the pit floor.

After a textbook victorious start, Neubauer now had to watch helplessly as the race completely fell apart for the Mercedes team, this time without any help from frenzied Nazis.

On the next lap, young Lang, who'd been leading, came in with terminal engine trouble. He stalked off to a corner of the pit and sulked. Then Rudi came in, doubled over with pain.

"My stomach! Can't do it!"

The mechanics helped him out of his car, and he stumbled over to another corner of the pits and sat rocking with pain, the result of some injudicious dining the night before. Lang had leaped to his feet and jumped into Rudi's car even before Neubauer had time to order him to do just this.

Seaman had been leading strongly, but then Manfred chose that time to begin a hammer-and-tongs attack on Dick when he should have held station according to team strategy. Neubauer had an uneasy feeling that the two boys, Manfred and Dick, were battling for something bigger than the checkered flag that day. Ignoring Neubauer's signals, Manfred pulled past Dick and took over the lead.

Neubauer threw his signal flags into the pits in disgust. It was obvious the prize that day, in Manfred's mind at least, was Erika Popp, the beautiful daughter of the head of BMW that both Dick and Manfred had been seen paying a lot of attention to recently.

Now Dick took the opportunity to harry Manfred mercilessly, sticking so close the cars might have been tied together with a rope. Neubauer knew what Dick was up to, but the tires of both cars were suffering for it. On the sixteenth lap both drivers signalled that they were coming for refuelling at the same time. Brauchitsch came in first and motioned Neubauer over for a talk.

"I've had enough! That fellow Seaman's driving me mad sitting on my tail!"

"Don't get excited, Manfred! You started it, remember. But don't worry, I'll talk to Seaman." Manfred might have been in the wrong, Neubauer realized, but he did have a lot of seniority, and Neubauer owed Manfred for a lot of years of loyalty. Meanwhile, as Seaman rolled up, Neubauer ran to talk to him.

"Do me a favor, Dick. Let Brauchitsch have his lead. I know you're in the right, but just the same, don't stick so close to him or he'll wreck the car!" Seaman took a new grip on the steering wheel, took a deep breath and then said in a small voice, "All right, sir."

Neubauer ran back to von Brauchitsch just in time to see that one of the mechanics, distracted by Dick's crew, had waited too late to close the high-pressure fuel hose. Manfred, not realizing what had happened, reached for the ignition switch. Neubauer yelled, "No! Stop!" but too late. Manfred was engulfed in flames.

Without stopping to think, Neubauer rushed through the mechanics up to the burning car and pulled Manfred bodily out of the fire. Manfred was on his feet, but still burning. Neubauer and the mechanics flailed at the still invisible flames singeing Manfred's arms as men with fire extinguishers covered the car, the driver, the pits with a white froth of foam.

After the fire was out, Neubauer took stock of the battle scene and, with a yell of horror, saw that Dick was still sitting in his car — still waiting in the pits.

"Holy mackerel! What are you still sitting here for?!"

Dick looked up angelically. "I thought you told me to let Brauchitsch keep his lead!"

"Stop thinking and start driving!" Holy Jesus, what a day!

Manfred's car looked as if it had been on the losing side of a dogfight — blackened, covered with white splotches of foam, dented, and smoking. Manfred looked much the same as he patted his arms continuously to put out the invisible small flames still singeing him, looking dazed and lost. Then a figure in a Nazi uniform approached.

"Well Brauchitsch," he sang out like a drill sergeant, "you're not retiring, are you?"

Neubauer couldn't believe his eyes as generations of military training surfaced in Manfred.

"Of course not sir!" The watching crowd went wild with applause as they saw Manfred climb back into his singed wreck of a car. Zimmer, Brauchitsch's mechanic, was tugging on Neubauer's sleeve.

"Herr Neubauer, for God's sake don't let him drive in this state. He's trembling all over. I know him. He'll land in the ditch on the next bend!"

But before Neubauer could step in, Brauchitsch was driving off in the still-smoking car, the wheels blotchy with foam, the body dented, blackened and still dripping fire retardant — hell-bent for Ragnarok.

"I hope we see him alive again," Zimmer said softly.

Dick came past, building a magnificent lead. But no Manfred appeared when he was scheduled to. Zimmer and the crew looked glum, sending glances of hatred toward the N.S.K.K. men. Finally a police car pulled up in the pits — and Manfred got out, steering wheel in hand. He was quiet, but flames were licking around his eyes.

"Well, I suppose you're going to say a few words of sympathy, Herr Neubauer. Don't bother!"

Neubauer slapped him on the shoulder, delighted to see Manfred in one piece again.

"Don't talk such damned nonsense, Manfred. I'd rather hear what happened to your car!"

Manfred's story is quoted with a straight face in most histories. (Neubauer, of course, thought it was pure hogwash, but didn't care. Manfred was alive and unhurt.) According to Brauchitsch's story, he was just gathering speed at the rise where the cars left the ground that the drivers had christened the "Flugplatz" or "Airport" when the steering wheel without warning came off in his hands. With all his strength Manfred had gripped the center steering spine and kept the car straight as he pulled it to a stop. Whatever. Neubauer had learned never to quibble about explanations of happy endings.

After the race Rudi took Manfred aside, grabbing him by the shoulder. "Well, that's the way of it, I guess, old man. Up one day and down the next!"

Manfred didn't answer. Were there tears in Brauchitsch's eyes? Neubauer was heaving a sigh of relief. No one killed or hauled off by the Gestapo. Dick had won in brilliant style, and the only fly in the

Nazi ointment was that Huhnlein now had to telephone the Führer and explain why an Englisher had won the German Grand Prix.

"Herr Neubauer, you are to return to the pits," an N.S.K.K. guard said in his best command voice. Neubauer saw with a sudden sinking heart the same Nazi that he'd had the run-in with earlier, waiting for him. The Nazi was clearly out for Neubauer's skin.

"Herr Neubauer," he snapped, "you sent a damaged car back into the race. You are therefore responsible for Brauchitsch's running off the road!"

"But," Neubauer began to protest, not knowing if he were digging his grave deeper or not, "it was KorpsFührer Huhnlein who ordered the car back into the race, not I. If I had been consulted, I would never have sent that car back in." Which was certainly true.

To accuse a Nazi official of being at fault was not always the best way to get yourself off the hook, but just then there was a clearing of a throat behind him. It was Huhnlein, listening to the whole confrontation, and now looking almost apologetic,

"That's quite right," Huhnlein admitted.

But the other wouldn't let go of his prey.

"You should have examined the car more closely!"

"What? That would have taken half a day!" Neubauer replied, feeling it was his turn to get heated. "Just what, may I ask, was wrong with the car?"

The Nazi became icy again. "The brake hoses must have been damaged by the heat. That's why Brauchitsch lost control." Now it was Neubauer's blood that ran cold. The man might be right. He hadn't thought about the brake hoses. The next few moments, while the officials examined the hoses, Neubauer went through the gates of Hell and back again. But the hoses were fine. And Neubauer staggered off for a well-earned cognac before the victory banquet at the Eifelerhof, while Huhnlein went off to make another one of his phone calls to the Führer.

At the banquet table an empty chair next to Erika sat waiting for her escort. Dick Seaman suddenly made his entrance at the table to a round of applause. Erika was motioning Dick to take the empty chair next to her. Manfred meanwhile, was up in his room, sleeping off the day's mortifications.

Back up in their room after the banquet, Rudi had a hunch. "Go and see what the boy is up to," he said to Baby. (During race season, Rudi was the absolute dictator of the Caracciola family. Off-season

Baby ran the show.) When Baby didn't return from Manfred's room in a few minutes, Rudi went to have a look.

Manfred was stretched out on the bed having a good, open-faced bawl. Two close calls with death, escalating Nazi demands, and now Erika going off with that Englisher, Seaman. It had been a long day, a long season.

"Let's drive to Lugano tonight!" Rudi said in his dictator tone that was more of a decree than a suggestion. "Manfred will take the first stage so I can rest." The idea sounded wild but delicious to both Baby and Manfred. No more racing, no more Nazis' dirty looks, no more anything but sun and water and mountains. They drove through the night, and by breakfast, Manfred's only concern was that Anatole, Rudi's pet monkey, had eaten half of Manfred's boiled egg when Manfred had got up for a moment to steal just one more gaze at the lake.

Changes began to take place, and politics grew like a cancer nearer the heart of the drivers' beloved sport. The League of Nations had put up sanctions against Italy for Mussolini's play at becoming Emperor of North Africa. According to the League, Mussolini's efforts at reviving the old Roman motto "Carthage Must Burn" had been a mistake, and Italian racing teams had been banned from competition in France. Rule-makers rarely investigate all the effects of their supposedly well meant sanctions, and Rene Dreyfus, then driving for the Ferrari Alfa team, found that he suddenly couldn't race in France, even though he was Champion of France. Since nearly all the teams had become a well-mixed bunch, the effects of the rise of nationalism became more confusingly absurd with each new political edict.

More and more embarrassing was the growing pageantry around the sport. To celebrate the successes of his playthings and set a seal on the job they were doing to insure the party's popular power over Germany, Hitler had issued a command performance of the Auto Union and Mercedes teams, not at a race course this time, but at the Chancellery itself. It would be a wonderful opportunity for the Führer to show how chummy he was with his heroes, and how much racing knowledge he had at his fingertips.

Rudi and Bernd and the whole group had to drive their cars inside, and then race the engines until the superchargers made the marble walls echo with their screams in the night. Then the drivers all had to meet the Führer and shake his hand. Then the cars were led in procession to the Motor Show Exhibition Hall, where they were met with a Roman fanfare of trumpets. Neubauer said later he felt like a clown in a circus.

A word to the wise? As Bernd's name became more of a household-word in Germany, he also found himself treading on thin ice with the Nazi Party as it found itself increasingly frustrated in its efforts to mold Bernd into a good ambassador for the Reich.

photo: Auto Union Archive

The pomp and circumstance was placing a strain on Bernd's sense of humor as well. His eyes were darting, searching for some redemptive release from what had been a hypnotically compelling display, but not the sort Rosemeyer really enjoyed. Friends knew that restless look and feared Bernd would do something outrageous. He did.

With a kind of genius for bad timing, Bernd had decided it was time to do his Führer act and give everybody a laugh, once the formalities were safely over with. He combed his hair down over one side of his forehead, held a comb under his nose and then went into his strutting, shouting, and yelling in his hoarse Hitler voice. At that moment a party of visitors came around the corner and down the aisle coming straight for where Bernd was holding forth. It was Hitler and his entourage. Hitler stopped for a moment to appreciate the performance and then strode over to Bernd,

"SturmFührer Rosemeyer!" he began, using the SS title conferred on all his hero-drivers whether they wanted titles or not. "Changed your hairstyle, I see."

Hitler was smiling, onlookers were relieved to see, and shaking Bernd's hand. But Bernd was close enough to read Hitler's eyes, and there was more calculation than amusement there. The Führer strode off without another word, and for once Bernd was the one left without a clever comment.

Chapter 16

Hammer and Tongs

While new drivers were brought on board by both teams, Rudi and Bernd still kept at their feud on the tracks, never giving the other an inch. At the Swiss Grand Prix at Berne, Bernd had been on edge all morning before the race. He had tried to calm himself by showing von Delius the way around the track on a map, but the distraction hadn't worked and tension was slowly taking a visible hold on Bernd. For once, Elly was at a loss about how to calm Rosemeyer. Stroking his hand, as she felt like doing, would probably have just the opposite effect from soothing him. To keep the chatter going Elly was telling friends about the action at the practice the day before, when Bernd suddenly broke in dramatically to tell Elly to stop talking about things she didn't know about.

"The Goddess of Speed," a special gift from Hitler to the winner of the German Grand-Prix, with Huhnlein doing the honors and giving the obligatory salute for the press. It's not hard to guess just from facial expressions who won the Goddess and who's so mad he's going to stick a lighted cigarette in her mouth at the presentation ceremonies. From left at back, Neubauer beaming, von Brauchitsch not paying attention, Rosemeyer fuming, and Caracciola grinning like an art-nouveau satyr.

photo: Road & Track

Elly had never heard him like that. Elly was suddenly just as angry herself. She had been just trying to help, after all. She came back with a reminder that if she were to stop him every time *he* was talking about things he wasn't an expert about, there wouldn't be much conversation left around the house.

Elly instantly regretted her outburst. Von Delius tried to defuse the situation by making jokes in various languages, but it was a silent carful that drove through the dense traffic to the track.

Bernd went to see to his race car without a word to Elly. Surely he'd come back to take his leave of Elly before heading out to God knows what on the track. Then the announcement came for the drivers to get to their cars. Elly saw Bernd coming toward her through the pits with relief. But when he spotted Elly, Bernd stopped, shook his head as if talking to himself, turned and walked off back toward his car.

Elly couldn't believe Bernd could just walk off like that before a dangerous race. She swallowed her pride and ran to him. A few earnest words about Bernd's idiot behavior broke the ice. His old grin returned, transforming him back as he shook off the tension and laughed at his childishness and then asked Elly to wish him luck as usual, as carefree as if he were getting on a merry-go-round.

Bernd was slower than Rudi off the starting line this time, but stuck to his tail as the two flew toward the first turn. Through the corners of the back stretch Rudi's Mercedes, with its superb handling, was able to pull away from Bernd a bit. But back on the finish-straight, Bernd could use the flexible power-range of the big Auto Union to pull right back onto Rudi's tail again.

So it went lap after lap until Bernd began to get the gauge of the twisting back-stretch and began to stay a little closer behind Rudi at the start of each straight. Gradually, Bernd began breathing down Rudi's neck all the way around, looking for a chance to pass. The blue flag was brought out by the course marshal to signal Rudi to pull over and let Bernd past. Neubauer later said Rudi had pulled over, but that Bernd had refused to pass because he knew he couldn't hold Rudi on the turns. This seems unlikely since the marshal had had to bring out the "pull over" flag, after all.

Elly, on the other hand, said later that Bernd was waving his fist at Rudi to pull over and getting more steamed as the race went on. Another possibility that no one mentions was that Bernd had planned this race to be a repeat of that famous earlier race when Rudi had reversed the situation and had pipped Bernd at the finish and then had given Bernd that patronizing little speech and the swizzle stick to practice his shifting with. Bernd was, it could be argued, arranging things in reverse to show his complete control of the race — which could also explain the nervousness that just wasn't like him, before the race. This might well have been a very important race to Bernd in more terms than just championship points.

Whatever the explanation of his strange driving, Bernd kept on Rudi's tail but did not pass, whether Rudi was blocking him or Bernd was scripting his own dramatic finish. The denouement was spoiled, however when Rudi dropped out with engine trouble and Bernd coasted into an easy, if unsatisfying, first place. With his rival out, and to make things more interesting, Bernd sped up and set a new lap record, just to show he'd been slowed by Rudi. He was still burning when he pulled into the pits. Was it about Rudi's drive, or about missing the chance to pip him at the finish?

Bernd was growling after the race that he'd have an earful for Rudi when he saw him, going on to add that racing was a touchy enough business without having to play with these unnecessary risks.

Bernd had won the Championship of Europe a scant two years after that first test-drive for Willy Walb. His was a truly meteoric career fulfilling all his stated dreams that had seemed so preposterous just a short while before. But still, after the race in Bern, Bernd seemed uncharacteristically unsettled and touchy.

As fate would have it, after the postrace party Bernd and Elly headed toward the elevator to go up to their room. When the doors slid open there, displayed like storefront mannequins, were Rudi and Baby, also retiring after a long and, for Rudi, unprofitable day.

The Rosemeyers got into the elevator with a cold nod to the Caracciolas, and then Rudi proceeded to touch just the right match to Bernd's fuse.

"Well, young fellow," Rudi in his baronial way, "you did very well today. May I add my congratulations?"

"You think I did well, do you?" Bernd said, flying right off the handle. "Well, I could have done a lot better if you'd gotten out of my way sooner!" Elly and the others in the elevator tried to melt into the woodwork.

Afterwards in their room, Bernd was still fuming and defending his outburst, saying that he couldn't just act like nothing had happened, after cursing and waving his fist at Rudi for half the race. Now at least Rudi had an idea just where they stood.

Bernd's instant following of his instincts, blanking out all diplomatic second thoughts, as part and parcel of his success on the track. Second thoughts can kill you in a four-wheel drift when the most important tool to survival is an unbroken flow of instinctual, un-self-conscious reactions to follow the fast flow of action. But it was unnerving for bystanders to watch. Elly had learned to have complete confidence that, if anyone could make it, Bernd was the one who could do the job. But even Rudi said later that all of the drivers feared for Bernd's survival through every race.

By this point Bernd had retreated into a strange new cold reserve whenever Rudi was on the scene. It was cramping to Bernd's natural ebullience, and he came to dread being thrown in the same room with Rudi.

Also pulling Bernd in two directions were his inborn love of homeland and his natural distaste for jumped-up bureaucrats like the

Nazis. Though he was as acerbic about the Nazis as von Brauchitsch — when he was put on the spot to choose between his desire to make fun of the Nazis and his love of his country, he'd be swayed by the argument that until somebody else came along to challenge Mercedes, Germany needed him.

However, when Hitler had sent a nice bronze bust of "The Goddess of Speed" as a special prize for the winner of the German Grand Prix, and when she was won by Caracciola, Bernd burned. The bust was later seen with a lighted cigarette in her mouth, with Bernd standing nearby looking angelically innocent.

Bernd's fuming came to a fever point when he and Elly received a command invitation to attend a banquet to honor a mixed-bag of celebrities of the Reich, hosted by no less than Josef Goebbels. The dinner would provide a wealth of photo-ops displaying the luminaries drawn by the brilliance of the Nazi flame. Bernd was fretting before the gala. It was becoming impossible for Bernd to sit at the same table with Rudi when he'd been such a sore spot in Bernd's side. Then, Bernd-like, he popped his own tension-bubble without warning and began to talk about how it was a fine state of affairs when Germany's two top drivers couldn't stand the sight of each other. Bernd went on to talk about what a great driver Rudi really was. Perhaps at the race at Bern, Rudi just hadn't seen Bernd trying to get by.

"Typically Bernd," Elly would say of this reconstruction of reality after the fact. That imp-smile would always find a way to grab control over the seriousness that had taken over, no matter what feats of logic-jumping were needed to do it. Besides, Bernd might have realized that he was already on shaky ground with Goebbels. At a previous banquet Bernd had refused to wear his SS uniform that had come with the honorary Nazi rank Himmler had bestowed on him. Goebbels had had to go out of his way to make a joke about Bernd's showing up in a suit instead his SturmFührer outfit. But once again, for Goebbels' own party Bernd still wasn't wearing the uniform. He'd never even put the thing on, in fact, even as a joke.

After Goebbels' banquet, it may well have occurred to both Rudi and Bernd that their greatest threat might not be each other, but the Reich. Whatever the case, the two men, accompanied by von Brauchitsch and Henne, grabbed enough champagne to float a small boat and retired behind closed doors to discuss the Nazis, unpredictable tires, oil slicks, team orders, and a host of other threats to life and well-being that they both shared. They were each fast becoming the only other person on earth who could understand the pressures they were each separately, facing daily. By sun-up, Bernd had returned Rudi's swizzle stick and given him back the same little condescending speech he had gotten at Nürburgring: "Well done, young man. But in future don't just drive around the track. Use your head." They'd forged a friendship that was to last well beyond the limits of personal survival. Meanwhile the pan-Europeanization of the teams escalated until there was hardly a place left for young German drivers to get a chance.

Varzi, one of Italy's driving legends, had been on the Auto Union team for some time now. When he'd left Alfa Romeo to duel more freely with Tazio while driving a French Bugatti, the Italians had booed him and called him traitor. Varzi never reacted to the catcalls, of course. It wouldn't suit the icy sophistication and aristocratic air he adopted (he was actually from a modest middle-class background). But when a chance to drive one of the more powerful Auto Unions opened up, he jumped at it and had become an effective team member. He and his always-chic girlfriends added a touch of glamour to the modest nuts-and-bolts team that Porsche and Walb were running.

One day, as the drivers began gathering at the Principe di Savoia Hotel in Milan before the Monza race, Neubauer saw an act unfold that riveted his attention — one he never forgot.

Neubauer had been in the lobby, sipping his apertif and nodding a nod of greetings to the lanky, elegant Hans Stuck and his wife (a tennis champion who wrote lively articles for the Berlin papers) who were chatting nearby. With them was a young, aspiring driver who was hoping for a trial on the Auto Union team, and his wife — a stunning Marlene Dietrich-double, Neubauer couldn't help but notice. (For convenience, and to protect the characters in this little drama who weren't the trouble-makers, they have been named "Peter" and "Lil.")

Just then the revolving doors spun and in strode Varzi, cool, smooth, and cigaretted as always. He gave a wave to the party, and then stopped dead in his tracks, losing all his usual Varzi-like poise. He was staring openly at the driver's young wife. Stuck, to smooth over the embarrassing gap in the conversation, took the initiative. "This is Lil," he said, introducing her to Varzi, "and if you're planning on being her admirer, Varzi, you're going to have to take your place at the end of the line."

Varzi had recovered himself by this time, and the chatter flowed on smoothly.

"I shall be happy to be allowed to admire you, even from the end of the queue," Varzi said. Still, as Neubauer watched from his front-row seat, he noticed that Varzi couldn't take his eyes off Lil even as he left to go up to his room.

A little while later at the track, Neubauer watched as another chapter of this story unfolded. Manfred had set up a blistering lap time in his Mercedes at practice and the Auto Union gang was itching to have a go at bettering this. Walb was standing between Stuck and Varzi, who were arguing over who should have the chance at Manfred's new record. Varzi settled the matter by grabbing his windcap and striding off toward his Auto Union. Just then Peter's low-slung Horch drove up and out got Lil. When Varzi spotted this, like an eagle catching sight of a mink, he threw down his cigarette and said, "I've changed my mind. Let Stuck have a try." Moments later Neubauer watched as Varzi was kissing Lil's hand. A little later Neubauer could see Varzi arguing again with Walb at his car. Then the dispute seemed to have been resolved, for Neubauer saw Peter taking off his jacket and putting on his racing windcap. He then saw Varzi and Lil driving off together.

Lil was becoming a constant visitor at their apartment, Paula Stuck noticed. Such an amiable girl. Then she remembered, with a cold feeling of suspicion one day, that Varzi had an apartment just above the Stucks'. And that Lil's visits were always curiously short.

Paula confronted Lil with her suspicions at the next drop-in visit.

"What are you up to, Lil? Using me as an alibi? You come by, pass a few remarks, and then disappear. To room 410? We all know whose room that is."

Lil flushed. "So what? I don't deny I sometimes visit Varzi. We've simply become good friends."

"What's Peter have to say about your good friend?"

"Peter? He's only interested in cars and racing. Besides, Varzi says he can help Peter. He thinks he can get Peter a contract at Auto Union."

The next scene Neubauer was to witness came at practice where Lil was learning the intricate skill of timing a race. Varzi was turning in some hot laps as Peter and Stuck watched from the pits. Then the loudspeaker announced that Varzi's car had left the track and crashed. There was a noisy clatter, and the group turned to see Lil's watch and clipboard dropped on the concrete. Lil had gone white.

Then another announcement reported that Varzi was completely unhurt and returning to the pits. Everyone showed great relief, except Peter, who looked more than usually pensive.

Stuck and Varzi, while they'd never been the best of friends, had been effective teammates. But with Varzi's last adventure with Lil, Stuck lost all respect for Varzi, and all restraint from battling with the man tooth and nail, teammate or not. At the race start, three cars stalled out — all Auto Unions of Stuck, Varzi, and Peter.

Then began a self-destructive battle among the Auto Union team that even Neubauer (usually the first to applaud any weak points in the Auto Union effort) couldn't enjoy. The three drove atrociously, grinding gears, skidding brakes, slewing wildly as they battled blindly in an uncontrolled grudge-match. They all placed well down among the last of the pack at the finish, and nothing had been settled except the state of their battered racecars.

Lil's story was typical of what was happening to many young women in Germany. A family's social ambitions sometimes took advantage of a beautiful daughter. Blossoming overnight into a devastating young beauty, Lil found that her mother was soon making big decisions for her.

What Lil needed most, her mother decided, was a well-established husband to spoil her. A rich merchant from Frankfurt was found to fill the bill, and at seventeen Lil was married and showered with every mink coat, fancy car, and assortment of diamonds that might have been better appreciated later in her life. She had everything but the companionship of a young man to face challenges in life with. Then she smelled the scent of another woman on her husband's coat and the fabric of her faith in the old ways of marriage began to unravel.

She sought a divorce and then fell in with the racing crowd, attracted by the unspoken existentialism of their live-for-the-day attitude. Her first conquest had been the driver, Jellen. But she quickly saw that he (like Chiron) simply wasn't husband material, and when Jellen's friend Peter asked her to marry him she surprised everyone by saying "Yes."

Jellen's driving took a turn for the worse. His concentration seemed to lapse, and soon he crashed and was found dead by the side of his car. Peter's track record, on the other hand, took turn for the better, and he began to find himself mingling with the more established drivers, while Lil enjoyed the many, varied, and nearly always amusing personalities of the racing celebrities they were meeting. Peter's career was just getting to the professional stage when Varzi walked through those revolving doors and into their lives.

After Varzi's crash, when Peter began to guess why Varzi was being so helpful to his career, Varzi had asked to meet with Peter and Peter agreed immediately. Somehow this situation had to be resolved.

There was no gloating, or even much happiness in Varzi's bearing when the two met. On the contrary, he seemed almost sad as he took Peter for a drive in his car. These things happen. People don't plan them, and they only complicated life for everybody. But it had happened, and there was no going back. There was not much any of the three of them could do to change things now. Peter saw that Varzi was right and that he was acting as more than just a casual wife-hunter. For once, Varzi seemed genuinely spellbound by a woman, not just trolling the field as usual for easy prey. The men agreed to a civil solution to the situation, a quiet divorce.

Varzi began to drive as he'd never driven before, becoming more than the token Italian on the Auto Union team, and in no time won two Grands-Prix outright. He began to shower Lil with expensive gifts — diamonds, clothes from Rome's best couturiers, a lavish apartment, a new white American Packard convertible. If Lil were not at the track, Varzi was on the telephone. No one had seen Varzi so outgoing, so happy-looking.

As the couple began living openly together, Varzi was to learn more of this new woman who had made more difference in Varzi than any before. He was in the throes of one of his after-race headaches one night when Lil reached in her purse to bring out as remedy she'd found to be helpful: morphine. "Lil, what in heaven's name are you doing with that?" She'd been given it when in the hospital with kidney trouble, it seemed. Since then she'd managed to find it whenever she needed a little extra "help."

"But it's poison. It's terrible for you."

She only smiled wryly.

"What about your smoking? And the coffee you like so much? It's not dangerous if you just use your head about it. It's silly not to use it, just because a few people can't control themselves. Just try it. You won't have any problems...."

Lil's power over Varzi was prodigious, they both knew that. Varzi stretched out his arm with a sigh.

Why did she do it? Did she even know? Drugs are a lonely life. Perhaps it would help the couple share more. It was true that Varzi's personality had become more outgoing with the appearance of Lil in his life. But now Neubauer noticed others looking at Varzi closely in conversations. He was not only outgoing, he was becoming an approval-hunter — boasting and seeking to top every story with a feat of his own. And laughing too loud at any joke, however lame. The old Varzi hardly laughed at all. Now, it seemed, he wanted pals and loud conversations that he could dominate.

His driving was no longer the cool, minimalist, killer-instinct attack. He was wilder, more theatrical, showy. And his laps times were falling off. Drivers began talking about the New Varzi and how he was becoming a menace on the track — unpredictable, choppy. When friends visited Varzi's apartment, they saw other "friends," pretty lads in perfumed silk dressing gowns lounging silently like household cats — friends that Varzi never bothered to introduce. When Dr. Glaser went to Varzi's parents to see if they could shed light on his change of personality, they told him that Varzi had cut them off completely and dropped out of sight.

Dr. Glaser made inquiries around the rumor-mills of Rome and finally ran Varzi down at his new villa. Varzi was effusive; polite phrases poured out of him like a diplomat. Glaser had never seen a Varzi like this. The visit proved nothing concrete to Glaser, but somehow it had confirmed all his suspicions that Varzi had changed for more reasons than just a new relationship.

But there was nothing solid he could put his finger on and his report back to the racing department mentioned only a "change in personality." Still, Varzi's overfriendliness was what chilled Glaser the most. He would keep a close eye on Varzi, just as Neubauer was doing as well, from the other team's pits. A good team manager kept an eye on all the regulars at the track, not just his own men. At speeds over 150 they were all pretty much depending on each other, and everyone had to maintain a professional predictability for any to survive.

Meanwhile, Neubauer had his own problems. Manfred and Rudi had pulled still farther away from Lang socially, and Seaman remained aloof from everybody. But then, another time, Rudi and Manfred would make the fur fly in a duel of their own without warning.

Huhnlein was smiling less and less at the kid-stuff pranks and jokes and there was talk of a whole new program to "clean up the pits" and make them a more wholesome area for the world to see. All those occasional women that Manfred brought in. All the booze, the bar-nothing dress code. Schnurrbiber was bad enough in his bib coveralls and no shirt. But Bernd was just as likely to drive in lederhosen and no shirt and sandals as he was to be found in a proper racing suit. Von Delius and Bernd had sent Elly out on the course to drive one of the Auto Union team cars, and later Bernd was seen squeezing Elly into the race car cockpit to show her what a real lap was like (afterward she admitted it was more exciting than anything she'd done in a plane).

The whole show was devolving into a party. Something, Huhnlein realized, would be done about it. Just as Rudi had delivered the punch Kruppke was scheduled to give the Belgian officer, perhaps it would be better if Huhnlein did the clamping-down — before Berlin got it into its head to do the same thing.

Since the race teams had forced Mussolini's cars into the background, Berlin was, instead of being more solicitous to their champions, beginning to treat them like used ammunition. They'd done their job, some were saying. Why put up with their embarrassments and insolence? Still, some of these drivers were heroes from Hitler's youth. And everyone knew that Hitler, for all his shortcomings, rarely forgot his early heroes — giving special visits and positions to old teachers and figures of boyhood adulation. Better go easy, was the word.

Varzi was becoming a race team's worst nightmare. Berlin was keenly interested in keeping Varzi, a token foreign driver, on the track when needed as a seal to the Italo-German Axis. But Varzi had slipped into disregarding practice sessions, completely ignoring pit signals, and sometimes missing a race altogether without warning. Dr. Feuereissen, the new Managing Direktor of Auto Union's racing effort, felt the time had come when he'd better do something about Varzi before Varzi ended his career in a ditch. He paid an unannounced visit to Varzi's villa. Lil answered the door in a dressing gown, looking alluring, but a little embarrassed. He'd noticed that, on recognizing him, she'd casually, but quickly thrown a towel over something on the table.

Feuereissen apologized for the sudden visit and went on to explain how concerned he was about Varzi's poor showing in past weeks.

"And you think I can explain it?" Lil asked, surprised (and a trifle challenging).

"You know him better than anyone else."

Lil began to talk about how it's natural for everyone to have down periods. Every driver goes through slumps.

"I'm afraid there's more to it than that, " Feuereissen said. "Varzi's living too much on his nerves. Too much coffee. Too many cigarettes. And, if you'll forgive my saying so, he should keep a quieter life, at least during the season." Feuereissen braced for what he thought would be a fiery response, or one of Lil's lightning tirades. But she just took a quick involuntary glance at the towel and kept quiet. On a hunch Feuereissen took a quick step toward the towel and grabbed it off, revealing ampules and hypodermic needles.

"Ah ... Morphine. Now I understand."

The rage came now from Lil. Backed into a corner, she went on the offense. "You have no right to come spying on us!"

"There you're mistaken. Your private life, unfortunately is tied up with the survival of everyone Varzi races against. Already there have been complaints about his becoming a danger. The consequences of what you have here are going to be very serious."

Lil went pale. Feuereissen nodded.

"I mean that before long Varzi will have driven his last race for Auto Union. In fact he should have his license taken away."

"You can't take his livelihood away from him!"

Feuereissen looked at her coldly. "Whoever gave him this took his livelihood away from him."

When Varzi returned to find Lil in tears, he flew into a rage. He'd show those spies and busybodies whether he could drive or not!

Varzi got a letter from Italy's leading sports journalist in the days to come.

> Dear Achille,
> You must have no illusions. The path you've chosen to take has no end unless you can turn back now. Do you seriously believe that any firm or racing team could engage you as a driver so long as they know the kind of life you're leading? I beg you as a friend: forget everything — and I mean everything — and try to regain some of your discipline and self control.

For awhile nothing seemed to help, and Varzi found himself off the driving roster. He made no inquiry about this change in the line-up. But then there followed a terrific row with Lil, one of the biggest in a long series. Varzi moved to a smaller apartment. As the world raced on, Varzi made changes. Lil was sent to a sanitarium in Switzerland.

One day, as Rosemeyer and Feuereissen sat sipping their drinks in an Italian hotel, a page brought Dr. Feuereissen a card. He looked at it with raised eyebrows and handed it to Bernd.

"Achille Varzi," Bernd murmured, "back from the dead."

Varzi greeted his team-mates with his old, cool self-control (or at least a good impression of his old self). He launched immediately into a quiet apology for what had happened. And when Feuereissen protested that it could all start again at any time, Varzi went into all the positive changes he'd made in his life, ending with, "I'm still a young man. I'm not ready for the scrap-heap!"

"Youth is not just a question of years, Achille," Feuereissen said. "Look over there at the mirror and tell me if the face you see is that of a thirty-three-year-old."

Varzi turned and look at the lines that had riven through his face. He saw the face of an old man. He turned back sadly.

"Yes, I understand."

Bernd's eyes had been following back and forth from Varzi to Feuereissen like someone at a tennis match as this dialogue had gone on. He'd been thinking — sympathizing with a man who loved racing as much as he did. Perhaps he thought back to when his motorbike license had been snatched away, years before, and the following emptiness he'd felt in his life.

Suddenly Bernd blurted out, "Why not give him a chance, Doktor? Varzi deserves it as much as anyone!" As a result, Varzi was scheduled for future races, but Feuereissen remained skeptical and kept close tabs on his performance on and off the track.

The thing that both teams had been dreading for some time now happened: direct race choreography by Berlin. There was a race scheduled to be run at the grand new Italian race course at their new North African colony, at Tripoli. The colony's Italian government was part of Mussolini's new rebuilding of the Roman Empire. But the colony itself — its architecture, its new mechanized farms, even its new farmers, had all felt the touch of one man: Governor Italo Balbo.

Starting out as a teacher, a poet, and journalist, Balbo had been drawn into the Fascist movement by a romantic, neo-Garibaldean, almost chivalrous instinct to save his beloved Italy from the clutches of what he saw as the gray, anti-individualistic, materialist-based Communists. He had the personality and connections to be of help to Mussolini in gathering and managing forces for the counter-revolution — the Black-Shirts. After their March on Rome and the assump-

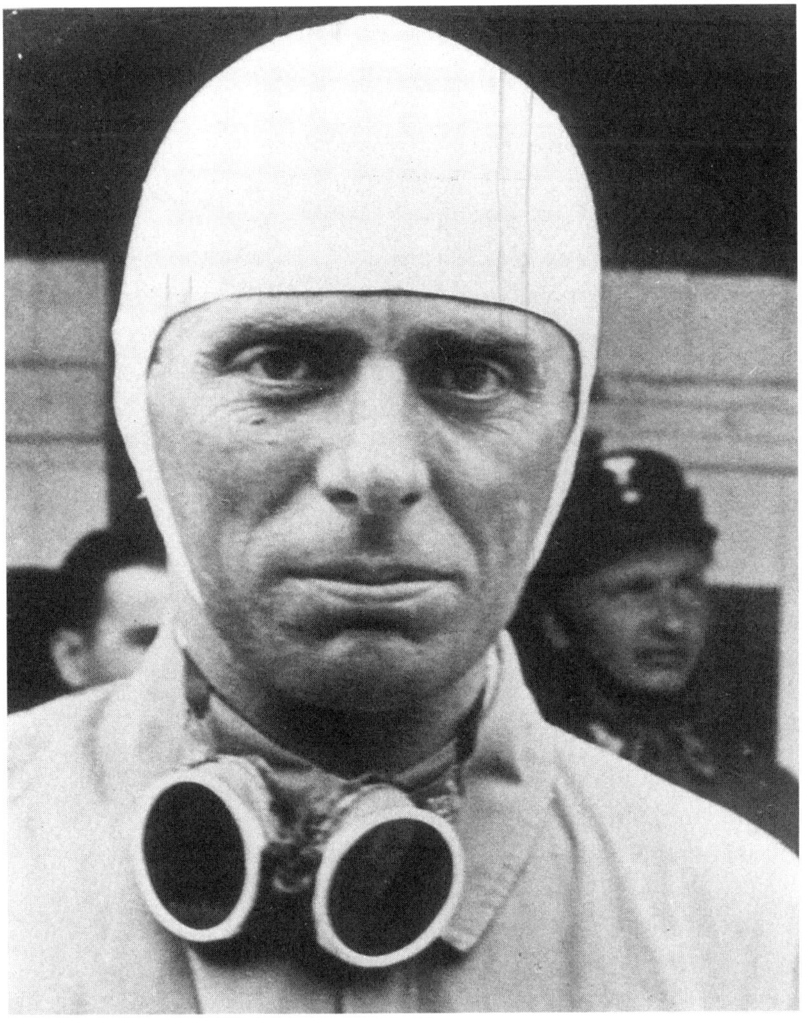

Achille Varzi, showing the scars of more than just many years of battling it out with Tazio. "Lil" may have shortened Varzi's career, but she paid a price, like a character in a Hollywood melodrama. Neubauer ran into her in later years, a physical wreck on the skids, and on the streets.
photo: Auto Union Archive

tion of power by Mussolini, Balbo emerged as an extremely popular leader of the new regime.

So Mussolini shipped Balbo off to the political hinterlands in the Air Ministry. Here, Balbo, with his usual energies, learned to fly, organized air competitions that drew the whole aero world to Italy, made record-setting flights to South America, and then Chicago — flying the lead plane in the formation himself. In Chicago, in typical Balbo-fashion, he charmed every one and was made an Indian Chief.

To reward Balbo (whom he privately called "the buried land-mine") for the fine job he'd done bringing the attention of the world to Italian aviation, and the Schneider Cup Air Races held in Venice, Il

Duce took his popular disciple and sent him to the far side of the moon again, this time to the barren, dusty hole of Tripoli.

Without a flinch Balbo bounced into action, this time organizing a huge mass emigration of landless farmers to North Africa. He even went on the ship with the immigrants himself, and saw to it a new Utopia would grow out of the desert (with taxpayer money, of course). By the time Balbo's excitingly fast new race course was ready, he was at the height of his popularity. But Balbo himself was wising up to Il Duce, was losing faith in his policies and anti-Semitism, and began to talk privately of dropping a couple bombs onto Mussolini's office in Rome. Interest for the race had built across Europe in the weeks before the event and much newspaper space had been given over to the preparation for the event. Perhaps too much.

News of the race had reached into the political backrooms of the Chancellery in Berlin. And one day, shortly before the cars were due to be shipped over to North Africa, Feuereissen got the call both he and Dr. Kissel had been dreading. It was no less than Hitler's Foreign Minister, Ribbentrop, on the line.

Since the race in Tripoli was to be such an important part of Balbo's launching of his North African colony, it would be nice if the Germans supported his efforts and saw to it that an Italian won the Tripoli Grand Prix. Do what is necessary so that Varzi should win. That will please Marshal Balbo — or so the official thinking from Berlin went.

Those who had any appreciation of what sort of man Balbo was knew this was the one course Berlin could take that would insure his rage. Balbo was extremely well-liked among the drivers of all teams. He'd socialized privately with both Hans and Paula Stuck, as well as the Rosemeyers. And the reason the drivers felt at ease around the man was that they knew him to be a performance-minded person who admired honest action more than guile. Berlin couldn't have picked a worse candidate to honor with their first race-fixing program.

Feuereissen shuddered when he realized what this new policy of fixing race results would entail. "Do what is necessary." If they only knew.

First, they would have to work out a strategy to induce the drivers to play along. And then they would have to move heaven and earth to make it possible for Varzi to win. In his present state, it would be impossible for him to win it fairly, Feuereissen knew. Berlin simply didn't understand. There would be no way to make a Varzi-win look like anything but a cheap carnival trick. No one but a Berlin politico would fall for it. Racing would lose its credibility, that would be the only result. And with it would go one of the Nazis' own most valuable propaganda tools.

Goebbels had realized that tact was needed when he dealt with the German film industry. They'd tried direct propaganda movies, the kind that were being produced in Russia, where the brave worker outsmarts the corrupt aristocrats. But Russia was still basically a backwater where the concept of movies was new to the public, and they seemed to sit still for heavy-handed propaganda messages. Goebbels had tried that and was met with hoots and catcalls from the more sophisticated German audiences. This was a cultural center of Europe, after all. You couldn't expect the same sort of message-films that thrilled Russian peasants who'd barely heard of indoor plumbing to meet with anything but derision in Continental Europe. So Goebbels had made a quick about-face and went to producing movies who's only propaganda message was that they were always upbeat and optimistic. Once in awhile a movie director, ambitious to make a beeline straight to Hitler's heart, would mistakenly bring out a propaganda saga, but it rarely met official enthusiasm. Hitler, for the one and sometimes two films shown at the Berghof every night, preferred the leggy musicals of Busby Berkeley, English Sherlock Holmes mysteries, and Gable's *Mutiny On The Bounty*.

Why couldn't Ribbentrop show the same laissez-faire attitude? These politicos who just drop in from Olympus to stick their thumbs in the works were like rich old dowagers with better ideas about how the younger generation ought to live.

What Feuereissen needed now was some plan to make this happen without exploding the whole tinderbox of politically incorrigible drivers into a full-scale public rebellion in front of the press of the world. Then maybe they could buy some time to think of a way to appeal to Berlin to follow a subtler course of action.

In the weeks before Tripoli, Stuck had been practicing extra hard, training his pit crew, checking every detail of his car's tuning. It looked like he meant to have his day in the sun at Tripoli, since Rosemeyer had been stealing the spotlight so long at Auto Union. It might be a good idea, Feuereissen thought, if he went to preside over the pits himself for this race. He'd be giving the pit signals and, as far as you could ever predict these drivers' responses to pit signals, calling the shots.

The pageantry at Tripoli was every bit as colorful as Berlin's Fascist Sunday best. Flags snapped in the wind. Bands marched, and the

Marshal Balbos's popularity made him a threat to the powers behind Mussolini, who privately called him "the buried land mine." Finally seeing Il Duce for the disaster he was, Balbo (also privately) vowed to drop a bomb on Mussolini's offices. However, before he could carry out his intentions, Balbo's plane was gunned down by Italian forces with Balbo and his family aboard.

photo: Archivo Caproni

Italian equivalents of the N.S.K.K. guards were resplendent in much more colorful uniforms, feathers, and staff braids. Ladies' hats blew in the grandstands like spring flowers, and Huhnlein (in the same uniform he always wore, even in official photos with Hitler) sat in the purring open Bianchi touring car with Marshal Balbo for the bigwig lap of honor.

Tripoli had always promised drama, and this season's rivalries were reaching the boiling point. After years of tension building between Fagioli and his team-mate Rudi, Fagioli had deserted the Mercedes team and taken up an offer from Auto Union. When the two drivers could finally battle it out from opposing teams at Tripoli, the fur really flew. And after Rudi had stayed ahead of Fagioli through the practice session using any means he could, Fagioli came looking for Rudi with blood in his eyes. Fagioli actually jumped the pit counter with a switchblade to get at Rudi, and after peace had been forcibly restored to the pits, Neubauer mopped his brow and declared that if Fagioli and Rudi were scheduled to race in the same heat against each other, Mercedes would withdraw from the race. Fans knew they could count on more excitement than just car racing at Tripoli.

The course was the fastest in the world at the time, with Stuck putting an average speed up near one hundred fifty miles an hour. It was also a tire-eater in the heat at those speeds, and if the hot, dry Ghibli winds blew, superchargers were also likely to blow once sand got inside them. Two adventurous Americans, the genial Pete DePaolo and Lou Moore, brought their cars over to see what they could accomplish after their experiences on a similarly fast autodrome at Indianapolis. Tripoli was another whole new realm of speed, they decided, after what seemed like the entire Alfa team blew past them on both sides through a corner, leaving them in a state of shock.

Practice lap times showed that Stuck seemed to be the driver whose sights were set most firmly on winning Balbo's prize and he rocketed away from the start of the race to control the whole event from the first laps on. Apparently Fuereissen hadn't gotten out the word on who Ribbentrop was counting on to win. Near the last laps of the race, Neubauer was not surprised when Dr. Feuereissen put out the "slow down" signal to Stuck.

"Playing it safe," Neubauer thought. No use pushing a car too hard once the race was in the bag.

But, consulting the three stopwatches that Neubauer always wore around the neck, he noticed that Varzi was catching up to Stuck, who was holding to the slower pace Feuereissen had ordered.

Fascinated, Neubauer watched the Auto Union pits more closely as a curious dynamic seemed to be developing. Sure enough, next lap Stuck was told to slow down even more, while without Stuck's being able to see it, Varzi (who was coming up on him from behind at a quick pace) was being told to speed up.

As he cruised on slowly around the final turn to the finish, Stuck suddenly saw Varzi appear out of nowhere in his mirror, going flat out for the flag. Before Stuck had time to recover his shock and make a move, Varzi had flashed past, heading straight for the finish. Stuck accelerated to catch him, but Varzi had crossed the finish line before Stuck could draw along side.

As Stuck's car rolled into the pits, Hans was white with rage. While his mechanic, Matthey, helped him out of his car, the normally quiet Stuck was yelling. This in itself was newsworthy, but what Stuck was yelling wouldn't have made good copy for the Berlin papers.

"That swine of an Italian broke all the rules! He stole the race!"

"No, Varzi had nothing to do with it," Matthey said.

"How come? He passed me after Feuereissen had given me the slow signal!"

"It wasn't quite like that. Feuereissen gave you the slow signal, but he gave Varzi the fast signal!"

Stuck, with fire in his eyes, marched off at once to see Feuereissen. He'd put out a lot of effort to dominate the Tripoli Grand Prix.

"My dear Stuck," Feuereissen said, looking profoundly mortified. "I find this very unpleasant, but I had strict instructions."

"Who from?"

"From high up. " He shrugged his shoulders. "From Ribbentrop! I hope you understand."

"I don't understand a damned thing!" Stuck roared for all the world to hear. "I insist on knowing who prevented me from winning!"

Feuereissen took Stuck by the arm and led him behind the pits, where he continued in a low voice, "All I can tell you is that certain circles in Berlin and Rome have decided that wherever possible Italians should win in Italian races, even if they're driving a German car."

Stuck stared at Feuereissen with disbelief, as the implications of this sank in. What an infantile, harebrained scheme! No one watching the race would be deceived by this sort of thing. Not only would it be a disaster for German credibility, it would also ruin the sport that the drivers lived for. Stuck was still carrying his car's removable steering wheel. Shocked onlookers saw Stuck suddenly hurl the wheel to the ground, and heard him yell at the top of his lungs, "To hell with the Rome-Berlin Axis!"

Balbo's banquets to celebrate his Grands-Prix at Tripoli had become the talk of the European race world. Teams without a prayer of winning the race would apply for a starting spot just for the sake of the banquet afterwards. Nothing in Berlin came close. Nothing even in Mussolini's Rome could compare.

Balbo, out of the sight of Rome's exchequers, let his neo-romanticism run amok for his Tripoli Race banquet. Writers have used the term "piratical splendor" in feeble attempts to do it justice. Elly

Hans Stuck, whose driving career spanned four decades, always lent a courtly air to auto racing, even though he was a self-confessed "failed farmer" who turned to racing mostly to find work. He was a great favorite of Hitler as well as Italy's Marshal Balbo, although he himself retired for a while to escape the constant political pressure and never seemed fond of power-people.
photo: Auto Union Archive

likened it to something done by an Indian Maharajah out of a fairy tale: marble floors polished to mirror sheen, dancing fountains, arched Roman colonnades, Moorish facades, crenelated roofs, a sheik of honor from each tribe in his best robes sitting atop his white Arab charger, scimitar drawn, a groaning board seating fifty chosen dinner guests (with dancing and partying for hundreds more), torches reflected on the floors and in the lighted swimming pools aswarm with naked girls (doing the backstrokes, as girls will in these circumstances). If Hitler had seen a Busby Berkeley musical set at the Tripoli banquet, he would have nodded with delight .

At this year's Tripoli banquet, when the time came for Balbo to rise and toast the winner, all eyes turned toward the Governor for his customary dramatic toast. The man had a magic about him (which was precisely why his hero, Mussolini, always managed to find obscure jobs for him). This evening, however, Balbo's toast was simple and direct.

"I raise my glass to the winner of today's race!" Balbo began. But then instead of saluting Varzi, he turned to Hans Stuck, and drank to his health.

There was a painful silence, and a tic shook Varzi's face.

"Your excellency," Stuck began with uncertainty, "there's some mistake. The winner is sitting over there." And he pointed across the table to Varzi.

Balbo smiled, then said in a loud speech-voice, "My dear Herr Stuck, I know only too well who won this race. I also know why my countryman Signor Varzi was first to cross the finish line. But it is my custom to drink to the true victor of Tripoli!"

There was a silence again, broken by the tinkle of a smashed champagne glass. Varzi was nowhere to be seen.

In his famous toast to Stuck, Balbo had lobbed a warning shot across the noses of the whole racing community that they couldn't ignore. By not winking away Varzi's prechoreographed finish, by telling Berlin that their clumsy diplomacy could never succeed with Italians, by bringing the whole affair out in the open and plopping it in the laps of the drivers, Balbo had forced them to come to terms with what was happening to their sport. He'd placed the drivers into a corner they probably should have placed themselves in before something like Tripoli could have happened.

Chapter 17

New Horizons

Dr. Porsche had received a summons to tea at the Kaiserhof again. This time, he guessed, it was his own fault. Soon after Hitler's Auto Show Speech, which had girded a new hope to the nation's automotive loins, Porsche had found himself motivated enough to write a lengthy treatise on one of his three favorite subjects: a really capable people's car.

Racing was fine and doing its job admirably, to make onlookers across Europe take Germany very seriously again as a source of new technology. It had also taught German engineers a whole lot about the kind of metallurgy, lubricants, supercharging, and fuel feed that would be needed for fighter aircraft, already in the works. Tractors, Porsche's third passion, could wait until Germany opened up larger farmland tracts that demanded machine cultivation (say, in the Ukraine?).

What was needed now, obviously, was a car that had the capabilities to open up a wider life for the German working family. Hitler had made big press by meeting with his head road engineer Fritz Todt and then digging the first shovel of dirt leading to a fabulous new freeway system to make commerce between far-flung areas of Germany a simple thing. The time had come for a capable family car to run on these lavish new autobahns that were now slicing straight across the new Germany.

Porsche outlined the parameters that the new car should meet in performance and economy. He'd already taken this same concept to nearly every auto manufacturer in Europe, but had met with nothing but rebuffs. Rich people were the only car market, they told him. In these days of Depression at least, why would anyone build a car for poor people? When Porsche had said all he had to say in his paper, the work was sent off to the new ministry of transport. Months went by, months filled with fierce racing action to distract the Professor. Now the call had come from Jakob Werlin.

Werlin said the ministry had been interested in what Porsche had to offer, etc. etc. — pleasant, glorious generalities, the kind only a politician or car salesman wouldn't wince at. When the Führer arrived and the two Austrian country boys got down to business designing the car, Werlin sat to one side and listened.

"It must be aerodynamic to have economy," Hitler was going on. "You only have to look to nature to see what shapes work in practice. Shape it like a beetle."

In later meetings of their Thursday afternoon design sessions, Hitler was shown sketches of the kind of body Porsche's team was evolving under the deft design hand of his young genius Erwin Kommenda. Hitler didn't like the lobbed-off short front end and made a sketch of how he thought the Volkswagen hood that we still see everywhere today, should look. The sketches have survived, along with the car that went on to become the most-produced auto in history.

They went back over the specs needed to get the Führer's approval: enough room for a family of two parents and two kids, plus luggage for a trip. Capable of all-day cruising speeds at 100 kph (62 mph). Getting forty miles to the gallon. It would be a small, full-size car, not a miniature that "would never be cheap in a sociological sense," according to Porsche's paper on the subject. Eventually they came to the limiting fiscal parameter. What price should the new car be retailed for?

"Any price you like, Professor. Any price at all as long as it's under a thousand Reichmarks." Hitler grinned, echoing his hero Henry Ford and his "You can have a Model-T in any color you like — as long as it's black."

A thousand Reichmarks! Porsche's heart sank. It could be the end of the project if the Führer arbitrarily placed this lunatic low price limit on it. You could just barely get a middle-of-the range motorcycle for a thousand marks. No car had been produced that cheaply. Privately, Porsche called the price stipulation "idiotic." Publicly, he got to work.

To make the enterprise seem reasonably fair, Hitler put out a contest for all manufacturers and design houses to bid on, following the specifications they'd put together. Porsche's design, with its clever all-independent torsion-bar suspension that became the darling of Baja off-road racers decades later, was the easy winner, needless to say, since some of the DAF people were already in love with his Volkswagen design before the contest ever started.

There are those who claim that Porsche for some reason would go to another design source to steal the layout that was finally used. There are similarities of the Volks design to both Mercedes and Tatra designs (with neither of these using the core-torsion bars that made the bug ride and handle so well, which were Porsche patents). But the center-spine chassis and rear-engine layout was current state of the art for the forward thinking European design houses at the time. It would be much the same as saying that copying had taken place just because most manufacturers went to the MacPherson-strut at roughly the same time, or adopted disc brakes at the same time. If we look at the daily development and testing schedules of the Porsche staff, we can see that they had to do an awful lot of experimental testing for a company that was copying its designs from lesser-known designers.

Once the fun of creating the basic design layout was over, Hitler turned the project over to the head of the German Labor Front, Dr. Robert Ley, to handle the details of carrying out the manufacture of the car. It would be Ley's responsibility (with the help of one of his lieutenants, Dr. Bodo Lafferentz and the RDA (association of German Auto Manufacturers) to see that all the German auto industry started preparing their plants to produce the new Volkswagen as soon as possible, while Porsche began building the first prototype.

This was easier said than done, for not one of Germany's auto manufacturers wanted to produce Porsche's new design. Most, in fact, had already turned it down on their own, as a project. Despite the power of Ley's Labor Front, which had usurped all the power previously held by not only the labor unions, but also the social-security, retirement insurance, and vacation-planning industries, the RDA was standing fast in their resistance to the VolksAuto plan.

On the nuts-and-bolts side, Porsche was beginning work on the new prototype, for whomever would end up producing it. This was an important project for Porsche — one he wanted to create a clear set of values for that would permeate throughout the whole design. The chassis, the engine, the interior, should all follow the same basic philosophy clearly. Porsche decided to remove himself from the distracting self-consciousness felt in a factory-based laboratory-shop milieu. He wanted to create this important new car, the most important car of his career, in a creative atmosphere, more like a studio than a factory. So he decided to build the first Volkswagen in his garage.

Just the right personnel was called to the garage — the kind of intuitive/scientific thinkers that could fill in the blanks creatively, with a certain amount of the artist's enthusiasm for this work. Also Porsche wanted the kind of worker he could trust to secrecy, which may explain why a quarter of the staff working on the new car were Porsche family members. He moved two lathes, a drillpress, and a mill into one end of the garage, and with twelve men, set up shop. It had to be done fast (ten months) and it had to be done right, what with every competitive manufacturer in Germany itching to tear the prototypes to pieces.

Meanwhile Motorshow time had rolled around again, and once again Hitler took the stand to send his message of the progress of Social-Motorization out to the airwaves. He began in his best proud-as-a-peacock tone:

"I am pleased that, due to the capabilities of the brilliant designer Porsche and his staff [if Hitler had only known about Porsche's brilliant aluminum-shaper who was drunk half the time when those 24-hour workdays started piling up] it has become possible to complete the first designs for the German Volkswagen and the first vehicles will be tested halfway through this year. It must be possible to provide the German people with a car that does not cost more than a medium-sized motorcycle and which is economical in fuel."

Hitler's scheduling was a little optimistic. With the first three cars being hand-built, it took another year before tests began. But a little back-pedaling smoothed that over. Instead of being skeptical, the German public was simply anxious, but understanding, when setbacks played havoc with deadlines.

When Hitler had brought out his idea to have all of Germany's auto industry build his Volkswagen, the battle began at once. The manufacturers had no intention of building someone else's design when they all had their own prima donna designers they'd been paying good Reichmarks for. Porsche had burned some important administrative bridges when he left Mercedes for the second time, and little sleep was lost at Mercedes over whether Porsche's feelings would be hurt if they balked at his new design.

While Hitler might have had a life-and-death "power image" over his people (and a demonic image in Hollywood), in actual practice, even after he'd taken over more powers during the war, he was never as omnipotent as he'd like to have been. Throughout the war his generals, designers, and advisers could be heard yelling at the top of their lungs, lecturing the Führer on mistakes he was making. In fact there is a surprising thread of short-tempered flying-off-the-handle that seemed to run quite through the fabric of German day-to-day working at many levels — a curious occasional anomaly of reckless individualism that at times rose above a clear sense of survival. Whatever the case, Hitler was running into opposition at this point. It seemed that the whole German auto industry was rejecting his plan to join hands together and make one car for everybody.

It was still essential for Hitler to show quick follow-through to the people at this point, however, but Mercedes and the other manufacturers were planting their feet and promising a long siege at the idea of all of them building the same car (a practice that was somewhat successfully adopted in the United States during the war when various auto plants built the same tanks and bombers). Time was passing and no progress was being made by the bureaucratic chain of command at Mercedes toward building the VW — nor at any other manufacturer, for that matter. Even Reichsmarshal Goering (as a good friend to Big Money industrialists) got into the act, confiding to Reichsleiter Ley, "I'll be honest with you. As you know I've always been opposed to nationalizing private industry, and that is what we're doing with Volkswagen!" But Ley stood firm against Goering.

Finally Hitler brought out his big hammer and declared that the Volkswagen would be built by the German Labor Front in a brand new plant and worker's housing and social facilities complex at a site to be specified later. They would call the community Stadt des KdF, standing for "Kraft durch Freude," a catch phrase that Hitler was trying unsuccessfully to foist on everyone. The idea had its start with the DAF Labor Front, which acted not only as labor arbitrator but also to provide leisure time activities to Germany's work force at bargain prices.

The phrase meant "Strength through Joy" but is better translated, possibly, as "Endurance through Fun." The job of the KdF was to make sure the workers had enough fun to keep them hard at it during work periods, organizing cruise ship vacations, sporting contests, etc.

Hitler settled the issue in his next speech announcing the new car. "It shall bear the name of the organization which is most concerned with filling the broadest masses of our people with joy, and thus with strength. It shall be called the 'KdF-Wagen,' the 'Strength through Joy Car.'" As snappy a name as only a simplistic linear-thinker could come up with, reminiscent of the Chinese "Jolly Hero-Worker Bicycle."

Dr. Porsche's son, Ferry, had said, "We were not enthusiastic about this name for export, since it meant nothing to other countries. 'VW' was OK and made good sense, but now we had to change thousands of advertising signs to 'KdF' and it had to be done whether we liked it or not. The name never caught on, however, and the people still called it the 'VW.'"

Hitler's demands for the placement of the new factory were more practical, however (and straight out of Henry Ford's placement ideas for the Ford plant). "It must be near the center of Germany, on a canal and near railway and autobahn connections." Dr. Ley's chief economist, Dr. Bodo Lafferentz, got to work at once searching out the perfect spot.

Count Werner von der Schulenburg was spending a quiet morning over his pilsner and bratwurst when his gamekeeper burst in full of excitement. A low-flying aircraft had been buzzing the property that had been in the Schulenburg family for over eight hundred years. The gamekeeper was saying the Count should complain to the authorities since the plane was upsetting the game in the forests. The Count thanked his gamekeeper patiently and went back to his quiet morning the way von der Schulenburgs had done for some time now.

Then the local teacher bicycled up to bother the Count again, this time with a story of large black cars touring the vicinity with men in both military uniforms and city-style overcoats. The Count made a note to himself to check into what was going on. Then a phone call came from one of his tenants reporting a strange car parked in her driveway. When the tenant told the driver of the car he was trespassing, the man had the nerve to tell her that he could go anywhere he pleased. If she'd realized that the driver was Bodo Lafferentz, she might well have left him alone to pursue his work.

The Count began to become concerned. A new autobahn through his property would be a nuisance. Still, the Schulenburgs had connections reaching way back past the present regime. There were ways to keep progress from cutting swaths through your holdings, even these days.

Then came the visit to the Schulenburg castle by Lafferentz himself, to inform the Count that two-thirds of his holdings were to be surrendered to the Reich for "an important national project." The Count went into action. He called people he knew far up in the Party in Berlin. But this "national project" was being sponsored by someone very, very high up. There was nothing they could do.

The Count went to the forestry department. There were some ancient oaks on the property that were national treasures. No luck. The Count brought in the wetlands conservations issue, claiming there were over seventy species of mosquitoes indigenous to the property that were unique to the area. Still no luck. Hitler had said to cut the trees and drain the swamp and that was apparently that.

Social-Motorization was on the move now. Parades of Nazi-laden Mercedes were making grand processions down the first lengths of the autobahn system, Hitler standing in the lead Mercedes and giving the salute every time they went through an overpass for the inevitable newsreel cameras. Seventy-thousand people attended the laying of the cornerstone of the Volkswagen plant. (It was quietly removed after the war and dumped in the canal for future treasure-hunters to search for).

The three prototype models, a convertible, a sedan, and a sun-roof were used to bring in Hitler and the royal entourage, including a boyishly enthusiastic Huhnlein in his usual uniform. Porsche and son, Ferry, were there; Ferry driving the beaming Führer for his first test ride in the convertible. Costumed representatives from the various trade guilds and legions of Huhnlein's N.S.K.K. youths paraded flags, bands marched, and all was well in the land of the Führer. The plant was going to cost a lot of money, but then Dr. Ley and Bodo had come up with an intriguing new way to pay for everything and then some.

Savings stamps could be obtained at your place of work, and when you'd filled out the "Sparkarte" or stamp-book, with its colorfully-illustrated cover showing a family outing in a VW, cruising through the Alps, your name was placed on a waiting list to receive your car. No banks involved. No parasitic middlemen (the kind the Führer made himself appear to hate) took their piece of the action. And no dangerous, bourgeois "living on credit" habits were encouraged. Yet a lot of money could be raised.

Over three hundred thousand German families signed up, raising over RM 67 million. To sell his car, Hitler made a point of riding into the most-publicized rallies and events, standing like a wooden Indian in the little convertible VW, saluting and looking more than faintly ridiculous posing so heroically in such a small car. This sort of thing never fazed the Führer, however. When stylists and image-builders sought to update his rather antiquated look, he would beat them off. "It's a matter of complete indifference to me how posterity remembers me." Good thing.

Dr. Porsche's patented trailing-link/torsion-bar set-up for the Auto-Union — the chassis layout that also formed the reason Volkswagens are so much fun to drive — it has a Grand Prix car suspension.

photo: the author

For some reason mainstream historians take this program as an opportunity to prove what a fraud the Führer really was (when there are so many better chances to do this that are actually based on truth). They claim that the party took the money after the war started, and that no one ever got his VW from the program. In fact, the money was stolen by the Soviets following the war, yet the renascent private VW company still made good on all claims for decades. The author interviewed customers who took their Sparkarte claim out in a nice new Karmann-Ghia version of the VW well after the war.

When it came to testing the cars, Hitler didn't mess around. The new VW's were given a test-run in actual road conditions that no private auto manufacturer had ever put its car through. Once the prototypes were finalized, the three cars were turned over to the German Auto Manufacturer's Association for testing, which scheduled the much-photographed prototypes for five hundred-mile drives six days a week.

Built in Porsche's garage with no facilities for materials-testing, they were bound to break. The job was to find out what would break (and break they did). Front wheel bearings went out, torsion bars cracked, brake systems failed, and even crankshafts broke, with all the breakage of other surrounding parts that went with a crankshaft failure. Bodo's man Vorwig had to write a report going into painful detail of every failure to determine remedies. But the testers were still enthused about the Bug. The faults were nearly always faults of material, instead of faults of Porsche's design concepts.

When these were set right, the new improved versions were summoned to the Berghof, Hitler's mountain lair high in the Obersalzburg. Herbert Kaes, Porsche's nephew, and two others drove the cars up to the Berghof where they were displayed by a proud Führer to top military staff, with an eye toward using the Bugs for jeeps. Luncheon was served on the terrace, while Kaes and his men furiously removed the entire body off one Bug to display its advanced chassis (which Kaes had hand-painted) to the generals, so they could see the obvious all-terrain potential of the car. Field Marshal Rommel later said he owed his life to the light-weight VW jeep, nicknamed the "Kübelwagen" or "Bucketwagon."

Then the Bugs were taken on an alpine trial, running side by side with four other competitive German small cars. This was when Porsche began to realize what kind of car they had on their hands. All of the advanced features (the trailing link independent suspension, almost exactly like Porsche's Grand Prix car, the unitized engine/transmission/differential unit, the spine-chassis with semi-unit body) had been added and developed over the months, with nothing to compare them with directly. Once they were driven over the same roads with other cars, and once drivers traded cars back and forth, it became obvious how superior these new features really were. Most of all, the Beetle was really fun to drive, with a supple agility and willing feel to it. That was what made testers want to sneak one home with them for the weekend.

Finally an order came through that Mercedes would now have to bite the bullet and manufacture a series of thirty of the new improved

VW's. These would be driven by both testing teams from Porsche's design bureau and SS officers, many of which had not had a chance to learn how to drive yet. The new test called for over a million and a half miles of driving by every kind of driver in all terrains and weather conditions. Test drivers took them out on Sundays to show off to their friends. SS men sneaked them, off hours, to run their own errands. Nazi officials winked at off-duty uses for the cars that would inevitably (and quietly) put them through tests never scheduled by the program. Jakob Werlin was seen driving a Beetle and Bodo Lafferentz had his own Bug for a daily-driver. This was not the kind of test program devised by a man set on duping the public with ballyhoo about a car, such as the much-vaunted Tucker (which had collapsed on its springs under the gruelling test of being wheeled out on stage for a photo op).

Hitler meant business with his KdF-Wagen. Afterwards Kaes and his men took the Beetles apart and measured the wear down to the smallest part, searching for weak points that needed strengthening. Before the new plant was built, Porsche was still using any room he could to carry out work, with Kaes doing the final wear measurements in a tiny shed in the middle of a parking lot.

All this was sapping the money and personnel from Hitler's own racing program part of Social-Motorization. Porsche had been pulled out of the racing pits at Auto Union and put on the drawing board for the VW project. And even Huhnlein was showing up at more milestone functions celebrating the coming VW than he was at races. In just about every photo-op promoting the Bug, from unveiling the first small wooden model to the setting of the cornerstone of the new factory, there in the background is our boy, Huhnlein, smiling with obviously unfeigned enthusiasm.

And the kind of research needed for high-performance combat aircraft was now going on openly at the BMW and Messerschmitt plants, once Hitler had gathered the power to renounce the Versailles treaty and was moving with much-ballyhooed programs to rebuild Germany's air force with Goering, Milch, and Udet at its head.

With a full plate of new interests, like the convenient dry-run of the civil war in Spain, and a new role to play as international statesman, rather than just national leader, racing was losing its raison d'etre for the Führer. He had bigger fish to fry.

The first rude awakening to this new status for racing happened in practice before the big race at Avus in Berlin. The teams had begun their practice runs with more than the usual rivalry between teams, and teammembers. Fans were looking forward to a real battle, as were the teams.

Then, from out of the blue, a Nazi staff car rushed past the barriers put up to keep the public out of the practice sessions. Word was passed to the team managers, who only gaped in disbelief at what they were being told: Reichsmarshal Goering was having an afternoon party and all this racket of the race cars was annoying his guests. Therefore practice was cancelled until after the last of his guests took their leave. The silence that the teams sat around in the rest of the afternoon could only be termed "a thoughtful one." Then came a reprieve.

Hitler himself had decided that it was time to take the message of German superiority to the whole world through the race teams, with trips as far away as Cape Town and New York in the works. A new honor for the successful racing program staff? Or were they being sent out of town to get them out of everybody's hair for awhile now that their objectives had been met?

Their forays to England were met with a stunned, awestruck disbelief. The sporting British had been following the amazing race records of the German teams, but they never guessed the effect the teams could produce when seen in person, on their own familiar tracks. Because of restrictive road-rules and a government unsympathetic to anything that resembled car racing, competition fanatics in England had been relegated to a few privately owned parks where an attractively cordial but largely out-of-touch mood prevailed. "The right crowd, and no crowding" was the motto at Brooklands, the huge car racing park built by landowner Locke-King. But ever since it was built back in 1909 to counter restrictive rules against racing on public roads, the banked corners had settled into dips and ruts that were becoming a dangerous chore to drive.

The Duke of Richmond and Gordon had opened up his driveway for a racing circuit and there were a couple of hillclimbs using private access roads. But the action, though it had its own heroes and heroics, was on a small, clubby scale.

When the silver monsters from Germany showed up at the first international event at the Donington circuit, they took the crowd's breath away. The bellowing roars, the supercharger screams, the cars leaping bodily into the air at the tops of hills, it was all something almost uncivilized, but completely fascinating to watch.

A Stuttgart surprise for the all-conquering new Alfetta 158's: the carefully-hidden new 1.5 litre W-165 Mercedes V-8's set out in formation (Lang in first, Rudi in second) to run away with the prizes at Balbo's Tripoli Grand Prix. The streamliner in fourth-place is Villoresi's 4CL Maserati (body by Farina).

photo: Mercedes Benz

The British racing fan was never the same again, and the trip to Donington had been the cause of much quiet rethinking on the part of those in England who realized how much modern warfare depended on mechanical expertise (and how expert the Germans were becoming at organized technology). This was precisely the message Hitler was intent on spreading, of course. "Respect for one's weaponry before battle is everything," Napoleon had written.

The Italians began to sense a weakening in the German solid-front that had wiped the tracks clean of serious competition in the first two seasons under the new racing formula. They began their counter-attack first by altering their race tracks to favor the nimble but less powerful Italian racers. They placed chicanes that required drivers to wind through a maze, replacing the longer straightaways where the German cars had previously left the rest behind. But these were quickly mastered by Rudi and Bernd and there were some bad accidents involving Italian drivers at these same chicanes as well.

Next, the Italians concentrated on their cars. They would, in future, put all their efforts into the smaller voiturette class, making this class of racing the arena of most interesting competition, just as the French had moved their motoring interest to long-range sportscar racing to enjoy a few victories away from the grasp of the German-dominated Grand Prix scene.

For their new voiturette the Italians turned to Ferrari, who had been managing racing efforts for Alfa in a separate, somewhat autonomous shop in Modena. Ferrari had never been able to stand the regimentation at Alfa (which had come under close Fascist scrutiny that took away the kind of majordomo power that a man like Ferrari demanded to get the job done). On his own, Ferrari collaborated with Alfa's best engineers on an outsourced basis to design and develop a truly remarkable little 1.5 litre-sized engine (a little larger than the VW beetle) that would eventually punch out well over 400 horses. It was called the "Alfetta" because it was so light and lithe-looking, not like the ponderous bimotor monsters Alfa had made to try to keep up with the beefy German racers. Besides, Maserati had long been the mainstay of voiturette racing. What the new Alfetta couldn't achieve, surely Maserati would supply in a strong field for the crowd to enjoy.

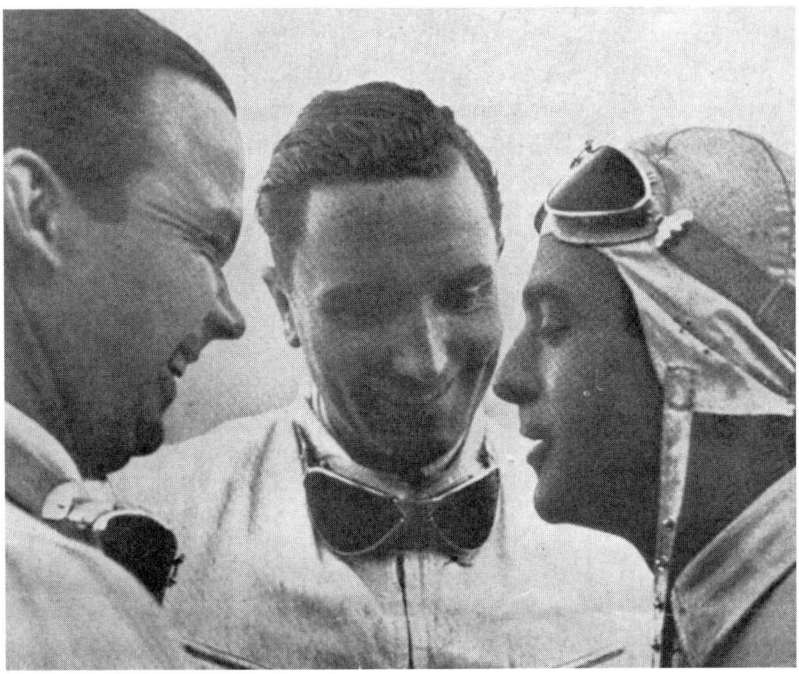

Inside joke (Bernd, at right, busily bursting the pre-race tension bubble for rivals Rudi and Manfred).

photo: Road & Track

Tests in Italy had brought smiles to everyone's face except the spies Neubauer had sent to see what all the hubbub was about. "The Italians have changed the rules so that the race at Tripoli is going to be limited to voiturettes only. If your car has a capacity over a litre and a half, then you can't compete," those in the know were saying. The race was in only eight months — not enough time for Mercedes to build a whole new car to this reduced scale. Or was it?

The challenge was too sweet to ignore. What if, after the Italians had effectively disqualified all German competition by limiting engine size to this new compact size, the Germans showed up with their own voiturette after all?

Partitions went up at Neubauer's racing department, complete with barbed wire and guards. Secrecy was their only hope to catch the Italians napping. With new worlds to conquer, the Mercedes design and fabrication teams worked day and night through the winter. But what came out of that shop was hardly a thrown-together "bitser." It was more like, as fans and collectors still agree, a little jewel of metal creativity, with the lethal-looking, flowing lines of a shark and a beautiful little V-8 nestled under the aerodynamic aluminum. But how well could a brand-new, un-race-proven car do, built for just one race?

Two of the V-8 prototypes had been built, and to the Italian crowd's horror at the Tripoli race they both led the way around the first lap. Then the next, and the next. At the finish they had led the entire race, finishing first and second, the young ex-mechanic Lang driving away with an easy victory. After the race, Neubauer went searching for Lang before the traditionally Balboesque victory banquet. Lang was asleep in his room. Worse than that, he didn't even own formal dinner attire.

"Wear a bathing suit, I don't care. Make yourself presentable somehow," Nuebauer snapped. "Governors don't like to be kept waiting!"

Chapter 18

A Glimpse of the Gods

To get a truly Martian's-eye-view of racing in the fattest days of the Third Reich, perhaps our best guide would be the relatively impartial viewpoint of one of the last of the line of the King (of the "King and I") of Thailand, Prince Birabongse. Sent from the tropical splendor and relaxed attitudes of the royal palace in Bangkok straight to the hallowed halls of Eton and then Cambridge, "Bira," as he came to be known to his racing pals, saw life in 1930s Europe as a culture shock rivaling a voyage to a nearby planet. Accompanying Bira had been his older cousin, Prince Chula Chakrabongse, his quieter, more restrained duenna in the curious West.

Bira quickly mastered life in England and went searching with boundless energies to ride every attraction this carnival, England, had to offer, in his own very earnest little-boy, Peter-Pan way. To Bira, the kind of endeavors we take as serious undertakings laced with drama, he saw only as another new world to explore, like a new kid's game.

When he became interested in the art world, he took a try at sculpting, finally ending up in the renowned studio of Malvina Hoffmann and winning prizes from the Academy. His bas-relief portraits were quite professional and are still on display in a day when few have the slightest clue who Prince Birabongse might be. When he decided to try the flying game, he ended up setting a new world's altitude record for sailplanes. "This is fun, I wonder if I can beat everybody in the world at it?" seemed to be Bira's motto. Bira always retained his schoolboy awe at the Western world, and in cartoons of himself Bira drew his racecars (named "Romulus and Remus" because the were twin E.R.A. racers) as almost-human, mechanical companions with whom he went adventuring. Bira and Chula were the kind of colorful newcomers to the racing world that made the touts and mechanics around the Brooklands scene scratch their heads and wonder, "What've we got 'ere?!"

Chula had introduced Bira to the world of car racing with a trip to Brooklands when Bira was still in school, and the young prince was entranced the way only young princes can be. "So this is motor racing! Well, it certainly makes a lot of noise!" was his first impression, arriving at the track between races with the cars warming up and creating a racket in the pits. When he saw the flight of the streamlined little "toys" around the track, however, he was beginning to feel the hook deep inside.

He ordered an M.G. Midget and tried his hand at this new game as soon as he could. Not surprisingly to those who knew him, he found he had a knack for it and better yet, found it was the most fun of any of the strange English games he'd tried.

On his twenty-first birthday Chula presented Bira with a gleaming new E.R.A., England's hottest new voiturette, a nasty-snarling, quick little beast. Bira painted it Siamese racing colors, light blue with a yellow stripe down the middle. When he bought a back-up car it was, in imitation of Scuderia C-C of Chiron-Caracciola — painted in the opposite color scheme: yellow with a blue center stripe.

When the shiny young prince appeared at Brooklands with the hard-to-get E.R.A., a car that everyone wanted, it couldn't have made him popular with the regulars, who were struggling along with aging, revamped machines, the sort Brooklands saw year after year.

When he did well with it, it must have driven the old hands wild with puzzlement. Possibly the most puzzled was Bira himself. He could never quite believe it when he found himself driving faster than one of his own heroes. And when he and Chula as a team walked away with the first place prize at their first Monte Carlo race, they just sat and stared at each other speechless through the whole night. This alien kid who seemed to treat racing like a child's game to be giggled over, clapping hands with delight and going into ecstasies over the appearance of racing big-shots — how could he slip behind the wheel and go out in his new silk racing suit complete with cunningly-knotted ascot and just beat everybody?

It is also a tribute to the young Prince's personality that, even after he went on to prove that his winning hadn't been a fluke, he began to gather friends. Drivers and mechanics alike found they couldn't dislike the little dynamo, even when they wanted to (and after Bira won the British Racing Drivers' biggest Gold Star prize three years in a row, you can bet there were some who would have preferred it if the Prince took up fly-fishing).

When he'd crash, coming as close to death as any of them, Bira would draw cartoons of his car in bandages, and vow to make it up to his "friend" the race car, as soon as possible. A curious Eastern/Western mechanical-age animism?

Reading about the German teams in full flight would never be enough for Bira. He would have to see for himself in what he called "A Glimpse of the Gods." While Bira was not exactly the sort who could become good drinking buddies, he'd found in Seaman a kindred spirit.

Seaman was going to be racing at the Nürburgring. Monkhouse, the photographer, would be there too, since his bosses at Kodak had placed him under the wing of Mercedes for a season of taking publicity shots of Neubauer's team in action.

"When I tell people I adore motor racing, it is not only the actual driving of racing cars round and round the circuit, but the whole thing," Bira wrote in his typically little-boy style. The race was only the climax of a whole step-by-step process of having a wonderful time in the Western world. With this existentialist's appreciation of "the process," then, the two cousins headed for Nürburgring, or as Bira called it, "Mount Olympus."

"My hyacinth blue open Bentley purred along those twisty roads quietly and easily," he later wrote during the long war years. Behind them, their mechanic Shura was transporting Romulus along hopefully in time for the race. Bira was fast becoming enchanted with the wald-country with its chalets and bell towers. "If one half closed one's eyes, it could almost have been a toy town," he commented. Bira loved toys and when he disappeared, as he sometimes did, Chula could usually find him at the nearest toy shop.

His reverie didn't last long as he caught sight of a silver shape approaching them from the opposite direction at high speed, heading right for the Bentley. It was Rosemeyer, driving an Auto Union G.P. car on the open road into on coming traffic!

"It would not have done at all to flatten out a god and his chariot the first minute I entered the kingdom. Rosemeyer, instead of being angry at the close call, just waved and laughed," as Bira watched with eyes the size of saucers. "I became fully aware that I was about to have four days of fun."

When he came down for dinner he found the lobby packed with people babbling away. "It might as well have been the Ritz bar. They

were odd looking people wearing odd costumes, ranging from smart town suits to Tyrolean lederhosen. A particularly tight-knit group stood at the bar chatting away loudly."

"When I got close to them, whom should I see surrounded? It was none other than that 'Golden Tortoise.'" This was the nickname of Tazio Nuvolari! The Italian Maestro was there in flesh and blood! This man, or rather superman, Nuvolari, had had a most renowned career, and every enthusiast of this sport must know his reputation like Napoleon is known to historians. Actually up to that moment I had not had the pleasure of speaking to him or being as close as six feet from him, so you can imagine my thrill on this occasion." Bira and Chula sat by themselves for a drink of water. Bira neither smoked or drank but claimed he could be ten times as drunk as anybody on this sort of excitement alone.

An Auto Union coming straight at you down a narrow mountain road is reason enough for anybody to feel a little shaken, but if you're the Prince of Siam, it can look like just another amazing attraction of that fabulous Carnival of Fun Rides called "Europe."

photo: Road & Track

Then there was a lull in the noise, and all heads turned as a kind of human tornado came into the room: Neubauer, "Looking like the god Jupiter," followed by the Mercedes team luminaries. Close on the heels of Neubauer was "the devastatingly good-looking" von Brauchitsch whom Bira had always admired, as much for his good looks as for his driving. (Time to note that despite their somewhat unmacho approach, neither Bira nor Chula was gay. Anything but, as a matter of fact, as Bira's wife later complained when she had to explain to the Prince why he couldn't keep his pet "dancing girl" in the family household, like they did in old Siam.)

While the Mercedes table was a constant uproar of insults, mock-toasts, and bits of food flying back and forth, making Bira feel like he was back in the third form at Eton, the Auto Union table was a quieter scene. Bira was to say, "Somehow I always had a soft spot in my heart for this team, largely due to the fact that I felt they were a very modest lot of people. When they beat up the 'Mercs' they never made much song and dance about it, but quietly celebrated the victory in their own sweet way."

A "Flugplatz" or "airport," as the drivers called the humps in the tracks that could send their cars airborne. Here Manfred brings his Merc in on final approach.

photo: Road & Track

Prince Bira in close conference with a driver who can show him the way around a race-track, Rene Dreyfus (wearing a coat made by one of his family's concerns).

photo: Bits And Pieces, by B. Bira

Realizing that he was actually a race driver himself (and a well-trophied one at that) and not just one of the camp-followers, Bira plucked up his courage and went over to where Rene Dreyfus and his entourage were sitting. Dreyfus, as always, was charming and Bira's clumsy French set the table rollicking with fun. They were joined by the trim-looking young Italian Piero Taruffi who wanted to know all about Remus and Romulus, since he'd be driving his Maserati in the same voiturette race against Bira.

Seeing Taruffi in such close consultation with the Prince excited the curiosity of the other Italian drivers in the crowd, and it wasn't long before Bira was surrounded by names he'd only read about in the competition journals — Dr. Farina (later the first post-war World Champion), the ebullient Marquis Brivio, and that medieval Italian knight who lived in a castle and had built his own aero-engined challenger to Mercedes and Auto Union, Count Trossi.

Bira, by this point quite "ten-times drunker than anyone," suddenly remembered that on one of his "frequent visits to the toy-shops" he'd found a particularly clever windup car that you could steer with a sort of flexible extension handle around a race course on the floor. There was plenty of space in the corridors outside Bira's room. Why not invite the world's top drivers to a little contest? Taruffi translated the offer, which was met by a typically Italian roar of approval from the chorus. They traipsed up to Bira's room. They met Stuck on the way who wondered what all the fuss was about. When they told him, he said they were all certifiable for wanting to play with toy cars, and then took his place in line for a chance to race the little car himself.

The car was a rather poorly turned-out version of a Mercedes saloon. But it performed like a champ, if a trifle hard to master. A course was laid out and Bira gave a demo lap, taking so long that the impatient Count Trossi grabbed the car out of Bira's hand to show how it should be done. Then a fight over the car started, each man grabbing for a chance to practice before the timed runs. Bira found it hard to break away from the melee, yelling that if they broke the car there would be no race at all. This, when it was translated for them, seemed to calm the Italians down enough to let some sort of organized practice begin before the event.

Lots were drawn to decide who went first, with Farina setting off first on his timed run. However, he was so nervous, he began knocking all the corner marker pegs down one by one.

Taruffi was next, cautious and studied (he later wrote the Grand Prix racer's bible on how to drive road races, showing much the same analytical driving style). At the end all the corner pegs were still standing as Taruffi crossed the finish line to a round of applause. Neither Dreyfus, nor Brivio could better young Taruffi's time.

Next came "B. Bira" who bore down with all the concentration he could muster in his first race against international Grand Prix competition. He was doing well, and at the end the Marquis Brivio yelled, "He's beaten him!" to Bira's delight as his time became the one to beat. The serious Count Trossi was the last driver, and Bira watched with nervous sweat as Trossi set out on the last run of the evening. When the flag dropped, Trossi tore off like a bullet. And with a fierce determination that took Bira by surprise, Trossi was never more than half an inch away from the corner markers, without touching a single peg. Over the finish, Trossi was a full fifteen seconds in the lead. A roar of applause went up that brought other hotel inmates out of their rooms to see if there would be any danger of being able to get some sleep that night.

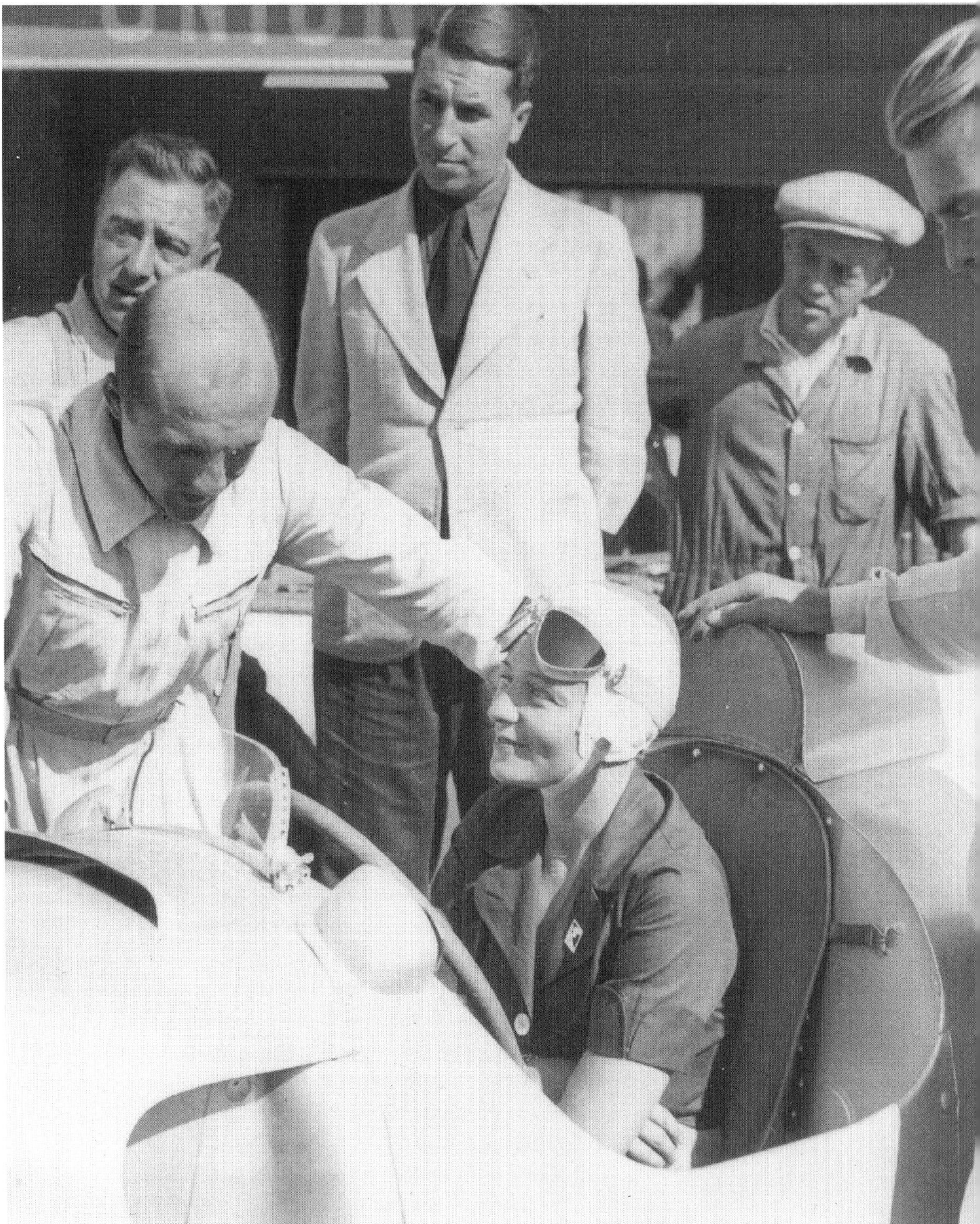

Chapter 19

Tomorrow, The World

Racing abroad in South Africa: Ernst von Delius's "adopted son" of Elly (in cockpit) and Bernd (standing) scored his first big victory on the trip. Elly's about to have a test-drive in the Auto Union here, with Ernschen and Bernd hovering nearby to offer advice, asked for or not.

photo: Auto Union Archive

Chiron was dropping out of the Grand Prix scene and leaving his spot at Mercedes. The news had come like a douse of cold water in the face to his many friends in the racing community. He'd had a high-speed crash, but had miraculously escaped without serious injury, and it was time for Louis to do some quiet thinking. The pace of racing was going well past the kind of lifestyle that fitted the needs of a sportsmen like Louis. It was becoming a job for dedicated heroes. Chatting with Monkhouse he'd said, "This modern motor-racing is all very nice. But I've come to the conclusion that it's much safer to be a spectator."

Dreyfus was moving his operations completely out of Germany, after having lasted longer than most thought he would. He was sad about the whole rotten smell of politics creeping into everything. As he drove through Nazi Germany, a half-Jew in a French car, he admitted he'd still found everyone friendly, and even felt welcomed by the locals. But somehow it just wasn't right. When Neubauer had toasted him at a dinner after racing, lifting his glass to say, "Vive La France," Dreyfus just couldn't bring himself to respond with "Deutschland Über Alles!" since he had orders in his pocket to report for duty as a draftee in the French army the following week. Italian teams couldn't race in France. French teams couldn't race in Italy or North Africa. Life was becoming complicated in Europe, thanks to the efforts of those living off the harvest of political turmoil.

To keep his racers occupied and out of his hair in 1937, while he went on to "simplify" things in Europe (by placing it under one flag), the Führer had approved a second year of forays to Africa and America, this time with an added race at Cape Town in South Africa. Always on the lookout for new adventure, Bernd had figured a way to make the African trip more of a memorable chapter in the Rosemeyer household, and not just a race date to meet.

Bernd had moved in with Elly after the wedding, bringing with him heaps of luggage and boxes of equipment. Having a personality like Bernd take over your digs was a daunting proposition Elly hadn't quite had time to mull over. And when Bernd gave his apartment to Delius, a strange despair came over Elly's sense of independence. But the future was sure to bring a house, the way things were going. And this trip would help them settle in their personality quirks, like bedding-in a new set of brakes.

By this time the British had established airline connections with their African colonies, flying their big, lumbering "Hannibals" to and fro, and Wilhelm Sebastian ("Bastl" to them, since he'd come from Rudi's team to become almost a member of the Rosemeyer family) and Ernstschen von Delius would have to come by this regular air service. Elly's sleek little Messerschmitt with its fold-away landing gear and low-drag fuselage would be cruising at an average of 180 mph, about twice the speed of the airliner. Bernd liked that.

A couple of days before departure, Bernd and Elly were setting out for a Christmas holiday party in full dress, when Bernd found he couldn't get "Manuela," their lowslung Horch cabriolet, to start. The more he cursed and fiddled with Manuela, the more Elly found she couldn't help laughing at the German champion fuming over his own car, helpless as a baby.

Taking off from Templehof on their African air safari, they had marvelous luck with the weather for that time of year, reaching Belgrade in four hours. After some rough stuff over the Balkans they reached Athens on the next leg. And from there they made the over-water flight to Cairo without a problem. They had to wait for the Auto Union crew's flight to catch up, spending the time in the cool bazaars of Egypt in winter. Next came the hop to Khartoum. The British airliner had already taken off at four a.m. to maximize the day-light flying hours on the leg to Khartoum. After a leisurely breakfast, the fastest couple in Europe set out in the Typhoon to catch the Hannibal. They found it sitting on the ground at Luxor; Elly swooped down and buzzed the Hannibal, while Delius and Sebastian on the ground waved their arms off. Stopping for fuel at Wadi Haifa they left a note for the crew inviting them to join the couple for a cool drink when they reached Khartoum.

By the time the airliner staggered in, it was after midnight and the Auto Union crew was in no mood to party.

Bernd never failed to enjoy turning the official greeting party away by saying he was only a passenger. The person they wanted to do their official business with was "Captain Elly." Then he'd enjoy watching their faces drop as they caught sight of Captain Elly's slim, chic, non-tomboyish looks. She'd been a fashion model at one point to pay for her flying, and much of the *haute couture*-look had stuck with her. A woman pilot was unusual in Europe. In Africa, it was unheard of.

In Nairobi, Bernd was struck speechless by the beauty that he'd only heard about from Elly. They stopped for romantic forays into the veldt, meeting old native friends that Elly had become close to on earlier flights. They toured the backcountry by car, searching for an elegant little French restaurant Elly knew about. It was, after all, their honeymoon and it was turning out to be one for the books, even from their somewhat gilded point of view.

In Johannesburg they were met by none other than Baron Claus von Oertzen. By this time he'd moved to Africa for the safety of his wife and was heading up marketing for Auto Union in the area. He had been instrumental during Bernd's early racing days in nudging Willy Walb to give this Rosemeyer lad a driver-trial, and he'd always been held in great respect by Bernd. Von Oertzen made available a fleet of little DKWs so the team would have the ability to run all the errands needed before the race in Johannesburg.

When they arrived at the track, they found out the rules of the race were not the sort of rules Bernd liked. It was to be run along British lines with a time handicap for the faster cars, which usually favored the wealthy amateur driver. Bernd went all-out in the race, and beat his car to a pulp, driving on flat tires, and taking all manner of chances to make up for the handicap time. When he rolled to a stop at the finish finally, the crew hesitantly told him he'd come in fifth. Fifth! All this trouble and risk just to place fifth. But then von Oertzen took over, reminding him to take a loss gracefully once in awhile when in a foreign land. He was driving for Germany, after all, not Rosemeyer.

The next race in East London, near Cape Town, was also to be a handicap affair, and Bernd found it hard to get enthusiastic. In the race von Delius managed to get past the Earl of Howe in the last lap to win his first international race outright. Bernd squeezed in a second, also in the last laps, and setting a new lap record in the process.

Elly had been invited by old friends to visit them in Windhoek, and by the time she found the field, she saw it was lined with hundreds of people waving bouquets of flowers. Bernd ground away with Elly's camera while she slid the Messerschmitt in for a quiet, soft landing on the turf. A shooting party had been planned, and Bernd couldn't wait to try out the shotgun Dr. Porsche had given them as a wedding present. Christmas, swimming in the warm, sparkling sea, it was all like a dream.

Then came the telegram to end the dream: Bernd's much-loved mother had suddenly died. They'd just gotten a wonderful letter from her two days before. Bernd was a great bouncer-backer and rarely let any tragedy keep him down for long. But then he'd suddenly burst into tears without warning or apparent reason. This was nothing new to Elly. She'd seen him burst into tears at the silliest things, although as she pointed out, it seemed not to change the fact that he was to her eyes the most masculine man she'd met on five continents. Bernd had other personal quirks that seemed to polarize his personality. A small boy at one end, an undauntable genius at the other. Watch a film of the man talking. He's definitely a little boy, perhaps even a little girl in gesture. Then watch him weave the 500 horsepower record car through the under passes of the Autobahn at speeds that no one had ever tried — and he's something more than human. A strange angel-like being? Even his eyesight was abnormal. He could race through the fog like it wasn't there. When the flag men couldn't see fifty feet in front of them, Bernd was breaking records.

One murky night when Elly had asked him to slow Manuela down for a pea soup fog, Bernd had replied that it was OK, he'd already seen the fellow on the bicycle. Elly couldn't see any fellow, any bicycle, anything. By the time the bicyclist finally appeared out of the gloom where she could begin to make him out, Elly began to guess at Bernd's extra powers. Where Rudi's genius was his uncanny ability to keep a car under control in the rain, to become the "*Regenmeister*," Bernd had become the "*Nebelmeister*," the Master of the Mists.

The next shock to Bernd's family came quickly. Bernd's brother, Job, had been killed in a car accident. Bernd made immediate changes in his life's plans: spend a lot of time with his father, since they were all that was left of the family now, and have an heir.

Hitler was not unaware, we can be sure, of the difficulties of enforcing his draconian decrees on highly self-generated performance-people. He knew that some looseness must be maintained between strictly enforced goals and the self-reliant types that are the only ones he could find to carry out these goals successfully. He was also keenly aware of the limitations of hired bureaucrats when setting out a task that required a lot of risk-taking.

He carefully sought out only people with an added motivational drive to do the really touchy jobs. "There's a limit to what a man will do for money alone," he mentioned in *Mein Kampf*. When dealing with people who did the job for other rewards than money, you needed a different approach, and no one knew this better than the Führer, as one of the master-motivators of our age. To loosen things up and maintain a token individual vestige of freedom, Hitler even had his propaganda staffs bring out "rebel literature" making fun of his own over-seriousness and often simplistic linear-thinking. Cartoons lampooned party bigwigs and less popular policies. This way, he could get the jump on the opposition and give the illusion of freedom at the same time, while making sure that nothing was said that shouldn't be said. It's a time-honored technique of propaganda-mills — to make sure you control both sides of a public dialogue.

Berlin knew that the racing program, with all its drama and colorful characters, had basically done its job. It was time to get them out of the spotlight and safely out of the way for a while. So the order came down for both teams to "make an important effort" at the coming Vanderbilt Cup Race on Long Island, New York. Tazio had stolen the show in his Alfa the previous year (after making a promise to his dying son to win it). Now it was time to show America how far they'd fallen behind Germany in technology.

At Auto Union, both Bernd and Delius were scheduled to drive in America. But instead of sending the "second-unit" team management that had been sent to Africa, the front-line crew was going. Everybody seemed to be going to America suddenly, as a matter of fact, from Bodo Lafferentz, as head of the Strength Through Joy club, down to the Sebastian brothers. Hitler's man at Mercedes, Jakob Werlin was going. Neubauer was going. Baby Caracciola was going, to act as timekeeper for the Mercedes team. (Neubauer had congratulated Rudi on having the foresight to marry Baby so Mercedes could keep her working in that job of confusing, awesome responsibility that no one else wanted to take the blame for.)

Dr. Porsche had arranged passage on the *Queen Mary*, fascinated as he was to see the ship's huge engines (foreigners were not supposed to visit the engine room, but a few phone calls to Europe had cleared that up). It seemed everybody in the German racing world, except Elly, was going. But then she was having a baby, although no public announcement had been made as yet.

When one of the Direktors at Auto Union heard that Elly wasn't on the list, however, he made changes on the spot to include Elly. She was, after all, Bernd's good luck charm.

On the boat, Werlin, as Hitler's representative, went out of his way to make sure the two teams had everything anyone could possibly need on the cruise. Rudi and Baby joined the crew on the *Bremen* at Cherbourg, and the next morning Bernd burst into the couple's stateroom with a beautiful pewter urn. He'd never given them a wedding present, so with typical Rosemeyer timing, he chose that indelicate moment to make amends.

The Mercedes crew took advantage of the fabulous food, and went right through the menu at each meal, before setting off to the gymnasium and the rowing machines. Ping-pong tournaments, and a special kind of billiards that seemed to bring out the worst expletives from Neubauer when he missed a shot, were the pasttimes of choice, along with the swimming pool, the shooting gallery, and the horse-racing games. At night there was a competent dance band and, off in a lounge, a wonderful Gypsy band that accompanied their after-hours talk-fests.

Back in Berlin, Hitler was enforcing rules to wipe the Gypsies off the map, but here on the *Bremen* safely at sea, the Gypsies were holding everyone spellbound with their music. It must have made Seaman smile, this typical Third Reich hypocrisy in the face of the impossible task of enforcing a strict racism in a complex, ever more interdependent modern world.

One of Dick's favorite jazz artists, Django Reinhardt, had just gone through a perfect example of this part-time racism. Reinhardt had been arrested from a Gypsy camp and sent, with the others, to a detention camp. When the general in charge (luckily a jazz fan, himself) heard that the great Django Reinhardt was in the camp, he raised holy hell. Wasn't the staff able to tell the difference between Gypsies and national treasures? Django was released at once and allowed to travel back to his haunts at "The Hot Club of France" in Paris where he continued to make music history, unconcerned about the politics around him. Today we can hear his rendition of "Lily Marlene" done for his German audiences, right next to his "Marseilles," done with equal genius for the French in the crowd. He was a Belgian, after all, and a Gypsy first and foremost. Cops of all regimes looked pretty much the same to Gypsies — trouble.

Werlin was pleased to see the two teams drawing closer together through the friendly rivalry of their American outing. They'd been pulling no punches through three hard years of competition. But now the old scars seemed to be healing over. When the cruise ended in Brooklyn, any remaining rifts were swept away by the appearance of a mob of cabbage-throwing leftists yelling anti-fascist slogans and calling the race teams "Dirty Nazis."

Neubauer was quite prepared to take them all on single-handed and was rolling up his sleeves to do so on the spot as he walked down the gangplank. But Werlin's better sense of diplomacy stepped in before Neubauer had a chance to make a worse impression on the press than the leftists were doing.

Monkhouse was amazed at the antiquated cameras the American crews were using. And Bernd flinched at the first question coming from the American Press, "Say Bernd — how's about a story on your speed record in Frankfurt?" Being addressed by your first name by a complete stranger! Well, this was America, after all. But all the press seemed interested in was Bernd's green Tyrolean hat, which they swiftly made into an icon and had to have included in every shot.

Elly was looking forward to touching base with an old flying friend, Antonia Strassmann, who'd come to New York to escape anti-Jewish pressures in Europe. She knew more about New York than the New Yorkers, Elly had heard, and she was looking forward to a grand tour.

But grand-tours were out. Bernd wanted to look at the course right away. There was a twenty-thousand dollar prize for this race (more like two-hundred thousand in today's dollars) and Bernd had a new household to furnish. Also with a new household to furnish was Caracciola, who had his eye riveted on the prize himself, so it promised to be a hard-fought race. Dick Seaman also had new-household plans for that prize. And who knew what miracle Nuvolari felt like pulling off? He'd been such a popular winner here the year before that he'd found he had to barricade himself in his hotel room to escape his new fans.

When Bernd returned from seeing the course, he was wearing a long face. It was a rough American guess at a road course, with the emphasis on rough. Bernd cautioned Ernst to fill his driving gloves with talcum to delay the blisters that would surely be felt after just a few laps on this brutal course. The only American driver who'd risen to the European challenge the year before had been Californian Rex Mays. This year his

In America at last! Continental Tire's Herr Dietrich (*Der Schnurrbiber*) and Bernd look ready to have a go at that twenty-thousand in hard Yankee dollars.

photo: Auto Union Archive

mechanics had grafted a new centrifugal supercharge onto his Alfa, and this was reportedly putting out more power than Tazio's. Mays seemed to have serious plans for that $20,000 as well.

The newspapers played up the German slant in a big way, and in one article a columnist said: "this Rosemeyer family seems to be monopolizing high speed, with Bernd driving down the roads at over 200 miles an hour (that kind of speed was only seen on the salt flats of Utah) with Mrs. Rosemeyer not far behind in her Messerschmitt. If this couple were to have a son, he'd probably have to travel by rocket ship."

Delius whooped at the article, reading it to Bernd, and making comments about how comical it would be to see Bernd actually holding a baby.

Elly blushed a deep red, while Bernd changed the subject. The official announcement of Elly and Bernd's new addition to the family was to wait until they got back.

Porsche's trip to visit Henry Ford had, not surprisingly, coincided with the Vanderbilt race. After his trip on the *Queen Mary*, where the Professor had met the cream of Hollywood movie stars, he'd gone on to Detroit to meet with Ford (and to steal some German technicians back to Germany for the Volkswagen project).

He and old Henry had hit it off from the start. Both had proved their own designs by racing them themselves. Both had had serious run-ins with Big Money. Both had proved their theories, scoffed at by Big Business, were right. And, as a man with a passion for peoples' cars, Porsche could have only a profound respect for Ford, the man who had proved in no uncertain terms the power of the Auto-Revolution. Aldous Huxley had imagined a world where the calendar years were called "the Year of Our Ford." To Porsche, this was more than just fiction.

When their meetings came to an end and the leave-taking finally was unavoidable, Porsche warmly invited Ford to visit Germany, where Porsche would give Ford a guided tour just as extensive as the one he'd just been shown. Ford's face fell. Didn't Porsche realize that their two countries would soon be at war? This time it was Porsche's face that fell. To him, they were hard at work crafting a new era of peace and achievement. How could war be coming again? Like Rudi, after his visit to Hitler's Brown House, Porsche was sobered by this thunderbolt. Possibly he should pay some more attention to politics in the future.

The drivers were driven grandly out to the course in a huge 16-cylinder Cadillac, where they found the elite of the American racing drivers waiting for them. Since women were banned in the pits in America, and since Baby was an important working member of the Mercedes team, the organizers had to put her in a special little tower away from the pits. Neubauer would have to telephone her to find out how his cars were doing when the lap positions got confusing. Elly and Dr. Porsche (no longer a part of the pits now that the Volkswagen project had been put in his hands) would watch from another viewing vantage.

In practice Rex Mays had done well, and found himself in the front row at the start, flanked by Rudi in pole position and Bernd on the outside. Second row was Seaman, Nuvolari, and Farina, with Delius, Ted Horn, and Billy Winn in the third row. Neubauer had discovered to his horror, doing his prerace calculations, that Seaman's car somehow was able only to carry enough fuel to get him to within one-half lap of the finish, even after one refuelling stop. He consulted with the crew, but no one could think up a way to squeeze in a few more gallons. Since the cars got around two miles to the gallon, you could run out in a hurry, even with their huge racing tanks. Somehow they would have to get Seaman to go extra easy, then he might just make it without that extra pit stop that would surely lose him the race.

When the starting flag dropped, Bernd shot out of the gate like a cannonball, then cut right across in front of Rudi heading into the first turn. Americans weren't to see acceleration like the Auto Union was capable of again until 1958, and then only with a specialized dragster. On the second lap Rudi was hot on the tail of Bernd with Rex Mays hanging on to third ahead of Seaman and Nuvolari. On the third lap Rudi pulled past Bernd and started to build a useful lead. By the eleventh lap, however, Bernd had fought his way back level with Rudi. Together they shot toward the turn, then Rudi eased off, letting Bernd take the honor. It could be fatal to try to out-brake Bernd in a corner. He seemed to delight in these situations where sheer nerve told who would come out ahead. And Neubauer knew the day was past when Rudi would hold firm to his position, risking both cars sliding off the track, just to stay with Bernd.

Nuvolari had been making a heroic effort to work his way past Seaman, but it was too much for his Alfa, which blew its engine on the seventeenth lap. A huge plume of smoke followed the Alfa around the track, then there was a scream from the crowd as they spotted flames shooting out from Tazio's cockpit.

The heat from the engine was enough to light Tazio's coveralls on fire. He'd brought the car down to about seventy, taking the opportunity to clamber back on the tail, getting ready to jump for it, when the car suddenly veered toward the stands. The spectators scattered. Steering with his feet, Tazio regained control, then sent the car into a harmless spin.

He'd always told Compagnoni that it was better "To smash into a wall rather than be fried like a chicken." Now he had a chance to prove his point. There was a scream of tires and the little man flew through the air. The car crashed into a barrier and burned itself out, while an ambulance raced for Tazio. By this time he was back on his feet, like a boxer, waving to a crowd that went wild with applause.

Then Rudi came in to the pits. The crew worked feverishly on his engine, but it was no good; a sheared supercharger-drive. Rudi threw his gloves against the pit wall in disgust, as his twenty-thousand dollars went flying out the window with the failure of one small part.

Bernd and Mays came in for tires and fuel, Bernd's stop taking 35 seconds, and Mays', a pathetic 78 seconds. This let Seaman into the lead — Seaman with the tank that was too small.

Nuvolari, meanwhile, had taken over Farina's car and was having the time of his life passing Delius, and then mixing it up with Mays, dirt-track style. Seaman was due for his refueling stop, which, if all went well might be his only stop. Rosemeyer was back in the lead once more. But after his stop Seaman was ignoring the fuel cautions and driving with abandon.

Lap by lap he whittled down Bernd's lead, while Sebastian nearly went mad wringing his hands and watching helplessly as Bernd's lead evaporated. Nuvolari, having sucked the juice out of another Alfa, limped into the pits and gave the car back to Farina, who grumbled something like, "I could have wrecked the engine without being the legendary Tazio!"

With reduced fuel in his tanks and better handling, Bernd began to increase his lead again. Then Neubauer let out a howl of rage that could be heard on the radio coverage. Seaman's car was spluttering as the last few drops of fuel were sucked into the carburetors. He pulled in for a quick slosh of fuel, but was 51 seconds behind Bernd at the finish — Bernd's most publicized win of his career. Mays finished a well-earned third with Ernstschen coming in fourth.

Over the seasons Hitler had gotten his money's worth from racing. With his customary tightness, the government subsidy he'd originally

Taking the show on the road, the German teams come to a real Grand Prix on British soil at Donington. The huge crowds were awestruck by the grand scale of the Continental teams, compared with their own amateur-sportsman-based efforts. Bernd (shown cornering here) took the cup, with von Brauchitsch and Caracciola second and third place in the German parade.

photo: Mercedes Benz

offered Mercedes and Auto Union was just enough to get them hooked into a committed racing program.

As racing costs escalated, the subsidy stayed the same, until Hitler's pump-priming money amounted to only about one tenth of what the two companies were spending on their racing programs. They did regain other benefits, of course: increased passenger car sales, and in the case of Mercedes especially, lucrative defense contracts. But once they had committed their energies to this racing program, how could they back down, with Berlin watching?

German victories, even with two teams running, had ceased to be big news. In fact, the cars had reached the point of superiority where they only made the front page now when they were beaten — and this wasn't very often.

The old German drive and energy to struggle seemed to wane when there was little to struggle against. Then there was that race at Pau, in Belgium. Rudi had showed up to drive the race, not in his usual helmet and spotless coveralls, but in something a lot more casual, wearing a regular English-style visored cap as if he were only going for a pleasant spin in the country. Rene Dreyfus was there with his stubby Delahaye, which looked more like a loaf of French bread with wheels than a mount worthy of the Champion de France.

Rene was happy to see the old gang again, and his wife Chouchou sat with Baby to watch the race at a slow corner where they could wave their husbands on. In practice, Rene had noticed something interesting. Rudi's Merc had so much power that he was spinning the tires a lot, seeming to have a hard time getting the car's power to connect with the pavement on that short twisting track. And there was another thing: the supercharged Mercs were using up over twice as much fuel as the stubby Delahaye with its big, but low-tech truck-like engine.

The Delahaye was a truly laughable looking car under any conditions — round like a drain-pipe with bulbous ends, ugly scoops grafted in place, and a grill that looked like it had been taken from a screen door. Next to the Mercs, which were looking more like hungry sharks every year, the French team looked like comedy relief. But then, they *were* there, while Auto Union had opted just to sit this one out and not even show up.

In the first laps, it was just as Rene had thought. The big thumping Delahaye was grabbing the pavement with each piston — while the high-revving Mercs seemed to do nothing but raise clouds of tire smoke, as their wheels spun trying to grab the road. Rene stayed close

The very successful British driver Kay Petre whose good lap times made other drivers grind their teeth, but whose good looks usually convinced them to forgive and forget.

photo: Auto Union Archive

to Rudi to see what tricks Neubauer might have up the Mercedes, sleeve. To the crowd's delight, Dreyfus pulled past Rudi. He had no intention of trying to hold the lead. He just wanted to see the look on Neubauer's face when he passed Rudi in his clumsy-looking bucket. Neubauer was waving his black and red "get a move on!" flags that Rene knew well from his racing days in Germany, and this made Rene laugh, which only made Neubauer all the more furious. At the slow turn, Rene could see Chouchou getting more excited with every lap, and Baby looking glummer and glummer.

Rudi shot in for fuel, but then a roar went up from the crowd as he got out of the car. His leg hurt, he said. Let Lang have a try. Lang vaulted in the Merc and tore off after Rene. Lang broke the lap record, hunting down Rene, lap after lap. But the dumpy Delahaye was perfectly powered for Pau, and there was nothing Lang could do to make up the time before the finish. The plodding Delahaye had beaten the Germans at the peak of their power, and there was an unforgettable party in store for Rene and Lucy O'Reilly Schell's little "*Ecurie Bleue*" racing team that had been struggling along through the seasons, mostly just for the fun of it.

Chapter 20

Swords Are Drawn

Huhnlein had made a mistake. He realized that the minute he got out of the staff car that had brought visitors from Berlin out for a visit to the racing pits during practice. The mistake had happened gradually over the years that the two teams settled in to do the job of beating the world; gradually and imperceptibly.

Huhnlein had always known that when people had a job to do that had anything to do with machinery and luck, that all the carefully manicured ideas of the staffroom often went out the window. He'd seen the trenches in the Great War, where the protocols of military base life slowly sank into the mud of the trenches and disappeared, leaving men and goals to deal with each other.

But on that warm summer morning of practice, he could see that, understandable or not, the mistake would be his to own up to. And as he swept his squint around the panorama of the pit lane, he was surprised to find that even he felt a little shock at the sight that met his eyes.

Schnurrbiber from Continental Tires was taking the temperature of tires on one of the Mercedes, wearing his hillbilly bib-overalls and nothing else, it seemed, but his clodhopper boots. Rosemeyer, standing nearby, was little better as a fashion standard, in his lederhosen and sandals. He looked twelve, maybe thirteen years old, as he joked with the Sebastians at the fact that someone had fixed a learner's-permit "L " sign to his Auto Union.

Nuvolari, stretched out on the Alfa counter, was fast asleep despite the roars and din around him, like a tired farm-hand — his brandy flask hanging around his neck like a talisman. Brauchitsch was better dressed, but hovering over a covey of young girls he'd met at the film studio and paying scant attention to the racing business of the day.

Pit conditions were a trifle laxer than in the Land of the Free, as the camera catches Bernd restoring the tissues with a relaxed snort, while Der Schnurrbiber, sans shirt, in the background oversees the tire-fitting for the next run. A young German's dream of paradise.

photo: Auto Union Archive

Brauchitsch's starlets shrieked like school girls when a smoke-bomb went off nearby, upsetting the gourmet breakfast Neubauer was snacking on off the pit counter. Stuck, tall and respectably German-looking, was behind the counter smiling at the smoke cloud and mixing himself a scotch and soda. Seaman had his phonograph going, playing those incessant Benny Goodman jazz music records again.

The visitors from Berlin were silent, faces set like granite. Through their eyes Huhnlein suddenly saw only disarray and laxity, like a back street in Berlin's nightclub district in the twenties. The visitors turned and went back to their car. This would get back to Berlin. Huhnlein knew by the silence with which the car was started and slipped it into gear. The engine revved high, but Huhnlein felt no movement of the car, only a vibrating that increased when the engine was revved. The visitors looked at Huhnlein with poorly contained exasperation. He looked out and saw that they weren't moving.

The transmission? A broken axle? What a time for car trouble! They jumped out of the car, its engine still running. The rear wheels were spinning some inches above the ground. Someone had used a racing jack to lift the rear wheels up so the car would be stranded. Huhnlein knew, without a word being spoken, that a new era would be coming to the racing scene.

In the days that followed Huhnlein scared the wits out of the regulars around the pits with a whole new approach: he was being fatherly. It created a new eeriness about the man that was far more frightening than his shouting rages and barked orders whenever things went wrong.

He was seen taking various figures aside for lengthy chats, maintaining all the while (with an obvious effort) a kind of chilling smile. When the victims gathered later to compare notes, they found that Huhnlein's little man-to-man chats had been much the same for all of them.

He had talked somewhat wistfully of his days in the War: of the trenchline informalities that would never be tolerated up at staff headquarters, of the changing roles good soldiers had to play at different times, of Hitler's conviction that the individual was nothing compared to the needs of the state and his homeland in times of threat, of the conviction that the world was being duped by Organized Big Money and that their generation would have to be prepared to do some ugly things, and even be reviled by later generations, if they were to reverse the enslaving trends of this new Babylon. When he saw their eyes begin to wander, Huhnlein would make it personal: a word to the wise should be sufficient.

"A lad as bright as you should have no problem figuring out what he should do next."

Huhnlein wasn't worried if half what he said wasn't understood — if the lads went away with a perplexed look on their face. It would all be crystal clear to them very soon.

It wasn't as though the drivers despised Huhnlein. Almost the opposite was the case, in fact. Over the years each driver had taken his own gauge of the man, seeing him through losses, victories, crashes, deaths, at rest, and on parade. He'd become a fixture, and an almost-wanted figure of authority to rail about, something solid to push against. And slowly there had surfaced a general consensus about Huhnlein: here was one Nazi who wasn't feathering his own nest with Reichmarks from his position of authority. He was a modest man. Hitler set himself to be a modest man, sleeping in a cell-like room on little more than a cot under a photo of his mother, eating only vegetables and never drinking nor smoking. But behind the curtain we see Hitler's weakness for the perks of office — his lengthy cars, his cafe-society daily routine. His private Berghof was hardly the simple mountain cabin it started out as (what with the world's largest picture window and sumptuous furnishings). Goebbels had his rafts of girlfriends, and Goering had simply let himself go at taxpayer's expense the way few in history have. But Huhnlein was still a simple major with a very middle-class lifestyle. His work was interesting for one of his background, and he let it become his whole life. And now, to carry out his work, the time had come to do some of the nasty business that goes with most jobs: discipline.

Huhnlein's notice on the bulletin board at the pits had drawn at first just the usual smattering of passersby, then a snowballing effect set in as the readers of the notice stayed on to argue over what it meant. There on the board usually dedicated to practice schedules and personal notes, was an order from the N.S.K.K., complete with letterhead, eagles, swastikas, and all: "Effective immediately, there will be observed a strict dress code in the pit area. No alcohol is to be consumed in the stalls. No music is to be played other than the marching bands scheduled for each race. The pits are not to be used for sleeping purposes. And at no time are women to be allowed in the stalls or pit lane, nor will any displays of affection between drivers and their women be tolerated. — ObersportskorpsFührer Adolf Huhnlein, N.S.K.K."

What! Is this America, where they think they can outlaw even alcohol?! Where women are banned from race tracks!? Words to that effect came from nearly every corner of the pits.

The furor was a grand one, as each individual realized which little pre-race jitters-blockers of his own were now illegal. Only Christian Kautz, the new driver from Switzerland, took it quietly. As a squeaky-clean youth of the Reich, he needed none of those props the others had grown used to. And as a loyal Storm Trooper, he would be able to report back to Berlin the exact details of the drivers' reactions to this brave new order around the pits. But then just as suddenly, as Huhnlein hoped it would, the tempest blew over, and the pits settled back down to business as usual, but quietly.

Too quietly, Neubauer realized uneasily. How could the drivers accept this new role as puppet-figures for Berlin after the gantlet that Balbo had thrown at Tripoli? After Tripoli no driver could rationalize away any other description of this new role Berlin was creating for them but "puppet of the state." Neubauer had joined in the outrage with the rest of the crowd, but gradually he was beginning to feel kept out of something. The international gestures of disgust had disappeared, and a quiet reigned over the pits — but not the sullen quiet Huhnlein had expected. This was a very self-contained quiet, as mechanics winked at each other silently, drivers nudged each other, and supressed giggles could be heard, always off-stage.

Neubauer didn't like it. He didn't like being left out, but then he realized he was in no position to be trusted by the men. They knew he wasn't the enemy, but they also knew he could be put in a very dangerous position if he did know what was brewing. Something was up, and he kept his eyes peeled for trouble.

Huhnlein, now more absent from the pits these days tending to the Volkswagen project, had missed all the signs of mutiny. And the young N.S.K.K. men he'd sent in to the pits to outnumber the drivers and set a good, German marshal tone were, half the time, trying to get autographs — too starstruck to notice anything not quite right about the pits. But to Neubauer it was clear as day: the drivers had given in too easily. It just wasn't like them. He mopped his brow like he did when a car was overdue at the pits.

The races in Germany were becoming more like folk-festivals — more of a regular celebration of a successful social movement than a hotly-contested battle for dominance between national cultures. The jolly marching oompah bands with their colorful uniforms, the aerial displays, the *Dirndl*-dressed maidens bearing bouquets of mountain flowers, the ponderous barrels of beer, the smoking cook-outs, the Hitler-Youth camps — racing was becoming just another component of the yearly schedule of folkish festival-outings for everyone, race-fan or not.

The media coverage had multiplied over the years with Huhnlein facing a battery of a dozen microphones to give the congratulatory speech and present the huge wreath of laurel branches, and to give the final Nazi salute, of course. It all cost the taxpayer a pretty penny, but it hadn't been long since the taxpayer was facing the distinct possibility of a complete Communist take-over. In which case the taxpayer wouldn't have any pretty pennies to begin with, judging by what was going on in Russia where the government was busily starving whole villages out of existence if they didn't toe the line of new programs that happened to be the pet experimental plan of Moscow that month.

We need to realize, from our vantage point in history, that it hadn't been a question of choosing between a Fascist state and American-style democracy; to the view of the time (after much Communist upheaval and some actual revolution), it was one of choosing between Hitler and a Bolshevik state led by someone like Stalin. And at this point everyone, even the liberals, admitted that had Hitler dropped dead at that moment, he would have gone down as the twentieth-century's most popular German leader. Even the English ministers were saying nice things about Hitler at this point.

So it was a content crowd that saluted Huhnlein as he took his lap of honor with the usual visiting bigwigs from Berlin in the *grossen* Mercedes. Since this whole pageant in front of three hundred thousand people with every radio station tuned in, every newspaper there with its cameras, was Huhnlein's show, his chest could be seen pressing against his Sam-Brown belt in pride. Especially now that the pits looked decidedly more squared-away. No sleeping Italians. No booze. And none of Brauchitsch's assorted women.

The drivers looked amazingly smart as they marched out each beside his car. Flagbearers marched in between the ranks of cars pushed by the mechanics in precise parade-ground order.

Huhnlein smiled to Kurtz, his aide, in approval. The Nazi nabobs in the VIP tribunal seemed to approve as well, he could see by their enthused nods. It was hard, no matter how high you were in the party, not to respond to the excitement of this spectacle in front of them.

He should have made his little talks to the drivers before this, Huhnlein decided. On this morning all was very smart-looking he thought. But in the Mercedes pit Neubauer mopped his brow. He could hear a time-bomb ticking somewhere.

The drivers got in their cars and the engines roared to life in a frenzy of echoes. The starting cannon was prepared to fire the starting shot. Then suddenly it was all stopping: the revving engines, everything. The crowd stared hypnotized as the last engine echoed to a stop and silence fell over the whole scene with a startling completeness. The officials looked at each other in confusion. Next, the crowd saw a sudden busy movement down at the cars. Every driver was jumping out of his car as if it had been a hot-seat. The crowd strained to see what was going on. The drivers were all running. They all seemed to be running toward the stands, to where their wives and girlfriends were sitting, now that they'd been exiled from the pits.

Then a roar of approval went up from the crowd, and Huhnlein stood transfixed to see what was going on. Each driver was giving his woman a huge, protracted, Hollywood final-scene climax, Clark Gable, bend-over-backwards kiss.

The applause grew to a roar, as the drivers waved back at the crowd, which had somehow understood the meaning of it all. The drivers, taking stagey bows and laughing to each other, put their goggles back on as the crews restarted the engines, and the starting countdown recommenced. It had been just a prank, a poke in the ribs of the powers that be. Teasing only meant sort of a form of approval, Neubauer was thinking, trying to turn the drivers' action into a less serious matter that it might be taken for.

In a few seconds the cars were gone in their usual thunder, and Neubauer strode uncertainly out into the pit lane to sneak a look up into the Nazi tribune to see what the effect of this demonstration by the drivers had been. Had the Nazis enough savvy to laugh at the gesture? It was worse than he feared. Huhnlein and all his officials and aides had disappeared from sight. This was more than Berlin could ignore. Swords had been drawn.

Neubauer was realizing just what the Big Kiss Rebellion had meant, just as Huhnlein undoubtedly was. The Boston Tea Party had been just a prank, possibly, at the time. Now we see it as the tip of the iceberg, the fuse that lit the bomb that helped to change the world.

Huhnlein knew his military history. A bloody nationwide mutiny had started in India over how bullet cartridges were wrapped. Tiny

Neither rain nor Auto Unions keeps Caracciola from enjoying the winner's last laugh after beating the competition.
photo: Mercedes Benz

sparks started big fires, if the fuel is already in place. And growing realization of the sort of police state Hitler would need if he wanted to carry out his plans was stacking more fuel on the pyre everyday. Any ruling regime can't get through a single working day without making enemies on one side or other. And enemies, like Count von Schulenberg, were growing in numbers as adventurous programs bruised a lot of people who rubbed up against them.

The Communist Threat was slowly fading from view as the Berlin Threat of centralized rule-by-edict touched more and more lives. There would come a time when the barricades would be thrown up and the nation would be forced into polarization: You're fer us, or agin us, with no space for anything in between.

Whether they realized the consequences or not, these drivers were playing a dangerous game taunting Berlin in front of the whole world.

But what worried Neubauer was the realization that some of these drivers seemed to be always on the look out for new dangers — new ways to tests themselves and compare each other's skill and daring. At one time Rosemeyer had gone so far as to qualify for the Olympics in his off-hours on the German bobsled team before the Direktors at Auto Union roped him back from taking extra-curricular risks. If the taunting of Hitler's life-and-death wrath became a popular sport, as it very easily could among a bunch like this, all hell could come down around their necks.

Neubauer had seen men like Rosemeyer go too far into a corner to chicken-out another driver too often. He knew that to some of these drivers, life itself was a chip you played to win a certain kind of persona. To seek to boss them around like children was asking for trouble.

But he'd seen the effects of Hitler's temper, too. The "Night of the Long Knives" when Hitler, outraged that some of the leaders of his own private army were exploring homosexual practices at their retreats, had acted with an unpremeditated ferocity that took the nation's breath away.

When word of this reached Hitler, there might well be some decisive retaliation. Just because many of the drivers like Stuck and Rudi had been heroes to Hitler since his early days, you couldn't count on him to look the other way. Would he crack down on his own personal heroes? He'd been just as infatuated with his niece and had let her get away with the most obvious peccadillos and foolishness that directly threatened Hitler's credibility. Perhaps the racing community would fall into that gilded class of Hitler associates who could do no wrong.

On the other hand, the S.A. leaders that Hitler had disposed of so completely had been old Communist-fighters, street-fighting buddies from the old days of the Beer-Hall Putsch. And he hadn't hesitated a second in pulling the trigger on them. Neubauer mopped his brow. It was anybody's guess what the reaction from Berlin might be. The season was drawing to a close. Perhaps this would give some drivers a chance to cool down before next year. Maybe some would take the hint and quit while they were ahead in the game.

Hitler had set an example with his Night of the Long Knives. The worst offenders had been sliced out as a message to everyone else in the organization. A scapegoat might be chosen from the drivers to send an unmistakable message the same way. Neubauer could see who that scapegoat would be, the lad who'd vexed Neubauer himself so many times, but whom he come to regard as his prodigal son: Rosemeyer.

Rosemeyer had always been the sparkplug of absurdity around the racing community, defusing the hypnotic spell of fear with his corny jokes that everyone had come to depend on. Without the constant push of Rosemeyer's mirth, the others would easily slip into a more serious tone. But with his impish humor around, they would join in, some even trying to out-Rosemeyer Rosemeyer. If a disciplinary example were to be picked, Rosemeyer would be the one. The others would then be an easy task for Berlin. With him, they faced the unknown of the man's wild imagination, and worse yet, possible public embarrassment for the Reich.

It wasn't a simple issue, even for Berlin. Rosemeyer had become wildly popular in Germany, especially with the youth. There was hardly a boy in the Reich who hadn't memorized every detail about Bernd, down to the license plate number on Manuela that made her recognized wherever she went. He'd become a household name, his picture put up by mothers to encourage their boys to try harder and put up by boys to encourage their mothers to give them a little more breathing space.

There was another complication, one deeply seated in Nordic cultural memory (so dear to the heart of the Führer): that of the much-worshipped Huck Finn rebel-boy icon. In Scandinavia he was Peer Gynt, the taunter of authority, the popper of pompous balloons who always just skittered out of the way of official discipline. In Germany the boy-rogue figure was *Struwwelpeter*, the one with the unruly hair who refused to hear, much less obey, commands of father-figures. In England, Peter Pan reached back to that old northern memory in Victorian days.

Bernd, whether it was realized or not, was the embodiment of a large portion of the collective memory of Middle Europe, dating back to the early Fasching Festivals where all authority was openly taunted on special days. Bernd, as a rebel in nature was just as firmly rooted in the culture of the Reich as Hitler was as the tribal king/father-figure. Perhaps it would all sort itself out in the long run. And the winter holiday was coming. Something would release the building pressure, Neubauer could only hope.

Meanwhile, with the season safely over, Bernd and Elly went home to plan their new family. Bernd had started talking once in a while about what he would do "after his racing career," much to Elly's delight. He was beginning to see there were many interesting avenues open to him, besides racing, to keep him full of life.

Rudi and Baby were absorbed in their new villa on Lake Lugano in Switzerland, set in just the sort of mountain grandeur that he said he never got tired of gazing at. They'd settled in to the kind of calm life Rudi always said was essential as a stable background to anyone really interested in making a mark on the world.

At the villa Rudi could plan his days at just the right pace. He was a full ten years older than Bernd, and the hard-fought battles of the last year had taken their toll. But now, a long stretch in the mountain sun seemed almost too good to be true. It was.

33
33

Chapter 21

Totentanz

Berlin had come up with a new brainstorm, a whole new kind of motorsport to be seen for the first time on German soil. It was to be called *Rekordwoche*, "Record Week." It wasn't a natural outgrowth of the events that private motorsportsmen had made popular, like the hill climbs. It wasn't the creation of the drivers, like the ice-racing. The manufacturers hadn't dreamed it up as a publicity stunt. It was the direct inspiration of Berlin, authorized by official order from Huhnlein.

Once a year in October, portions of the Frankfurt to Darmstadt Autobahn would be closed so that teams could run world speed record attempts, not on the salt flats of Utah (used by teams from all of the rest of the world) but on a *Reichsautobahn*. These events, to be staged like tournaments, would pit the team's best drivers against one another in a one-on-one joust right out of the Middle Ages. (We have to remember that jousting was still going on by reenactors in Germany up to just before the U.S. Civil War.) This, everybody saw at once, meant a battle of Mercedes' champion, Rudi, against Auto Union's champion, Bernd.

"Whoever heard of records being run like races? It's murder," Caracciola was quoted as saying.

Dr. Porsche used the same term to describe such madness, and some wondered if this weren't a suicide mission that could put a conveniently heroic end to Rosemeyer's pesky gadfly humor that was becoming a state embarrassment. Running record runs like two gladiators seeing how far they could test the fates seemed to spell the distinct possibility of the end of the career for the driver who was forced to go too far. And everyone knew just which driver it was who never let up in a turn when someone else was trying to go deeper without braking — Bernd.

"Metropolis" at play. Even today, well over a half century later, this scene of Avus still looks like something out of the future.

photo: Auto Union Archive

The Big Time: on the 1-in-1 banking of the futuristic track at Avus, Rudi overhauls Bernd on the North Curve. Average speeds rose over 160 mph, creating a whole new kind of auto racing that was to lead to Rekordwoche.

photo: Mercedes Benz

Record-setting was limitation-finding — a little like two people playing Russian roulette. One would try once too many times to test his luck. It was racing with an added degree of danger, and little of the sporting give and take. And the only time it could come to an end would be when one of the champions fell.

Rudi was none too enthusiastic at this new racing form. "For a second I could see it like a vivid picture: two armored monsters racing against each other until one of them was vanquished."

If the mano-a-mano format weren't lunatic enough, making record runs on the Autobahn was pure folly. For one thing, there were the overpasses. These were not extra-wide in those first Autobahns, with only a few yards leeway on either side of the roadstead. At speeds above 250 mph (not kph) these overpasses would shrink to the drivers' eye to the size of needle-holes. It's one thing to drive on a salt flat and try to follow the black line put down to keep you straight. If you wander a little, no harm is done. And since the wheels grab the earth only about as much as a normal car at normal speeds can grab black ice, the slightest side breeze will blow you off course a little. A little off course going under one of those Autobahn concrete overpasses meant a big splatter mark on the cement buttress and no more runs for the day.

Then there's the aerodynamics. When a car starts pushing 300 mph it's doing a respectable fraction of the speed of sound, say around Mach .4. Shockwaves build up. When a car goes by at fifty or a hundred, we see it go by, hear the noise, and then feel the breeze as the wind-wake hits us. Watching a car go past at 250 you'll notice the breeze of the passing car differently than you're used to.

If we watch the films of the record attempts on the Frankfurt-Darmstadt Autobahn we see the little marker flags by the side of the road give a sudden jump, before the car has even arrived. This is the shockwave beginning to build. From the driver's point of view, you're forcing that shockwave through those tiny holes at the overpasses. The result is a quick silence, followed by a thunderclap that hits you in the stomach, as the shock wave cannons you out the other side of the bridge.

Lining up for those overpasses was a nightmare task. "I couldn't understand that my brain should be slower than the speed of the car," Rudi said after the runs. "Again and again I had the strange impression that I had to aim my car in order to get through."

The cars used for the Rekordwoche runs came directly from the high-speed track at Avus. This is the '36, Type-C Auto Union. Note the increase of uniformed, happy helpers from the N.S.K.K. The sound of jackboots was getting ever louder around the racing pits.

photo: Auto Union Archive

Perhaps the most unnerving feature, from a spectator's point of view, is that if you stood on the overpass to watch the car run underneath, the car is on you before you're ready to absorb it. And then when you spin around to watch it continue down the road, it's already a small shape in the distance.

Another problem with running the cars on autobahns was purely Berlin's fault. October was too late in the season for this sort of thing. Each morning the road surface was covered with either slippery dew or more often, hoar-frost. If you went too early, the roads were slippery. If you went too late, the morning breezes will have sprung up, making the runs decidedly dicey. There was only a short interval when it was "safe" and if you have two teams making runs in only one week, somebody's going to get the short end of the scheduling stick.

Berlin had decided to make the most of Rekordwoche. The military was everywhere, for some reason. Some were helping out blocking off the Autobahn, others setting up the timing stations and laying phone lines between observation huts. But there always seemed to be twice as many soldiers and N.S.K.K. personnel as needed. Tent-like pit pavilions were set up for the teams and large press facilities were erected.

The cars that were being prepared for Rekordwoche were quite different looking than the kind of Grand Prix cars used for the tight corners of road courses like the Nürburgring or the streets of Monte Carlo. The new cars were to be based on the envelope-bodied speedsters created to take advantage of the long straights at Berlin's futuristic Avus track. The high-speed cars were built to go in one direction, with long fish-like bodies that swept over the wheels hiding them and restricting the turning radius radically. Driving the cars took the utmost of precision. At the speeds they planned to reach, the steering wheel could only be turned less than half-inch either way, or disaster would follow.

The wheel had to be held lightly, like a fencing foil, to keep body sway from sending the car off its narrow path. The usual ka-bump ka-bump rhythm of the highway concrete joints at that sort of speed melded into a resonant vibration, blurring vision. The brakes could not be used at speed under penalty of complete loss of control, and a driver had his hands full just to prolong his survival long enough for the car to slow down on its own to normal braking speeds at around 160. For standing-start records, gear-changes had to be made instantly and faultlessly. These were not machines for the weekend racer. A driver had to be in what he hoped was "mid-season form" with his reaction-times honed to a fine edge, his instinctive, unpremeditated moves accurate, his nerves as solid and dependable as he can make them.

The record cars had another difference to them: a large swastika plastered on the headrests right behind the driver's face, so that any press coverage would leave little doubt who was behind this technological trump that Bernd and Rudi were to jockey into the world's papers and history books.

When Rudi and Bernd realized the rules of the gladiatorial match they'd been entered in, willy-nilly, there was little to do but show the kind of willing that helps you survive, and get it over with. If t'were done, t'were well t'were done quickly, so they could get back to the winter holidays they'd been looking forward to, a rest that they'd been fighting to survive long enough to enjoy.

As Rudi put it, "In that hellish tempo we imposed on each other everything was mercilessly hard. We did not give a second to each other. It was his wild stormy, youth against the experience of an opponent ten years older."

Rudi appeared at the runs in October, all professionalism. With an almost sleepy calm he and Baby drove past the barriers on the autobahn and went directly to where they could see lights had been set up so the crews could work through the night prepping the car for its early morning run. It was bitterly cold as they stepped out of the cozy warmth of their Merc cabriolet and Baby put on her warmest fur. Rudi could hear Neubauer's battle-command voice seeing to every detail himself, as usual.

The cars, reflecting the early grey of morning on their polished aluminum, looked like huge sleeping dragons, and the fringes of the pittents hung limply in the cold predawn stillness.

Bernd had shown up full of bubbling fun, Feuereissen was relieved to see. He was going to make a game of this Rekordwoche nonsense, instead of moping through it because his holidays had been postponed. Auto Union had a surprise waiting on the pavement for Bernd. Instead of one car, they'd brought two: a second, identical car with one of the old V-16's. Now he'd be able to go for records in twice as many classes. And twice as many chances to flatten himself against one of the overpasses, Elly couldn't help but think.

When attending Bernd's record runs as his good luck talisman, Elly would have her hair done up in the bandana she often wore in the pits with the little thirteens embroidered all over it for good luck, her outfit looking minimalist and futurist next to Baby's furs.

Rudi's 3-litre, 12-cylinder rekord-rocket, that took him to 247 mph on the Dessau Autobahn.

photo: Mercedes Benz

Neubauer couldn't help noticing Sebastian eyeing the Mercedes pit tent curiously as he walked past.

"Bet you'd give a pretty penny to see what's going on inside, eh?" Neubauer chortled.

Sebastian put a finger to his chin thoughtfully and said, "Why don't I take a guess? I'd say your mechanics are having a hell of a time figuring out how much ice to put in your new heat-exchanger cooling system. Am I right?"

Neubauer's face fell. He'd thought Mercedes were the only ones on earth using ice as a coolant. And now he finds Auto Union's people had hit on the same new wrinkle.

Dr. Porsche had showed up, of course. No activity of this magnitude could go on without the Professor in the middle of the action, watching over every detail.

The cars would take a couple of trial runs before their engines could reach working temperatures and then the tournament could begin in earnest.

On his first runs, Rudi was looking none too happy. And when the engine had warmed and he could try raising the speeds, he found an unsettling characteristic of his car was showing up above 200 mph: the nose was beginning to lift, reducing steering effect of the front wheels to zero. At 230 Rudi found that the front was lifting so much that he could hardly see where he was going! He didn't want to think about what would happen if the wind got well and truly under the body. It wasn't a pretty image.

Neubauer stopped their runs at once. They'd have to transport the car back to Stuttgart and revise the aerodynamics, hopefully in time to return by Wednesday, in time to wipe out any records Bernd had managed to set in the meantime.

A narrow double-lane roadway that would scarcely pass for an on-ramp today, with concrete bridge supports only a few feet from the pavement. Fine for driving your Volkswagen at its 100 kph cruise limit. But not so fine for aiming your racer through the gap at four times that speed, when the shock-wave smashing against each overpass creates a deafening clap of thunder for the driver.
photo: Auto Union Archive

With Mercedes making such an ignominious start, Bernd decided to have some fun with the Autobahn all to himself. As a little boy he'd dreamed about being given the chance to drive the world's fastest car. Now he had all the chance in the world to push records out of reach of Mercedes for many years to come.

On his first test drives in the original record setter, he had put the entire crew on edge on his return run to the pit tent. All at once his hurtling car swung widely off to one side. Then it veered wildly off to the other edge of the pavement. Then back again, and again: ten times before the careening car finally rolled to a stop. The crew ran to rescue Bernd from the cockpit. But he was chuckling to himself when they arrived. Just a little demonstration of Bernd's driving mastery to liven up the day.

The crew looked at each other with a mix of disgust and relief. On another early run he drove right on past the barriers and out onto the

open Autobahn, knowing he'd have to drive to the roundabout at the next village before he could turn his monster around without help. Bernd enjoyed bringing his drives close to his public.

Now he attacked the official runs with the same sort of aggression, seeing how far he could go before disaster struck, not just "trying to hold on" like some brooding record-drivers he'd seen. Bernd found the top speeds of the two cars very similar, despite the different engine sizes, and both were fast enough to set new records for their classes. On the first day, Bernd became the first man to drive over 250 mph on a regular paved road.

The next day he set out with the lighter, open-wheeled racers to set acceleration records that would last for decades. Bernd was eating up the Autobahn and having himself a ball. First, becoming Champion of Europe only two years after entering the Grand Prix world, and now these new records, seven in the first day of driving.

On Wednesday Mercedes Benz showed up again with altered bodywork to keep the nose on the ground. Rudi set out, the complete professional as usual, and this time there was no feeling of lightening in the nose as before. But the power just wasn't there. Neubauer was throwing his hat, stomping around, anything to help. But the big dragon-like Merc just couldn't push its way to the top speeds needed. This, of course, made Bernd even harder to live with, as he went on to try every possible record the team could shoot for. Although he'd a certain number of broken records already that week, he'd decided to make another try to raise his new marks even higher.

It was like having a whole race course to yourself, but with all the pit crews and officials in place. He'd seldom had such a good time, Huhnlein saw, as Bernd chatted happily with the uniformed guards. If the world was calling these record runs on regular roads "calculated murder," Bernd seemed to be the only one who didn't think they were. He was surviving every test as if they were new carnival rides to try. Or was he?

Toward the end of the runs his car was coming back to the pit area none too steadily. When the cockpit was popped open Bernd's giggle could be heard, but it was strangely high and strained, as if he'd just had a damned good scare and was trying to laugh it off. He sat in the car awhile instead of hopping right out triumphantly. He'd set a new record, but complained that he'd smelled oil, the same smell that had almost gassed him at Avus earlier in the year. His voice sounded squeaky, boy-like. Once outside in the fresh air, he'd recovered his old

By the time of the Rekordwoche runs, Bernd was maturing from his little-boy gadfly role. He was becoming a father himself of another little-boy Bernd.

photo: Auto Union Archive

composure, but everyone was realizing that even Bernd was reaching his limit.

Talking about that run, Bernd said he couldn't quite explain exactly why he'd acted that way. Possibly simple "Speed-Effect" as he put it — an overdose of that excitement we all feel at speed, taken to the limit and overwhelming the mind with a sequence of events too rapid to process.

One run of two or three minute's driving at those limits, and you're more worn out than after a 300-mile race, according to many drivers. And Bernd, with his teeth in the bit, was going wholesale for every record the cars were capable of, Huhnlein was gratified to see. Bernd seemed intent on spending every minute that he could on the same road that Rudi was beginning to dread. "Those tiny holes at the overpasses. Before you have a chance to tell what has to be done, you're through and out the other side," Rudi had described them. Now a punchiness was setting in with Bernd, a little like the rapture of the deep — a rapture of speed.

Then another sloppy finish, Huhnlein noticed, and Bernd had to be lifted from the car bodily. Dr Glaser found Bernd's pulse racing off the clock. When he recovered, Bernd admitted that he hardly knew how he finished the run. But he simply wrote off the lapse as the effects of the speed again. If Bernd lasted out the week it would be a miracle of tenacity and very quick, automatic reactions that seemed to function on their own, whether Bernd was consciously at the helm or not.

Huhnlein noted he was dealing with a very strange human, and it would take more than normal challenges before Bernd started making the same sort of mistakes most mortals would make.

Elly had been surprised by the uniqueness of Bernd's strange mind, the more she got to know it behind the scenes. Bernd had learned how to fly her Typhoon, and even how to stunt it, like no one else she'd seen. But this was to be expected in a man who made his living physically outperforming the rest of the world in machines. But then she noticed, whenever Bernd read a book, he knew every detail on every page in one quick reading. It was as if she hadn't read the same book at all, when he would recall all the details that had slipped past her.

With languages, she came to realize with some envy, he seemed to learn "by ear" and though his grammar was sometimes not exactly textbook, he could get to carrying on conversations in new languages in no time at all. In England at the Donington Grand Prix, he'd even given a speech in English and she had no idea where he'd picked it up. It was maddening to Elly, as a professional lecturer who had to take lessons to learn languages. In analyzing her husband's strange gifts, she laid a lot of emphasis on his ability to focus his entire being on one subject, like a hypnotic suggestion state, or crisis-induced adrenal state. No matter where he was, he could blot out everything else in the world except what he needed to concentrate on at the moment. If a person wanted to eliminate Bernd for any reason, he'd better make sure Bernd didn't get wind of it. Given a survival challenge, Bernd could become a difficult case for any assassin.

By Friday Bernd had toppled three world's records and sixteen class records. Score: Auto Union: 19; Mercedes Benz: 0.

Later Elly was to wish fervently that Bernd had not rubbed it in so hard. If Rudi had managed a better showing in the faulty Merc, or if Bernd had just not gone out of his way to break every record in sight that week, everything might have turned out differently in the end. As it turned out, his successes were to have serious repercussions.

With Rekordwoche successfully in Bernd's pocket, the Auto Union crew drove home a happy bunch. The weather was closing in on the Autobahn for the winter, and with every test met and conquered, they could now enjoy the winter holidays with even more relish than after the end of the regular season. Bernd had been in the cross-hairs of Fate, but he'd challenged it, forced its hand, and had come up winners. Those who weren't giving odds on his chances of surviving October were scratching their heads. What would it take to kill this man? According to the Chinese, "The courage of your enemies does you honor." Bernd was fast becoming a very honorable man.

On the political front, there was his constant Nazi-baiting, his refusal to join in the Nazi fun of the uniforms and the salutes, and of course, his public mockery of Hitler in front of Hitler. Then, as an SS officer (drafted), he became the target of a Nazi attempt to get him to renounce his religion.

"Fine," was Bernd's reply, "right after I renounce my commission in the SS!"

And Elly wasn't helping either. But, as she later said, she thought that with Bernd's status behind them, that they could get away with it — not realizing, perhaps, that she was only adding to a cumulative effect and that every resistance to the party line was being rung up on a big political attitude-register in Berlin. One of these days the bell was going to ring.

The Nazis hadn't just fallen into power. It had been a decade-long, bitter, dirty fight, first with the Communists, then with Big Money when the anti-Communist partners turned on each other with a fury. These were no cream puffs that Bernd was standing up to.

Rudi had said about Bernd, "He does not know fear and sometimes that is not good. You have to know where the real danger lays." On the sports front there was his relentless attack on Mercedes. Mercedes was having problems, and as much as Neubauer was fond of the lad, he cheerfully would have seen Rosemeyer take up golf or some other field of conquest. Mercedes had always been the darling of the party, and there was really only one man continually upsetting the glorious plans of that darling: Rosemeyer. Without Bernd around, a lot of powerful factions would breathe easier, and this was not a reassuring thought to those around Bernd who did know where the real danger lay.

Without realizing it, perhaps, Hitler was setting a bad example for Bernd. Hadn't he himself taken a shortcut to rock-star status with the use of his immensely popular Social-Motorization programs, in order to free himself of the big power-wielders? Consciously or unconsciously, Bernd was following the same path. If unconsciously, it's perfectly understandable.

Try living a life where everyone treats you as "the Lord God Almighty," as Elly described the role people assigned to Bernd, and see how long it takes you to start thinking of getting away with murder.

If it were a conscious decision, then it might well have been Bernd's Big Mistake. Hitler had run a calculated course to an amazing popularity, even in international circles. But he was, as we can see in his writings, so indelibly marked by his early misfortunes that he could never, even for a minute, forget the tenuousness of his own position. As a result, Hitler backed up his rise to power with a breathtaking ferocity in reprisal.

Bernd's own happy childhood, his close family, his rafts of kidding friends, his warm and constantly attentive (even jealous) attitude toward his wife, all added up to a very untroubled outlook. Bernd was basically, to many minds, a "nice person" with the normal repertoire of open human emotions. A trifle arrogant, some might say, but basically warm-hearted.

The game he found himself playing now, however, was one better suited to those who saw a moment's hesitation in revenge as a chance to slip in the knife. Bernd had been playing with sportsmen. Hitler had been playing with people who saw the sacrifice of human life as a simple technique of the power game. His rival totalitarian, and in many ways colleague, Stalin, had said, "One death is murder, but a million is History." Men who already had the painful deaths of many of their own people on their consciences when they went to bed every night, were Hitler's playmates — on both sides of the Channel, both sides of the Atlantic.

Even then, Hitler had correctly counted on the bourgeois hesitation of some of his foreign rivals to give him time to slip in his own knives (while his opponents would play the role of shocked innocents, even though every one of them had played chess with the lives of their own people, and not always successfully). Hitler had counted on this bourgeois hesitation, and made history with it. Yet he'd stated a fair warning to people like Bernd who might be tempted to test him: "Do not mistake me for bourgeois," Hitler had said, plain and simple. A word to the wise, as Huhnlein was trying to point out, should have been sufficient.

This time Rudi and Bernd went to their respective winter holidays with a new determination to forget official policies and duties. No more record runs, no more state dinners. No more public life for awhile.

But even in the peace of Switzerland's Lake Lugano, Rudi was still prey to the bureaucrats. Word had come from Stuttgart that certain officers of the N.S.K.K. had been nosing around Rudi's contract with Mercedes. The notice had come from the N.S.K.K., not Direktor Kissel or Sailer. "It has come to our notice that you have taken up permanent residence in Switzerland. Under such conditions the funds accrued to your retirement cannot be paid unless you plan to return to take up permanent residence within the Reich."

So the old bone of contention about his love of the Swiss lake country had risen again — in a most convenient way for the Nazi accountants. They would have to watch their pennies, he and Baby, if war really came, for Rudi had no intention of giving the Nazis any more help than he already had as a by-product of his lifelong drive to race.

For Bernd, the Rosemeyer family was cruising into 1938 riding a wave of good fortune that even he hadn't counted on to be so cooperative. Elly had been convinced that her first-born would be a daughter. To prepare Bernd for the event, she had gently slipped into his mind the advantages of being the father of a beautiful little girl. In a few weeks, Bernd had joined in enthusiastically, seeing himself squiring the captivating (and enchantingly bright) Fraulein Rosemeyer from pillar to post. They'd even named her "Eva." But when little Eva turned out to be young "Bernd Junior," Papa Bernd, having lived in nothing but a "guy's world" his whole life, wasn't exactly disappointed. He took the young Bernd to visit his trophies, explaining what would be expected of him, and envying him for being able to drive much faster in his day than Papa Bernd was able to in his own time. Privately, Elly vowed to show young Bernd more about life than just racing.

Bernd was impossible as a father, driving nurse Hedwig mad with his constant new ideas for "better ways" to raise children. Impossible, as everyone knew he would be. When Elly arrived home from the hospital, she got the surprise of her life. There, on her office writing desk, was a neat stack of all the household correspondence all attended to — the bills paid. All done by Bernd, who always professed a horror at paperwork, red tape, and bill collectors. Bernd had always preferred to spend a half hour on the phone rather than three minutes to write a line of correspondence, so Elly was expecting chaos when she arrived back home. This was, to Elly, more touching than flowers or candy could have been.

With her convalescence over and the nurses gone for awhile at least, Elly glowed with the prospect of having her two Bernds to herself over the holidays, with no outside world to make puppets and advertising-tools out of them. Bernd had refused flatly to let the photographers in to flash their bulbs at young Bernd. But then, just a little while later, Bernd completely reversed himself, just as if he'd never taken such an adamant stand, and let himself be photographed with young Bernd. Elly knitted her brows, trying to figure her husband out.

During the peace of the Christmas holiday, Elly noticed that Bernd still went at every task with the same relentless, 100-percent focus, just like the way he would drive a race car. Could a man who got so much out of every minute, to whom each year was a life time long, could he, she asked herself soberly, ever reach the age of seventy or eighty?

The New Year's holiday of 1938 was to bring a wonderful surprise, a visit from the Nuvolaris. Tazio had come as the only human Bernd thought was appropriate to be little Bernd's godfather. And Tazio had accepted the post with more than his usual warmth and good humor, so the Nuvolaris were to spend New Year's Eve with the Rosemeyers at the Esplanade Hotel in Berlin.

Nuvolari had never let mere politicos cloud his view of the sporting life. He'd socialized with the top echelon of Mussolini's regime, being photographed with Signora Mussolini when he was still a young motorcycle racer. He'd been championed himself by the poet Gabriele D'Annunzio for providing Italy with the perfect, chivalrous champion, for setting such a clean, capable example for Italy's youth, and for not sullying his position by selling himself like a prostitute to advertising campaigns.

Tazio was a man of enthusiasm who admired people who got things done against long odds. But while he admired them, he never feared them, nor let any sort of authority cloud his own hard-won instincts. And this strange bilingual bond that had grown up between the two drivers seemed to reinforce Bernd's simple disgust with the world of politics where a forthright man is looked on as a fool and duplicity is the name of the game. Duplicity never helped anybody driving above 250 mph. But conniving politicos were getting a tighter grip on the world with every techno-invention that increased their ability to keep tabs on the people and to wield the awesome weapons of propaganda.

Chapter 22

The "*Sippenhaft* Effect"

Bernd was not exactly the first to rebel against the wrath of a reign of terror. Nor was he the first who held very little importance to the risks of this wrath to his own safety. So those who have imposed reigns-of-terror have worked out, over the years, a very effective way of controlling those who don't fear for their own safety: they shift the punishment from the rebel who is taking the risks to his family. In this way the rebel's own courage becomes a danger to those he holds dear. The more he fights for what he believes in, the more he threatens those he's fighting for.

In America, there's a phrase that means that the power wielders are willing to make the rebel's family pay for his action: "We know where you live." In Germany before the Second War, the term was "*Sippenhaft*" and it was a powerful enough tool to make anyone search their mind to see if they'd done anything that could possibly be interpreted as rebellious. *Sippenhaft* created the kind of terror that made people turn in their neighbors in order to escape suspicion themselves.

Sippenhaft was what came into effect when the young Count von Stauffenberg tried to bomb the Führer, resulting in Stauffenberg's family being threatened, with the retribution of choice being slow-hanging with piano wire. And like all hostage systems since the birth of conflict, it is extremely effective.

"*Sippenhaft*." In English, it loosely translates into "clan-warrant," the kind some Scots clans suffered under the English when children were taken from their parents for "re-education," when any woman who consorted with a clan member had her cheek branded, and when any felon bringing in the head of a clan member would receive a royal pardon. In Russia, it was used more recently to keep their celebrity athletes and artists from defecting when traveling in the West.

Hitler was a frequent user of *Sippenhaft*. It not only quelled the courageous, but the ripple-effect had a marvelous way of spreading a reign of terror throughout the less-than-courageous. When Bernd had badgered his way into the risky, high-visibility world of Grand Prix racing, he was a young buck with little to lose but his own skin. Then he became a husband, and then a family man. The rules were changing, Bernd's position was changing, but was his attitude changing?

"Happy egotists" was the way Elly would describe their early life together, flitting about the world with a host of good friends. They were the prototype jet setters, wrapped in their own world of excitement and new horizons to conquer.

This new, forward looking crowd with their mobility, their stylishly informal dress that fits the last part of the century better than their own decade, their streamlined conveyances that bore them around like magic carpets, has hardly been improved on now in a new century. When we see photos of this casual crowd contrasted with the formal officialdom of the day, we feel like somebody stumbled onto the wrong movie set. The Nazis look laughably out-of-date, with their late-nineteenth century romantic militarist garb and their backwards-facing pomp and circumstance processions.

Both Hitler and Bernd may have been making an end-run to rock-star status to grab themselves some room to maneuver, but there had been a difference in timing in the two men's reach for celebrity immunity. Hitler had used his car programs to bring tangible changes to people already tired of the rhetoric after a long line of nonachievers. Hitler was grabbing popularity by dismantling an already unpopular regime.

Bernd on the other hand, had won the popularity of the people, but not at a time of fading power of his enemies, but during a growth of a new reign of terror. Instead of giving him celebrity immunity, the times were becoming ripe to make him into a perfect example that no one is above the power of this new reign of terror. Perhaps, from Berlin's point of view, the timing was becoming perfect for letting it leak that they were no longer granting immunity because of celebrity; that no individual, no matter how popular, was above the community goals of the Reich. Hitler had even seen his own end coming in the same way, often repeating that "The individual is nothing; the state, everything." It was the old contrast between the *Gemeinschaft* ideal and the *Gesellschaft* context of the behavioral psychologists, with *Gemeinschaft* representing the attitude reached when an individual

The "Happy Egotists," as Elly called herself and Bernd, now parents with a new generation of Rosemeyers to think about.
photo: Auto Union Archive

realizes that his welfare and the community's welfare are one and the same; and *Gesellschaft*, where individuals work together, but only as long as it suits their individual goals.

In *Mein Kampf*, Hitler had gone on in detail repeatedly about what trouble genius can expect when working within a social context. He seems sympathetic to the lone creator striving against dullard rule-makers. On the other hand, he never goes so far as to say that genius has a right to dispute a state when that state is surrounded by unfriendly international neighbors.

Hitler seems to commiserate with individual creators, in a peacetime context. But when the state is at war (which his would always be, for just this reason), then genius has no right to work for any goals but that of his country. And war was coming.

Chapter 23

Berlin Surprise

Rudi couldn't believe the letter he was reading. It was getting so he dreaded opening anything with a German Reichspostmark. The dreaded (by the drivers) Berlin Auto Show would be happening again as usual in February. So, incredibly, Huhnlein had given his O.K. to the harebrained idea of running another Rekordwoche in January to give the teams (obviously, Mercedes) another chance to raise international speed records just before the opening of the show, so the cars could be on display, etc. etc. It was a new degree of craziness to come from Berlin, straight from the Mad Hatter's Tea Party, as anyone who knew the facts about driving fast in those conditions could see at a glance.

With the shortened sunny hours of January, everyone knew that by the time the hoar frost had melted from the pavement, the winds of morning would have been well underway. There would be no "window of safety" at all.

Rosemeyer got the good news in a call from Dr. Feuereissen. Bernd objected right away to the runs on the basis of the rules, pointing out that Berlin had stipulated that all record attempts were to be made only during Rekordwoche in October. But Feuereissen said strings had been pulled "in high places" to organize this impromptu run in the middle of winter. Then Bernd objected for practical reasons, pointing out that there would be no time to design a new car to raise the records. Feuereissen replied that, as a matter of fact, they'd just come up with a quick way to modify the aerodynamics of the old car to add another 30 mph. No, Dr. Porsche hadn't thought up the changes. Dr. Porsche hadn't been in on this new modification scheme, as a matter of fact. Porsche had been pulled completely off racing to attend to the Volkswagen project. Bernd didn't like the sound of this. No, Dr.

A joke's a joke; but Berlin's next bit of heroic lunacy was anything but funny to those who had to carry out the whims of brass-hats in comfy offices. The faded swastika tells the whole story.

photo: Auto Union Archive

Porsche wouldn't be able to attend these record runs. Bernd liked this even less. He'd never made a record run without Dear Onkel-Doktor there to keep rein on the goings-on.

Elly reported later that Bernd was very unhappy about the way his usual crew was being kept out of things.

As a matter of fact, Elly wouldn't be at these winter record runs either. She'd postponed a number of lecture dates in the fall to be able to be in on Bernd's *Rekordwoche* runs. With the certainty that no one would be driving in January, she'd rescheduled the lecture dates for then. She couldn't back out now, not a second time.

When Bernd saw what they'd done to his faithful record setter to add to its top speed, he was even less enthusiastic. They'd simply bent a sheet of aluminum over into a long inverted channel and attached it between the graceful rises that flowed over the tops of the huge wheels connecting them into one long upside-down trough on either side of the cockpit. Bernd wouldn't be able to see out to the side, but worse than that, the new fairings made the car an obvious prey to the slightest side-wind.

Porsche had seen rough sketches of this idea and had advised against it, because of this obvious side-wind danger. Fins extending down to the pavement along both sides of the car added even more to its vertical profile and side-wind vulnerability. It was a hasty lash-up to keep pace with Mercedes, which had gone right to work after its fiasco in October to build a proper new record-setter. Mercedes had also responded to its poor showing previously by placing an engineer, Rudolph Uhlanhaut, behind the wheel, who could both design and drive (Auto Union trial and error style). The new car not only didn't lift its nose, it had loads of power and was smooth to drive.

Every time Bernd raised a logical objection to the runs, on political or practical grounds, he was talked out of his objections. As Elly set out for her lectures in Saxony, Bernd had said that his only option was to count on the fact that during the few days scheduled for the runs, the winter weather might force a postponement. Here was Bernd, the man who usually loved a challenge others balked at, publicly trying to get out of it (and not caring who knew it).

But then, very suddenly, with his usual Rosemeyer unpredictability, after refusing the assignment twice in a very loud and public manner, oblivious to all criticisms of his nerve, Bernd made one of his instant about-faces. From then on, for some reason, no one could talk him out of driving in January.

Bernd flew himself to Frankfurt alone, and almost didn't make it. The weather had closed in, and he'd circled waiting for a break in the clouds. When he finally spotted the airport and swooped down in the last light of the afternoon, he'd nearly wiped out a hedge that suddenly appeared in his path. He had to call for a ride to join the team at the hotel. Both team's cars were being rushed to completion for the runs. Neubauer had made an emergency call to Stuttgart to see why the Mercedes record-setter had been delayed.

"It has to be here by six a.m.!" he'd yelled into the phone. There was a silence on the other end. Then a voice said they'd do what they could. The Mercedes showed up on schedule, but the Auto Union team wasn't ready to run until later. Much later.

On January 28, 1938, Rudi once again headed his Mercedes through the barricades to where he could see activity at the timing tents in the early dawn light. But if it was chilly in October, it was like the South Pole in January. It looked very much like winter maneuvers as he drove up. Soldiers in great coats hunkered down next to the roadstead, testing phone lines and trying to keep from freezing in the boredom of waiting for someone else to risk his life. He could see little clouds of white at every utterance the soldiers made. There were an awful lot of uniforms milling around the tents that day, more than he'd ever seen at an event, even at a Grand Prix, much less dawn at a record run.

Rudi was always reserved, even in the best of situations. Always the "baron," whether he wanted to be or not. But this morning he felt an icy indifference to the warm greetings he got from the uniforms. Why were there so many uniforms there that day? If it were up to him, he'd be back at the villa thinking about getting up to feed Anatole and Moritz. He noticed the flaps of the tent pavilions were blowing like flags. The morning wind was already here, and no sign of the frost melting off the road.

The Auto Union team was nowhere to be seen. Maybe something went wrong. There was a rumor about Bernd having a plane crash or something. Well, it would be great to have the place all to himself, just like Bernd had in October. Well, almost great, if that wind would only die down a bit.

Neubauer was on him like the impresario he was, bubbly before the big performance.

"Feeling right, Rudi? That's fine," (before Rudi had a chance to answer). "I nearly lost weight last night worrying about the car. Could they get it done and delivered in time? But it just arrived a few minutes ago. We'll have it ready for you soon," he said, shrugging toward the transporter that was unloading Rudi's dragon like some secret weapon. "It'll be ready for you in fifteen minutes. When do you want to have a try?"

Rudi looked at the morning objectively for the first time, from a driver's perspective. It was bitterly cold, but clearing, with only passing clouds. The wind was already up before the sun. Better make it a quick and early run.

"As soon as the frost is gone. Probably about eight."

"Fine, fine. It'll be a great day."

Not if Rudi had anything to say about it. He wouldn't even be here if he'd had anything to say about it. But with Mercedes' miserable showing in October, and questions about his loyalty to the Reich constantly cropping up where he least expected it, he didn't have a lot of choice. A great day. For whom? What did all this prove? It was a far cry from the old days in Monte Carlo with Chiron and Dreyfus and Charly. This was a bunch of boys playing at war — a game they might wish they'd never started.

With a chill Rudi realized that the time had already come for his first run. Already. What about stalling a few more minutes? But then, what about playing with that nasty wind that was rising with every minute? Better get it over and done with, one way or another.

A pleasant surprise hit Rudi, the first of the morning, and perhaps the most important of his career — the car handled beautifully and there was plenty of power on tap. He felt a thrill of hope. Maybe it could all be over with in just a few minutes. Then no Hitler on earth would have the nerve to ask him to go again!

The warm-up runs went smoothly with no nose-lift at all. Now just concentrate on those awful, tiny black holes under the overpasses, and time his steering against the side-wind at the Morfelden clearing. It shook Rudi to realize that no matter how he forced it, he couldn't make his mind keep up with the flow of events at that speed. Line up for the hole, Kaboom! in the stomach and we're through. But then there's another one coming. Better line... Kaboom! Next one. Better... Kaboom! He was getting farther and farther behind the game at each over pass. But now it was over. Just turn the car around and do the same again. He might as well shut his eyes, he was getting so far behind the aiming up for the holes. Pure, unconscious reactions were saving him. But these were holding true, at least.

But how could he trust something he couldn't grab time to think about? Like playing the drums, if he began to think about it, he'd start making mistakes.

Kaboom! Don't try to think. Kaboom! Just go with your eyes wide open watching everything like a jungle animal hunting and being hunted. Kaboom! It was over. He let his beast (now his faithful beast) coast down to 200, 175, a mere 150. To touch the brakes too soon would have ripped those paper-thin treadless speed tires, and the results Rudi didn't like to think about. Under a hundred it seemed like he could get out and run along side. 80, 70, brakes, stop. People running up laughing and yelling. The car had done magnificently. He knew it had more speed in it. With a higher ratio, they could go a lot faster. Neubauer, with his usual gusto, bulled his way through the crowd.

"Wonderful, Rudi! Wonderful! 271! That's faster than any man ever drove on a road! It looked very steady. You want to have another run?"

"No! No ... Let's see if we need to. Maybe tomorrow." (Another night of dreaming of those overpasses? No thanks!) "There's a nasty side-wind out there, and it's not getting any better."

Manfred fought his way through the crowd.

"Time for a glass of something, Rudi. Come, I'll drive you back to the hotel. We can take our time over breakfast now." Food! It sounded like a fantastic reward, just to be able to think about breakfast.

The meal was a loud one, with neighboring diners glowering at them. But what did Rudi care? Then a telephone call to Manfred. He came back to the table with a concerned look.

"The Auto Union gang is out there."

A wave of shock brought Rudi back once more from his comfy retreat from those overpasses.

"I'm not going out there," he said.

"That's a late start. Especially in today's wind."

They tried to keep the banter going when Neubauer came past their table, but — who were they kidding? There wasn't a chance of relaxing when Bernd was out there making a try at Rudi's new record.

"Um, do you think, ah, we ought to sort of…?"

"My thoughts exactly!" said Manfred, and they made a hasty retreat and dashed for their car, leaving the heaps of eggs and steaks they'd ordered. Neubauer wasn't far behind.

Sure enough, it was more than just one of those rumors that flashed through the racing teams. There were the tall, boxy transporters of Auto Union parked near the pit pavilions. By this time the flaps and fringes of tents were snapping in the wind, and the great coats of the army staff had to be held closed or they'd blow open. At the tops of the surrounding hills, the tree tips waved with a restless insistence, almost as if they were trying to signal someone.

"Driving in a wind like this! Can you imagine such a thing?!" Rudi was grumbling to Manfred as he pulled his Merc through the crowds of soldiers.

Manfred only shrugged. Scudding clouds changed the lighting from bright sun back to overcast and then back again in moments. Rudi, with Neubauer-like determination pushed his way through the crowd up to the newly modified Auto Union. Bernd was already in the cockpit of the car. When he saw Rudi, Bernd's face lit up and he tried to reach Rudi's hand across the wide bodywork.

"Congratulations, Rudi!" Bernd said with his characteristic grin. "Now it's my turn!"

Flustered suddenly, Rudi just said a "Thank you." He wanted to say more, but only he and Bernd knew what those overpasses were like. Part of him wanted to rip Bernd out of the car and shake some sense into him: to grab him away from the hypnotic pull of this crazy game that Bernd seemed to feel tugging him; to warn him about that gust that hit from the side at the Morfelden clearing. Bernd could always try early tomorrow. There was plenty of time left in the week for setting new records!

The other part of Rudi knew, as no one else but Bernd knew, exactly what was buzzing through Bernd's mind, and how little anyone could help him. Rudi would only distract him. He could never talk him out of driving at this point.

"I wanted to say something more too, a lot more," Rudi said later. "All rivalry was forgotten at that moment. He was my comrade, exposed to the same dangers as I." But Bernd only laughed his little-boy laugh and looked at Rudi closely for a moment,

"Don't worry, Rudi. Remember, I'm one of the lucky ones!"

Then Bernd left Rudi behind, turning to the work at hand gruffly. The engine wasn't warming fast enough for him. Sebastian pushed through the crowd, and caught Bernd's attention,

"Look here, Bernd, I don't like these gusts of wind. Look at these tents. Look at the way they're blowing!!"

"Then get a move on! It's not going to get any better while we sit here!"

Sebastian didn't move. His face changed and suddenly he said in a completely different tone of voice, "Bernd, to Hell with the records. Let's wait until tomorrow!"

"Nonsense. I know what I'm doing! Let's go!"

Now it was Dr. Feuereissen who pushed his way up to the cockpit. "I'm told there's a 40 kpm crosswind," he said. "Wouldn't you rather postpone it?"

Bernd was curt, as if all these distractions were ganging up on him.

"What for? There's only one point where the wind could be dangerous. I know exactly where it is. All I've got to do is bring the wheel round a fraction and nothing can go wrong."

It wasn't until 11:42, almost high noon, before Bernd's car was ready for a real attack on Rudi's new record. But Bernd's car just didn't seem to have the push that day to do the job. He'd have to pull some sort of rabbit out of the hat to beat Rudi. Bernd no longer had the unclouded look of a boy playing with challenges with an aggressive mirth. No longer *Struwwelpeter*.

Bernd's face, the onlookers saw, had changed into a bitterly determined old man, almost magically. It was as if Bernd had been replaced

Bernd aging visibly under the pressure. He was not even thirty when this shot was taken.

photo: Auto Union Archive

by someone else in the cockpit. An old man facing the answers to life and death, with no choice but to go head on and find out what Fate's verdict would be that day.

The old man drove off, his foot down hard. The phone reports at the kilometer checkpoints started coming through. Neubauer was finding it hard to breathe.

The staccato reports came from the soldiers, one following the other almost immediately.

"Kilometer three, he's through."

"Kilometer four, through."

Then at Kilometer nine a voice was yelling hysterically. No one could understand what was being said by the garbled words, but there was little mistaking the message.

Feuereissen went white as a sheet and ran for his car. It wouldn't start.

"Take mine, Doctor!" Neubauer was yelling, throwing him the keys. Sebastian had already driven to the end of the course before the final run. When Bernd hadn't appeared on time, he knew. He ran to his car and drove down the course from the other direction.

He saw the car, just a bare chassis now, driven into the embankment next to the roadstead. A trail of torn and crumpled aluminum led up to it. The car was empty. Feureissen drove up while Bastl was searching the area for Bernd.

There, under a tree, Bernd sat, not a scratch on him, not a trace of blood. Someone sent up a cheer of relief. But Bernd wasn't moving. They ran up the bank to him expecting him to leap to his feet and say something stupid — some Bernd-joke: "Well, I had you fellows going that time, didn't I? I should like to see someone crash a car better than that!"

But no jokes were coming. As they neared Bernd the sun suddenly shown from behind a cloud, changing the shadows on his face. Bastl stopped dead in his tracks. Bernd had moved! No, it was the damned shadow-play! Bernd had gone on a drive and wasn't coming back, Neubauer realized with a shudder.

Accusations flew back and forth about the final cause of Bernd's death. The newspapers were crowded with headlines of rival theories, competing blames. The controversy became such a national issue that the remaining Auto Union record setter was to be modified like the one Bernd was killed in to restage tests to prove or disprove various theories.

Some said that there were photos showing disfigurement of the body. An English newspaper ran photos of a very mysterious skid-mark left after the crash that would never be there under normal circumstances. It showed a single wheel, locking up, releasing and locking up again. Had the engine seized? Neubauer pointed out that engine seizure would have torn the tires to shreds. But they were still in good shape when the bare chassis was found.

Dr. Porsche decried the whole insane process, of running records at that time of year, when the authorities clearly knew Bernd couldn't let himself resist the challenge. "Murder," Dr. Porsche had called it, pure and simple. Not much room for misinterpretation there.

If Porsche had been on the scene, Bernd would never have had a chance to drive no matter how he argued, everyone sensed. But Berlin had called him away.

Detailed, minute-by-minute weather reports had been retrieved from a nearby airfield. They showed a spike of wind velocity of almost hurricane force at 11:42. This led to Neubauer's theory. The wind pressure at 270 mph on the thin aluminum skin was considerable. Add the grafted-on sheets they'd used to smooth out the airflow between the wheels, and then add on top of that the pressure of a suddenly vicious gust at speed, and you have an awesome amount of pounds per square inch on the body. A tiny rip, a flap lifting into the airflow, and the body could have been peeled off like a cornhusk in a split second. And then, without its streamlining, the car would have been uncontrollable. Not even Bernd was that good.

The papers ran photos which showed flaws in the car (which Bastl swore were forgeries) and condemned Auto Union for killing Rosemeyer. The only witnesses were two foresters working nearby. They had been found mute with shock after the accident. They'd looked up at the roar of the approaching car to see it lifted as by some unseen hand. Then it disintegrated into small parts, the chassis driving into the soft soil of the banking. The driver? Thrown like a doll.

The 1938 Mercedes Rekordwagen of 5.6 litres which Caracciola drove to 268 mph.

photo: Mercedes Benz

Perhaps the greatest mystery surrounding the death of Rosemeyer was not the physical "cause" of the car's careening out of control and disintegrating. Everybody on the scene knew something like this would happen eventually as they neared the breaking point. Sooner or later limits would surely be reached as certain as the turning of the Earth. When those limits were reached, something would let go and a man would die. The higher the speed, the more certain the probability.

The real question about Rosemeyer's death wasn't "What broke?" but rather "Why did Bernd drive that day?" How could a new father with such warm connections to his wife and son, head off into what everyone watching, especially Bernd, knew was an uncommon risk above and beyond duty? As spectators, we're filled with an anger that he should be so determined to be "stupid," just when a happy ending was so close. It was as though Robin Hood, in the last reel, should say, "Oh, to hell with it. The Normans are going to win anyway," and let himself be captured by Prince John.

The personal/professional-pride argument falls flat when we realize he'd already blithely abandoned the role of hero when he first ridiculed the record runs and sought any logical excuse to postpone them. The professional-rivalry theory falls flat when we realize that this was not his last chance to beat Rudi. In fact, his engine wasn't really on tune that day and could obviously have benefited from a day's delay. He had the whole week left to beat Rudi.

Why was Bernd so impatient with those who were practically forcing him to postpone the run? A side-wind is more than just dangerous — it also very effectively scrubs off speed, like a bobsled slewing sideways, making beating Rudi's speed even harder.

Bernd always found a way to get his way. Why would he force his will to go when conditions were so poor for success, let alone survival? It was clear to Rudi that no one could talk Bernd out of what he had set his mind to do. Talk would only reduce his chance to survive. But what chance was there? Like two boys seeing how far they could lean out a window, the game would only be over when one of them fell.

When we watch the films of the run it's obvious that hours after the time that Rudi had driven, the winds had become stormy with insistent gusts. It was clearly madness to drive. Yet this genius-ability mind with a perfect new family chose to drive. Did he realize Berlin would keep hunting him, hounding him until they began to touch his new family? Was the Sippenhaft Effect to be considered?

Last run.

photo: Auto Union Archiv

At this point Bernd had become valuable to Hitler in a new way — now more as a dead hero than as a possible future embarrassment. AT other times Hitler was quick to pull heroes of the Reich out of combat to keep them safe for further use. Now he was throwing heroes to the wolves with what was clearly a suicide mission. And another consideration: What would happen if a fiercely focused mind of Bernd's capabilities became political? Bernd had a popularity that amounted to idolatry in the youth of Germany. Even today, every January 28, they still gather at a small monument placed at the Morfelden Clearing where his car hit the bank. A yearly vigil is still maintained well over a half century later to celebrate this strangely brilliant mind.

If he'd suddenly gone political, wouldn't thousands follow wherever he led? Hitler had seen the man face to face, making a mockery of Hitler's archaic style. This ultra-modern human at the cutting-edge of so many technologies, familiar with new worlds that had become locked away from Hitler as he slowly became surrounded by an insulating staff — did Hitler think Bernd had his thumb on a new pulse, the same way Hitler had when he started out?

Just a few phone calls could create a fatal challenge that Bernd, Hitler knew, would find irresistible. A few strings pulled and Bernd would be flogging down the Autobahn at insane speeds, as certain as the dawn. But something would be needed to make sure Bernd took a challenge that was basically mad. A direct challenge from Hitler? By staging the runs under unsurvivable circumstances, Hitler would be coming out from behind the mask and challenging Bernd to live through what no normal mortal could deal with — just the sort of bait that would make the tips of Bernd's mouth begin to turn up in his angelic imp-grin.

Motive, means, and opportunity were what Hitler held in his hand. Bernd had been irritable, not coy, at the end. Uncharacteristically gruff with those trying hardest to help him survive the insanity. A man committing suicide when he has everything to live for can't be expected to be in a good mood. He took that drive sooner rather than later in the unstopped growth of a reign of terror. Was this what he meant by calling himself "One of the lucky ones"?

Next came the funeral. A state funeral with all the military trimmings of the death of a Hero of the Reich. Elly had publicly warned the world that if the Nazis turned Bernd's funeral into one of their propaganda acts, she would find a way to shut the whole show down.

A short, formal, predictably opportunistic message had come from Hitler:

"Let the nation be consoled in its sorrow by the knowledge that Bernd Rosemeyer gave his life in the cause of the Reich." A Hero's death in the best Teuton tradition, and not a photo-op to be missed.

Rudi felt a sudden disgust for the whole spectacle of this public display, celebrating a tragedy that didn't have to happen.

"What was the sense in men chasing each other to death for the sake of a few seconds?" Rudi was asking himself. "To serve progress? To serve mankind? What a ridiculous phrase in the face of the great reality of death." And twenty years later Rudi was to add, "The gap Rosemeyer left behind has never been closed."

Neubauer put it more poetically, in his usual romantic style. "For me, young Rosemeyer with his fair hair and laughing eyes is still alive. He simply climbed into his silver car one day and drove off to an unknown destination, a destination we must all make for sooner or later."

At the funeral, Huhnlein stood to give his official speech. There was no look of triumph, no sound of the strong soldier in his voice. Elly also stood at the same moment and started to shout at Huhnlein, as she'd promised she would. Huhnlein only folded his speech and sat down quietly, looking shaken by the death of the boy he was going to "set straight" with his little talks about public obligations. Public obligations didn't seem to have much of a grip on Huhnlein that grim winter's day.

AUTO-UNION

Chapter 24

Aftermath

Racing changed completely for many of its leading characters from this point. Auto Union abandoned Rekordwoche, leaving the field to Mercedes. They almost gave up their racing program altogether, if it hadn't been for Tazio, who'd suddenly appeared on their doorstep. He would take Bernd's place on their team, he announced. He would wear a special red windcap as a mark of remembrance for his friend. Tazio, like a few other drivers who needed racing in their lives as mortar for their bricks of stability, kept on racing for his own reasons.

War was approaching. This was brought home forcefully to the photographer Monkhouse as he visited his friend Dick Seaman's father-in-law at the family's alpine chalet. A little trout fishing had been organized. When he reached the chalet, however, he was greeted with the news that a general of the Luftwaffe would be staying with them that weekend. When Monkhouse's face fell at the news, he was told that this general wasn't the usual sort of Nazi general. It was Ernst Udet, third in command of Germany's new Luftwaffe, an old ace from World War One, who seemed as young as he did when he flew with von Richthofen's Flying Circus. Monkhouse was told that this was one general that Monkhouse would enjoy talking to.

To fill the gap left by Bernd in Dr. Porsche's Auto Union team, Tazio doffed his leather jerkens, yellow jerseys and baggy pants to put on the team uniform of Auto Union. His only nonconformist talismans: his tortoise pin and a red wind-cap to honor Bernd. Once on a mission, Tazio was a hard man to beat. And to help the maverick Auto Union team (more and more on the outs with the Nazis), Tazio won a lot of races in the final, D-type Auto Union.

photo: Auto Union Archive

Monkhouse found Udet to be charming, full of life, and a perfect storyteller over wine after a long day's chasing the fish. As Udet grew to like Monkhouse and his wry, English comments, Udet's eyes began to shift with nervousness, as though something big were about to happen — as though he had something important to say, but didn't know how to get it out. With a silent hand-sign Udet and Monkhouse's host held a hasty conference to one side. Then it was announced that they would play a game now, where they all would stop drinking and look for Udet's lost car keys. What they were searching for were hidden microphones. Udet had a growing number of enemies in high circles in Berlin.

They all turned to and searched behind every picture frame and under every table. When the room was declared "clean" their host brought out new wine and the group sat down to enjoy some open conversation, the kind they used to enjoy out in the open-air beer gardens.

Udet went on with great skill to regale the group with stories of the growing madness in Berlin: the Mad-Hatter paranoia of high command, the "off-with-their-heads" single solution to all political problems. Even though Udet had at first been enthusiastic about building a strong air force for a Germany surrounded by nations already caught up in an arms race (even Poland had bought more arms than they could ever use, much to the delight of the war profiteers), he was now beginning to see it was a mistake.

It was he who had invented dive-bombing and developed the nightmarish sirens attached to the Stuka landing gear to frighten their enemies with a little *Schrecklichkeit* (warlike fearsomeness). Now, it seemed, Germany was to take over the role of the aggressor, and he'd had enough.

Monkhouse wondered privately how one who had climbed so high could just one day call in sick and leave it all behind, secrets and hidden-skeletons and all. It would be a tricky process, this disentangling oneself from the Reich — even for Monkhouse who as a foreign photographer had seen behind the scenes, he realized with a shudder.

Udet became suddenly serious. International pressures were changing daily. Tactical ploys were playing havoc with people's lives, as "Phoney Wars" came and went, while real ones grew all the while backstage.

"There may come a situation soon when you will want to leave Germany quickly," he said to Monkhouse. "If this happens, I will give you a sign. I know you're very familiar with Germany, but you must follow the route I give you exactly, and you will have no problems. Keep a full tank of gas in your Bentley. When the time comes I will knock on your door before sunup. Do not answer, for I will say nothing. Just leave at once."

Far in the Alps in a hidden chalet, the possibility of war seemed fantastic. But one morning Monkhouse heard a sharp rap on the door announcing that Germany had invaded Poland and the war was "phoney" no more. Udet's route to freedom proved as safe as he said it would be. But Udet's own route to freedom could only be suicide.

Neubauer had received word that racing should continue, as if this Polish problem were a minor scuffle to be ironed out without disturbing real life. But when he began to round up his team, von Brauchitsch was nowhere to be found. Neubauer finally ran Manfred to earth at the airport, just about to board a plane.

"When the war trumpets sound for Germany," Manfred told him, when Neubauer finally found him, "a von Brauchitsch must heed the call."

"That's fine, Manfred, but now we have races to be run." And he pulled Manfred off to a waiting taxi. It wasn't until the taxi was underway that the scene he had just gone through with Manfred was replayed through Neubauer's memory. It was then that he realized the crowd was waiting for a plane bound for Switzerland! Manfred was "heeding the call" all right. Now Neubauer almost regretted having finally found Manfred, for who knew what future lay in store for the no-longer-needed racing community in a highly utilitarian police state?

Fittingly, Tazio won the last race of this titanic era of racing. Dr. Porsche had approached Tazio to test their new Type-D racer, pleading, "Only you can tell us whether our new cars are fit for anything besides the rubbish heap."

Tazio had tested the new car, suggested extensive revisions, and then drove the resulting design to a fine string of successes. Sensing a last-minute remission from the political tone that racing had taken on, Stuck was back on the team again, after having quit for the sake of his wife Paula.

The parting between Porsche and Nuvolari before the war was laced with an undertone of deep emotion. Porsche, as a parting gift, promised Tazio the concession for the Volkswagen in Italy after this war madness had died back down again. Tazio promised to help in any way he could. He was to make good on that promise in spades. Rudi, with his customary cool counter-punching clarity of mind, had successfully made his way to back Lugano with Baby, where they spent the next few years doing a lot of gardening. After the war Mercedes needed Rudi back to rebuild their racing image, and he got his pension, despite the predictions of the N.S.K.K. official. Louis Chiron eventually made it to Switzerland as well, living dangerously by helping downed Allied pilots to escape through Spain (the "railroad" that Chuck Yeager was to take before becoming the pioneer of supersonic flight).

The shark-like flowing lines of the Mercedes for the 1938–1940 formula. The last of the pre-war cars resufaced at the Buenos Aires Grand Prix after the war (to be driven by a new driver named Juan Manuel Fangio) and one made a try for Indianapolis. But they were simply too complex for the non-works mechanics to deal with and they never reached their potential in later life.

photo: Mercedes Benz

In time Elly married a nice, sane doctor and raised young Bernd out of the public eye. After the war, not unnaturally, one of Bernd Jr.'s pals was Wolfgang von Trips, a dashing driver for the new Porsche company.

When von Trips was killed at Nürburgring, the wisdom of Elly's efforts to keep him out of the racing limelight began to sink in on young Bernd.

Manfred, in his checkered way of slipping through the cracks, ended up after the war running the German Sporting Commission, becoming a sort of Huhnlein himself for (of all people) the East German Communists.

Huhnlein was promoted to head of Military Transport during the war, but then was mysteriously wiped out in a purge of Hitler's favorite henchmen who'd fallen under sudden suspicion for some paranoid reason or other.

The ever-popular Marshal Balbo was also killed by "friendly fire" and removed once and for all from the worries of his messiah, Mussolini.

Neubauer was placed in a boring desk job at the Transport Ministry. But after the war he was called back into harness at his old job at Mercedes, where he wrote another, just as historic chapter of racing for Mercedes with Juan Fangio and Stirling Moss, finally laying his (and Mercedes') racing career for that generation to rest under a dust cover.

After the war Rudi tried some racing with Neubauer again. But a head injury at Indianapolis (attributed, by some, to anti-German sabotage) and a later crash put an end to his career as a real contender. He spent the remainder of his career as a very popular liaison to the American military for Mercedes — back selling cars again, but enjoying the process this time.

Varzi went to Argentina after the war, one place where anti-Fascist feelings did not make life difficult. He raced in Peron's events and discovered a new driver whom he helped bring to Europe, the eventual five-time world champion, legendary Juan Fangio. Varzi had lost his old coldness and became a great help to restarting racing after the war for a new generation. Even Fagioli seemed to lose his old aggressive self-absorption, apologizing to the whole racing community for his ruthless driving and becoming an asset to newcomers to the sport.

Dr. Porsche didn't have it so easy. During the war Porsche had been put in charge of the Peugeot factory in occupied France. There he repeatedly stepped in to prevent the Labor Front from exporting local French workers to slave labor elsewhere in Europe. At one point he prevented the Gestapo from carting off Rene Peugeot on sabotage charges. It was made clear to Porsche that he had not impressed the Gestapo with his cooperation when a warning came: "A cell has been reserved at a concentration camp for Dr. Porsche when he finally goes one step too far."

After the war, the French were busy accusing each other of cooperating with the occupying Germans. A favorite way of escaping accusation was to accuse someone else, so Peugeot accused the man who'd saved him from the Gestapo, Dr. Porsche, of war crimes.

Captured in the last days of the war and completely cleared of war crimes by both the American and British occupying forces, he was invited to Baden-Baden to talk over the design of a new people's car for Renault by the French Minister for Industry, Communist Marcel Paul, who promptly had Porsche arrested. Porsche and his son, Ferry, were paraded through the streets in chains, then thrown into a primitive dungeon where they awaited news about a pending million-franc ransom that had been set by the French government.

The beautiful Cisitalia postwar version of the Auto Union, designed by Dr. Porsche and developed by one of his ransomers, Piero Dusio, industrialist and ex-race driver who spent his fortune trying to help racing and the Porsche family after the troubles in France. The car, shown here before its final paint and trim was finished, combined the genius of forward-thinking German design (including four-wheel drive) and the exquisite execution of Italian workmanship.

Tazio himself came to the effort to help publicize the car. But lacking the backing to field a full race team, Dusio had to find another race-mad dictator to make the dream happen: Peron. In Argentina, however, schedules lagged, and the car slowly drifted into oblivion, resurfacing on display for a spell at the Briggs Cunningham Automotive Museum near Los Angeles.

photo: Shell Oil of London)

A French driver, Raymond Sommer, the French race organizer Marcel Lehoux, and the Italian Industrialist Piero Dusio (with Tazio's help) worked to raise the ransom, and after Dusio's mortgaged his wife's villa and virtually ruined his own fortune, the ransom was paid — but not before Porsche's health had been permanently ruined. He retired to the mountains of Austria where the family built a new sportscar in what was little more than a barn. The car was to be called, not unreasonably, the "Porsche."

By the time the Professor was able to be taken out for a ride, just before he finally succumbed to his condition, there were enough new post-war Volkswagens on the road to bring tears to the Professor's eyes.

Tazio emerged from his gardening during the war, still foremost in the minds of his countrymen as their champion. However, he'd had a slow start to begin with, and by now was in his fifties. Despite lungs that had been permanently scarred by the constant inhalation of the high-test fuel that had hypnotized him as a youth, Tazio went back to driving. When he walked away from Alfa Romeo before the war to take Bernd's place, it was for good. They'd risked his life once too often with their helter-skelter pitwork. Still loyal to Rosemeyer's team (virtually the forerunner of the later Porsche team), Tazio had joined with Dusio to try to rescue the Professor. To help publicize Dusio's small sportscar manufacturing efforts, Tazio drove a little, Fiat-based Cisitalia sportscar in the Mille Miglia after the war, facing the powerful big new Ferraris and the powerful post-war Alfas (rebuilt out of old Grand Prix car chassis), two- and three-times the size of his Fiat-engined Cisitalia.

The race was wet that year, but the ageing Tazio had proved his magician's reputation by pushing the tiny Cisitalia up into first place before he finally hit a puddle that completely drenched the electrics. The car stopped dead, and it was twenty minutes before he and his mechanic could get it running again. By this time the leaders had all repassed him before Tazio set out on another of his famous demonic drives. At the finish, Tazio had flogged the little car back up into second place — probably his second most legendary drive in his extensive collection of history-making races.

Tazio continued to race as the grand old man of Italian sports until his retirement in the early fifties. He'd been wrong in his interview with the reporter years before. He died peacefully in bed surrounded by his family and mechanics, not at the wheel of a hurtling race car as he'd prophesied.

They've all gone down that same road Rosemeyer took that blustery noon in 1938. Huhnlein and Hitler. Rudi and Bernd. And so the tales of their struggles have been covered over by later battlers, fading under the tide of newer heroics and champions to follow. Then one day a newer generation of race-struck youths stumbled across the old tales and found something in them to stir their imaginations.

Epilogue

Full Circle

The world was a different place after the war, the one single event that had involved more humans than any other happening in the history of the planet. It had been an adventuresome few years, and the stories, both funny and sad, went on for years as the fighters gathered with drinks in hand and cigars at the ready around the glow of barbecues in the darkening evening.

The older generation had had just about enough government intervention in their lives. First the Depression, the New Deal programs, and then the War — too many ugly orders to be followed. And worse yet, too many ugly orders to pass along down the line. They'd seen the tranquil, warm orange groves of Southern California in glimpses on their hurried way to Okinawa or Leyte Gulf. And now they wanted desperately to take a much longer look. A fellow could keep himself alive raising oranges with a little luck, it seemed.

A sudden glow of a cigar in the night signalled that somebody was about to make a pronouncement.

"The hell of it is, when I made admiral, I thought I'd have a little say-so in things. But there's always somebody above you. Hell, even Truman can't make a move without getting an OK from somebody." The orange groves looked better all the time. The song was "Mañana, mañana, mañana is good enough for me!"

The older generation just wanted, demanded a rest in the sun to listen to the waves. They'd been too close to politics as advisors, close to espionage in the OSS. The whole family had played the political game: cousins in what became the CIA, uncles running campaigns, more cousins on Rockefeller's staff. They been up to their eyebrows in the movements of political power, the tidal ebb and flow of dominance, and they were tired of it. The farther they could get away from

Washington, the better. Recruiters from younger generations of Roosevelts were turned away. "Mañana's good enough for me."

They'd had kids, of course. All the movies said you should have kids. But kids could take care of themselves, and we did.

It was a glorious freedom to have parents well satisfied with being just left alone and leaving everybody else alone. We made the most of it, left free to roam the hills in search of adventure and freedom from orders to follow and orders to give. And so, as kids will, we became interested in cars — race cars, of course.

We read every word in every hotrod and track racing magazine we could scrounge. If an Allard J2 were to stop in our little town, even for a brief soda on a weekend tour down from L.A., word would go out like tom-toms and the car would soon be surrounded by a crowd of awestruck urchins.

"Don't touch that fender, kid!" We wouldn't think of it. We weren't so isolated that we didn't know the body of a J2 was made from thin, fragile aluminum. And we'd no more hurt this holy relic than spit on a Christmas tree.

We were desperate for sporting machines in our provincial lives stuck away in the rural coasts of post-war Southern California. Even hotrods could begin to look good if we squinted our eyes a little and pretended you didn't look stupid sitting upright with your knees around your ears with no hope of getting around a corner quickly.

The movies started showing traces of the MGs and Jags that the GIs were finding so interesting in postwar Europe. We were struck by the use of wire wheels in high-performance cars. We hadn't seen wire wheels in this country since the Model A of the early thirties. Wire wheels were something you covered up with wheel discs to look cool. But our few glimpses of European racers showed elegant-looking high-profile wire wheels that caught our starved imaginations.

Road racing was making its first clumsy, but charmingly hospitable, efforts on the new continent. Kids like us could still wander through the pits unhampered by guards and passes. Being the kid brother, it fell on my shoulders to create a perfect deportment record for weeks before a race in order to scrounge a ride to the course with the big guys with drivers licenses. It was a fine new form of extortion that they quickly perfected to an art, complicating my life with a new need for tact and diplomacy. When true sportscar magazines appeared, we haunted the mailbox until our monthly connection with the world of performance machinery finally appeared.

At one point a bit of magic fell into our lives: an older kid with a lowered and much customized '49 Mercury lead-sled was going to make the run to L.A. to the Autorama in January. Would we like to come along, since we obviously were so nuts about cars? Our deportment record hit a new high in good manners, for nothing, nothing could jeopardize this trip. To the Big City without Mom and Dad, to the Autorama, a pageant we'd only seen pictures of in the magazines.

We left in the afternoon of the big day, reaching the city after night had fallen and the city lights had turned the night smog pink. Where we came from, the sky was black at night, and this new pink glow set a magic mood on the evening. When we wound our way to a parking place and got out of the candy-apple maroon Merc, it had somehow turned pitch black in the strange arc lighting. Curiouser and curiouser, we wound our way to the lighted pillars of the entrance, paid our arm-and-a-leg fee, and entered Oz, drenched with flashing lighted tinsel and echoing loud music. There were models that seemed very much like they were smiling right back at us — punk kids with our collars turned up and string-thin leather belts, worn low.

We made our way through the maze of displays, cars turning on tables, spinning in air, flapping their doors automatically. Chrome and more chrome, models, tinny echoing music, garbled loudspeaker announcements. And then the hotrods, cars we knew we'd be seeing in magazines soon, with chromed undersides of running boards, chromed axles, upholstered bottoms of hoods, tuck and roll, flame and lacquer, with hours and hours of painstaking skill lavished on every component but one: the basic concept of the car (which nearly always looked stupid to us). We saw cars that were blocks long, cars with coffins for hoods, cars where you sat like a clown to drive them, cars that could obviously never make it around a corner fast. Subtly, but quickly the energy of our pent-up enthusiasm turned on itself, and became critical, even bitter. We began to scoff at the miles-long idiotic futuristic Lincoln imitation rocket on wheels, at the absurd General Motors version of a rocket on wheels (with after-burner tail lights), at the ludicrous Packard speedboat on wheels, complete with nautical hardware. Wasn't anyone interested in creating a good looking car in its own right?

Had our entire country forgotten that some roads have bends in them? Our enthusiasm had been turned into an energetic mockery of Detroit, as well as some marginal hotrods we almost liked at one time out of desperation. We didn't even try to collect smiles from the models anymore, but sadly wandered off into the back aisles where small aftermarket equipment suppliers had their modest stalls. It was quieter there, and we couldn't come all this way without getting our exorbitant entry-money's worth.

Parked along one of these back aisles was a small display of car books, "Floyd Clymer's Popular Motor Books." We'd seen his full-page ads crammed with tiny titles of all the books he had for sale in the back of nearly every car magazine. But no one, of course, had taken the time to read what he was offering. Now the books were arranged for our inspection on the counter right in front of us. And in our effort to waste time before heading back down the coast, we picked through them.

They had strange cars in them, with tall wire wheels like we'd seen on some European racers, but even taller. We began taking a closer look, our eyes caught by the fact that this racer seemed to have sixteen exhaust pipes, while that one was covered over completely with flowing bodywork, even though it was obviously racing on a track. The glint of eyeglasses reflecting the spotlights shone in our eyes. It was Floyd Clymer himself, coming over to help us pick through the books to find something that moved us.

"Interested in race cars, boys?"

We mumbled an assent.

"How'd you like to see one that did 271 on a highway?"

"Oh right," we answered in our best teenage sarcasm. "The best they're doing on Bonneville is 180. How can it do 270 on a highway? You mean 271 kilometers an hour, don't you?

"You're talking about Bonneville," he said. "That's hotrods. This is different," he said, and then rattled off speed figures (in miles an hour, not kilometers) that confirmed our guess that Floyd was a trifle touched in the head.

"A dragster can't even do that in the quarter," we protested. "How can a road-racer beat a dragster in a standing start?"

Floyd smiled indulgently, like the Ancient Mariner. He'd hooked his fish and successfully riveted our attention with glittering eye as he opened page after page of photos showing cars doing speeds we'd never thought possible, judging from the speeds being set by our favorite specialist hotrod record setters that we were familiar with. The books seemed legitimate. It was all there in black and white and we looked at each other in dumb awe as the process of scales falling from our eyes began.

The gateway to a new perspective on the racing world was found in the small print of Floyd Clymer's ubiquitous ads for "popular motorbooks" that American youth were turning to for technical pointers. In among the nuts and bolts books, was a whole world of history largely forgotten by the post-war world.

author's collection

The hotrod magazines had led us astray. The kind of speeds they were raving about were eclipsed by something that had gone on before. Way before.

"But, well, when did these cars, you know, do all these things?"

And he mentioned dates in the mid-1930s that were ancient history to us, "Before the War," even. Before we were born. Before most of our parents had even met. We took another look at these books to see if we could catch some clue of a hoax.

"Look, this one's got its engine behind the driver," one of us said with suspicion. "How can a road-racer have its engine behind the driver?"

"Someday, " Floyd smiled from behind his glasses, "All racers will have their engines behind the drivers. Look at these little 500 jobs from England." And he showed us tiny motorcycle-engined racers (the forerunners of all Grand Prix cars of today) bouncing around small British tracks in gloomy weather. They looked incredibly fun to drive, like they would go around a corner and be fun at the same time. Not like a hotrod.

We stood and gazed at each other in mute confusion. Here were books showing facts that had never been dreamed of in our philosophies, nor our hotrod magazines. There were other books with beautifully sculpted cars in front of castles that made the chrome-slathered clown-cars from Detroit look like a study in abnormal behavior. We'd been disgusted by Autorama when we saw it up close and personal. But now we were feeling cheated by the whole automotive press. I pulled out a wad of carefully-saved cash with the determination of the newly converted. I suddenly wanted to set right a long period of misapprehension.

"Let me have some of these books. "

Floyd smiled broadly and guided us in an organized method for delving into this new world of study.

"You can start out with this," and he held up *The Boy's Book of Racing Cars*.

"That's a kid's book!"

He just smiled patiently. "Have a look at what's inside." And we saw a nicely chosen array of incredibly potent-looking machines covering the history of European road-racing. We bought it. That, and a book about the account of some English photographer's year chasing around with the Mercedes racing team.

"I thought Mercedes only did big sedans."

"That's after the war. Before the war they pretty much ran everything in Grand Prix racing. Mercedes and Auto Union. "

"Auto-what? Never heard of them."

There was a book written by some driver. Must have been an Italian judging by his name, "Caracciola." And one about another Italian with the wild name of Tazio Somebody. It was written by a Count, and that impressed us with visions of brooding castles emitting evil noblemen in strange, lethal machines. Perfect.

The Boy's Book of Racing Cars (The Church Army Press) was crammed with incendiary shots like this, taken by Fellowes at Pescara.

We drove home in a brooding silence, broken only by disgusted outbursts at the motoring press that we'd been following like the true believers we were. They hadn't told us half the story, and the cars they touted and the drivers they went on endlessly about were puny compared to these new giants.

"Look here, it says they were averaging 158 at this track. And what are they doing at Indianapolis now? 125? And that was back then! And with real turns. Right and left-handers!"

We poured into our new studies, learned about the cars, formed our own favorites, and met the characters that made up this new world we were living in. Two-stage Kompressors, nitro-hydro-benzol-toluene, down-force aerodynamics. We were catching up to the nineteen-thirties!

Just as there'd come a certain polarization between the student body and ourselves over the preference of "You Ain't Nuthin' But A Houn'-Dog" to the Mulligan and Baker quartet, there came a deeper more serious rift between us and mainstream education, now that we realized how much the mainstream was leaving out of their picture of big-H History. Theirs seemed to us to be a conveniently moralistic, neatly dovetailed-together little fairy-tale that was nice to listen to, but hardly useful. It was History-Lite, with all the confusing contradictions removed. Our essays in History began to get lower and lower grades as we brought in elements that didn't agree with the tales as told. And gradually, we began to understand more and more of what our OSS and CIA-trained relatives were talking about when they brought up subjects at family gatherings that were so contradictory to what our teachers were teaching. (As mere kids we had great security clearance because, as everybody knows, kids never listen.)

And what was the "mega-message" that we were to glean from the story of the battles between Hitler and his own heroes?

Could it be, we wondered, that political monsters beget still more political monsters? If it hadn't been for the epic apathy of the Romanovs for the needs of their people, Lenin might have had a hard time finding anybody to listen to him. And if it weren't for the fear generated by the bloodthirsty murderousness of Lenin's Bolsheviks, Hitler in turn would have had a hard time getting enough people to follow him to get up a soccer team.

Then one of us stumbled across a bit of writing that seemed to sum up our new faith in the power of positive indifference. It went: "This planet once moved through the ether for millions of years without human beings; and it can do so again some day if mankind forgets that it owes its higher existence not to the ideas of a few crazy ideologists, but to the knowledge and ruthless application of nature's stern and rigid laws."

The dilemma that faced us at this point was that these appealingly skeptical lines were written by one of history's most accomplished "crazy ideologists" — a youthful Adolf Hitler.

The more we learned, it seemed, the less made sense. And it became hard in retrospect to find any human who couldn't be smart one minute and an imbecile the next, from Hitler, to Rosemeyer, all the way to Dwight David Eisenhower (who abruptly dropped his Ozzie Nelson role in his final speech, to warn the world about the perils of buying into the Daddy Warbucks jingoism of the military-industrial complex).

Nothing was adding up the way it would in History-Lite, in a world where Robert McNamara, the genius who created the Edsel could be rewarded for his efforts by being put in charge of the Vietnam War, and then be rewarded for that by being made a director of the World Bank.

Real history, arousing as it does a suspicion that there might actually be two sides to every story, was confusing.

But then slowly, as we took our new discoveries back out into a contentious world, we began to discover that we had learned something from Clymer's books and the perspective they brought with them. As we listened with new ears to the tales of atrocities of "the other side" (whatever other side it happened to be) we realized that those telling the tales were frightened of any evidence showing that their enemies might actually be less than crazed demons, and might actually be normal humans much like themselves, shivvied around by war-profiteering politicos. We talked to those who were there in the war with new interest; those who had been subjugated by politicos, those who had actually had their talents used by politicos, all sorts. They seemed suspiciously like everyday, normal human beings.

In arguments we could see our fellow debaters becoming frustrated at our new perspective. "Well, just which side are you on?!" they'd yell. And we slowly realised that we weren't on a "side" anymore. That once you're on a side, you're no longer free to look at any evidence that weakens your "side's" position. Your mind locks away ideas contrary to your cause, and you become afraid of something as out-of-control as the truth.

We were no longer putting ourselves up to be chosen for either side of any political kickball game. And from there on, when talking politics, or religion or theories on how to catch fish, we'd first ask our debaters, "Tell me, which side are you on?" And if they'd reply Side-A or Side-B, we'd wander off to talk to somebody else. But if they replied "Neither" or "Both," we'd stick around to hear what they had to say, and learning the value of what Mark Twain had said over a century before, "I never let schooling interfere with my education."

Year on year the old tales of Rudi and Rosemeyer lay fallow in our minds as other, more pressing details of living occupied us. Finally able to regain time to study the question and write about this rarefied little microcosmic world, we set about chasing down the photos needed to illustrate a book on the subject. The people at Audi (today's Auto Union) couldn't have been more warmly welcoming. Shell of England, with its vast archives of racing lore were helpful beyond all expectations, Mercedes-Benz was of great assistance, and *Road & Track* magazine did its part to help.

Picking through the many beautiful prints contained in the various collections we came across a strangely out-of-place photo that caught

We'd come full circle, Clymer and myself, from first getting youngsters like our gang interested in wider horizons, and then in this photo, caught in the act of consorting with the very heroes he'd introduced us to, without ever mentioning the fact to us that he knew them well enough to be hanging out with them all along. He probably guessed we wouldn't have believed a word of it.
photo: Road & Track

our eye. Mixed in with all the exciting pre-war racing action shots was a static pose of two men at the front of a small postwar Mercedes saloon. The car is artfully parked in front of a beautiful old castle rampart in what looks like the Italian Dolomites, or perhaps Italian Switzerland.

The two men look as if they're on a leisurely driving tour, ready to stop at any provocation to savor the scenery. There's no traffic in what (judging by the cut of the pants) is obviously the first part of the postwar period. The men look confident, like they've just had a wonderful lunch.

One of the men is obviously a more mature Rudi Caracciola, and the other I don't recognize right off. He looks American and very familiar. Then the glint of his glasses takes me back to Autorama in a second. The other man with Rudi is Floyd Clymer, the man who first poisoned our minds and made us unfit for mainstream education. He's wearing that same cat-who-caught-the-canary smile he wore back years ago when he listened so patiently to our extensively misinformed criticisms of his claims about the pre-war racers.

Appendix

Resources for Chapter 1

To find more details about Caracciola's flight from the Kakadu Bar as well as his early family background, interested readers are directed to Caracciola's autobiographical work, A *Racing Car Driver's World* (publishing details for all resources can be found in the Bibliography following this resources list).

Resources for Chapter 2

For a comprehensive account of Hitler's post-election encirclement by his own supporters, David Irving's work, *Hitler's War*, gives well-focused coverage.

Resources for Chapter 3

Readers are directed to Caracciola's A *Racing Car Driver's World* for a personal account of his link-up with the Round-Table Gang and his early racing adventures. Alfred Neubauer's *Speed Was My Life* also provides a personal look at Caracciola's early struggles to become a Grand Prix driver.

Resources for Chapter 4

Although both the content and significance of Hitler's speech at the Berlin Motor Show, given shortly after his rise to power, are barely noticed by popular history books, a good account of the importance of this speech is covered by David Owen in his "Porsche, The Man" and "Porsche, The Cars."

John Toland's *Adolf Hitler* provides an interesting look at the development of Hitler's oration techniques.

Resources for Chapter 5

More about the story of Caracciola's romance with Charly, as well as his early experiences driving for Mercedes, can be found in his *A Racing Car Driver's World*. Alfred Neubauer's *Speed Was My Life* also covers this period of Caracciola's career from a personal point of view.

Resources for Chapter 6

A comprehensive account of Hitler's gathering of Germany's racing talent can be found in David Owen's "Porsche, The Man" and "Porsche, The Cars," also see *A History of Progress* published by Audi. Owen also covers Stalin's wooing of Dr. Porsche, as does von Frankenberg's *Porsche, The Man and His Cars*. Von Frankenberg gives one of the best accounts of Porsche's family history, although this can also be found in a number of books focusing on Porsche cars. The influence of Mussolini on Italian motor racing can be found in Count Lurani's *Nuvolari*.

Resources for Chapter 7

A good portrayal of the social side of the European Grand Prix world before the period of German domination can be found in Dreyfus's book, *My Two Lives*. To find out more about Caracciola's victory in the Mille Miglia, check Neubauer's *Speed Was My Life*. This race is also covered in Caracciola's *A Racing Car Driver's World*. An account of Caracciola's visit to Hitler's Brown House can be found in Neubauer's book as well.

Resources for Chapter 8

More details about Caracciola's season driving for the Italians can be found in his *A Racing Car Driver's World*, as well as in Neubauer's *Speed Was My Life*. A slightly alternate view is found in Count Lurani's *Nuvolari*, as well as *Grand Prix de Monaco* by Rainer Schlegelmilch and Hartmut Lehbrink. A detailed account of Caracciola's crash and convalescence can be also be found in his autobiographical book.

Resources for Chapter 9

More on the meeting between Hitler and Porsche to hammer out the future of German racing is covered by David Owen in his "Porsche, The Man" and "Porsche, The Cars." And the subsequent organisation of the racing program is gone into in detail by Neubauer's *Speed Was My Life* as well as Monkhouse's *Motor Racing with Mercedes Benz*, and Prince Chula's *Dick Seaman, A Racing Champion*. Neubauer's visit to the convalescing Caracciola can be found in Neubauer's book as well.

Resources for Chapter 10

Details of the Mercedes Racing Department organisation can be found in Neubauer's *Speed Was My Life*, Caracciola's *A Racing Car Driver's World*, Monkhouse's *Motor Racing with Mercedes Benz*, and Chula's *Dick Seaman, A Racing Champion*. The racing scene at the Nürburgring can be found in Prince Bira's *Bits and Pieces*, and Monkhouse's book. The incidents of industrial espionage, the removal of the Mercedes paint, and the driver-tests of Nazi youth organisation members is also found in Neubauer's book.

Resources for Chapter 11

Details of Charly's accident can be found in Caracciola's *A Racing Car Driver's World*. The account of the appearance of Baby Hoffmann on the scene can be found in Dreyfus's *My Two Lives*. And Caracciola's unannounced appearance at the Mercedes speed tests was covered by Neubauer in his *Speed Was My Life*.

Resources for Chapter 12

Details about Italian design approach and Nuvolari's background is found in Count Lurani's *Nuvolari*. The failure of the German teams in their first outings is covered in Boddy's *The History of Motor Racing*, as well as *Auto Union Die grossen Rennen 1934–39*, by Gianni Cancellieri, Cesare De Agostini, and Martin Schroder.

Resources for Chapter 13

The appearance of Rosemeyer on the racing scene is covered in *Speed Was My Life* by Neubauer, *Rosemeyer!*, by Elly Beinhorn and Chris Nixon, *Great Racing Drivers* by David Hodges, and David Owen's

"Porsche, The Man" and "Porsche, The Cars." Rosemeyer's romancing of Elly Beinhorn as well as his reluctance to join in the Nazi programs is also covered in detail in these works.

Resources for Chapter 14

A detailed account of Nuvolari's great drive at Nürburgring can be found in Count Lurani's *Nuvolari*. The story of von Brauchitsch and Caracciola standing-up the Führer can be found in Neubauer's *Speed Was My Life*, as well a coverage of growing inner-team tensions. More about the German foray to Donington in England can be found in Monkhouse's *Motor Racing with Mercedes Benz*.

Resources for Chapter 15

A number of varying accounts of the pit stop in which von Brauchitsch's car caught fire (and of Nazi interference) can be found in Neubauer's *Speed Was My Life*, Monkhouse's *Motor Racing with Mercedes Benz*, and Prince Chula's *Dick Seaman, A Racing Champion*. Perhaps the most accurate account can be seen in the videotape, "Die Silberpfeile aus Zwickau" produced by Audi AG. The confusion overlayed onto the racing world by politics is covered by Dreyfus in his *My Two Lives*.

Resources for Chapter 16

The growing battles between Rosemeyer and Caracciola can be found in *Rosemeyer!* by Elly Beinhorn and Chris Nixon, and *A Racing Car Driver's World* by Caracciola, as well as Neubauer's *Speed Was My Life*. The story of Varzi and "Lil" can be found in Neubauer's book, while the Tripolitan extravaganzas of Marshal Balbo can be found in Neubauer's book as well as Monkhouse's *Motor Racing with Mercedes Benz* and *Italo Balbo* by Claudio Segre.

Resources for Chapter 17

Accounts of the early development of the Volkswagen can be found in Clive Prew's *VW Beetle*, David Owen's "Porsche, The Man" and "Porsche, The Cars," Ray Miller's *Volkswagen, The People's Car*, Ferry Porsche's *We At Porsche*, and Richard von Frankenberg's *Porsche, The Man and His Cars*. More about the rise of Lang can be found in Neubauer's *Speed Was My Life*.

Resources for Chapter 18

A more detailed account of the racing scene around the Nürburgring can be found in Prince Bira's *Bits and Pieces*, as well as Neubauer's *Speed Was My Life*, and *Motor Racing With Mercedes Benz* by Monkhouse.

Resources for Chapter 19

The effect of politics of racing on the drivers is well covered in Dreyfus's *My Two Lives*. The trips by the German teams out into the world beyond Europe are described in von Frankenberg's *Porsche, The Man and His Cars*, Elly Beinhorn and Chris Nixon's *Rosemeyer!*, Neubauer's *Speed Was My Life*, Rene Dreyfus's *My Two Lives*, and Count Lurani's *Nuvolari*.

Resources for Chapter 20

Descriptions of the continental pit-scene and moods (the pranks and rebelliousness) can be found in Monkhouse's *Motor Racing with Mercedes Benz*, Neubauer's *Speed Was My Life*, and Prince Chula's *Dick Seaman, A Racing Champion*.

Resources for Chapter 21

More details about *Rekordwoche* can be found in Neubauer's *Speed Was My Life*, Elly Beinhorn and Chris Nixon's *Rosemeyer!*, Caracciola's *A Racing Car Driver's World*, and *A History of Progress* published by Audi Ag.

Resources for Chapter 22

Differing accounts of Rosemeyer's last run can be found in Neubauer's *Speed Was My Life*, *Rosemeyer!* by Elly Beinhorn and Chris Nixon, Caracciola's *A Racing Car Driver's World*, and *A History Of Progress* by Audi AG. The effects of the shockwaves of the record cars on course marker flags can be seen in the videotape "Die Silberpfiele aus Zwickau" produced by Audi AG.

Accounts of Dr. Porsche's postwar ordeal in France can be found in David Owen's "Porsche, the Man" and "Porsche the Cars," von Frankenberg's *Porsche, The Man and His Cars*. The later career of Nuvolari can be found in Count Lurani's *Nuvolari*, the postwar fates of von Brauchitsch, Varzi, and Lang can be found in Neubauer's *Speed Was My Life*, and the end of Huhnlein is covered in Johannes Steel's "Mystery of The Nazi Generals." Udet's last fishing vacation was covered in Monkhouse's *Mercedes Benz Grand Prix Racing 1934–1955*.

Bibliography

Audi AG. A *History of Progress*. Ingolstat, 1993.

Bhanubandh, Prince Birabongse Bhanutej. *Bits And Pieces*. London: G.T. Foulis & Co,. Ltd., 1944.

Boddy, William. *The History Of Motor Racing*. New York: G. P. Putnam's Sons, 1977.

Canciellieri, Gianni, DeAgostini, Cesare, Schroeder, Martin. *Auto Union Die Grossen Rennen 1934-39*. Hannover: Schroder & Weise, 1979.

Caracciola, Rudolf. A *Racing Car Driver's World*. New York: Farar, Straus and Cudahy, 1961.

Chakrabongse, Prince Chula. *Dick Seaman, A Racing Champion*. Los Angeles: Floyd Clymer, 1948.

Chakrabongse, Prince Chula. *Road Racing 1936*. London: G.T. Foulis & Co., Ltd., 1946.

Dreyfus, Rene. *My Two Lives*. Tucson: Aztex Corp., 1983.

Dugdale, John. *Great Motor Racing of the Thirties*. New York: Two Continents, 1977.

Dunnigan, James F. and Albert A. Nolfi. *Dirty Little Secrets Of World War II*. New York: William Morrow, 1994.

Fest, Joachim. *Hitler*. New York: Harcourt Brace Jovanovitch, 1973.

Gentile, Antonio. *Eduardo Bianchi*. Milan: Giorgio Nada Editore, 1992.

Gillies, Mark. "Sportscar International." July, 1993, p. 42.

Hodges, David. *Great Racing Drivers*. London: Temple Press Books, 1966.

Irving, David. *Hitler's War*. New York: Avon Books, 1990.

Lurani, Count Giovanni. *Nuvolari*. New York: William Morrow, 1959.

Miller, Ray. *Volkswagen: The People's Car*. Oceanside: Evergreen Press, 1984.

Monkhouse, George. *Mercedes-Benz Grand Prix Racing 1934-1955*. London: White Mouse, 1984.

Monkhouse, George. *Motor Racing With Mercedes Benz*. London: G.T. Foulis, 1956.

Neubauer, Alfred. *Speed Was My Life*. London: Clarkson N. Potter, 1959.

Owen, David. "Porsche, The Man" and "Porsche The Cars." *Automobile Quarterly*, Vol. 9, #2.

Porsche, Ferry. *We At Porsche*. New York: Doubleday, 1976.

Prew, Clive. *VW Beetle*. New York: Smithmark, 1993.

Proche, "Varzi." *Road & Track*. Oct., 1960.

Rosemeyer, Elly Beinhorn and Nixon, Chris. *Rosemeyer!* London: Isleworth, 1986.

Schlegelmilch, Rainer W. and Lehbrink, Hartmut. *Grand Prix de Monaco*. Koln: Konemann Verlagsgesellschaft mbH, 1998.

Segre, Claudio G. *Italo Balbo*. Berkeley: University Of California Press, 1987.

Steel, Johannes. "Mystery of the Nazi Generals." *World At War*. Aug. 1943.

Toland, John. *Adolf Hitler*. Doubleday, New York, 1976.

von Frankenberg, Richard. *Porsche, The Man And His Cars*. London: G.T. Foulis, 1961.

Index

About the Author

Peter Stevenson, born a Navy brat while his father worked at the Pentagon in 1941, was whisked away to New Zealand where the family got a ringside seat for the war in the Pacific.

Back in the States after the war with a bit of an English accent, Stevenson and his older brothers had become fascinated with the sportscars that the G.I.s were bringing back from England. Stevenson was able to tag along to some of the earliest roadraces on the West Coast where Allards did battle against the big American Cunninghams.

Later Stevenson did volunteer work at the Briggs Cunningham Automotive Museum where he was able to talk with some of the visiting racing greats like Juan Fangio, Sterling Moss, Reid Railton, and Innes Ireland, as well as interview one of the characters in *Driving Forces*, Rene Dreyfus, in New York. At the museum, Stevenson was also able to get the cockpit feel and handling characteristics of vintage race cars before they became precious icons.

Stevenson has written vintage motoring features for national magazines including *Road & Track* as well as in his book *The Greatest Days Of Racing* with an introduction by Grand Prix champion Phil Hill.

Stevenson lives with his wife Susie in California where he continues to hand build replicas of his favorite historic cars.